The Irish Women's History Reader

The Irish Women's History Reader is an exciting collection of essays revealing the tremendous diversity of women's experiences in Ireland's past. This book draws together for the first time key articles published in the fields of Irish women's history and women's studies over the last two decades of the twentieth century, including contributions from Ireland (North and South), England, the USA, Canada and Australia.

The Irish Women's History Reader explores the lives of ordinary Irish women since 1800, looking at the key themes of:

- historiography and the development, and writing, of women's history in Ireland
- politics and the variety of political activities undertaken by women including suffrage, nationalism and unionism
- health and sexuality, revealing hidden histories of sexual activity, mental illness and attempts to control fertility
- religion and the experiences of Catholic nuns, Protestant evangelicals and salvationists
- emigration and the pattern of female migration to the USA, Britain and Australia
- work, including both paid and unpaid employ inside and outside the home.

Alan Hayes is Researcher at the National University of Ireland, Galway and Publisher of Arlen House and **Diane Urquhart** is Lecturer in Modern Irish History at the Institute of Irish Studies of the University of Liverpool.

The

Irish Women's

History Reader

Edited by

Alan Hayes and
Diane Urquhart

London and New York

First published 2001
by Routledge
2 Park Square, Milton Park, Abingdon, Oxon, OX14 4RN

Simultaneously published in the USA and Canada
by Routledge
711 Third Avenue, New York, NY 10017

Routledge is a imprint of the Taylor & Francis Group

Transferred to Digital Printing 2007

© 2001 edited by Alan Hayes and Diane Urquhart

Typeset in Perpetua and Bell Gothic by
Florence Production Ltd, Stoodleigh, Devon

British Library Cataloguing in Publication Data
A catalogue record for this book is available from the British Library

Library of Congress Cataloging in Publication Data
The Irish women's history reader / edited by Alan Hayes and
Diane Urquhart.
    p. cm.
Includes bibliographical references and index.
ISBN 0–415–19913–1   ISBN 0–415–19914–X (pbk)
1. Women—Ireland—History. I. Hayes, Alan, 1970–
II. Urquhart, Diane.
HQ1600.3 .I77 2000
305.4′09415–dc21   00–055338

ISBN 0–415–19913–1 (hbk)
ISBN 0–415–19914–X (pbk)

Publisher's Note
The publisher has gone to great lengths to ensure the quality of this reprint
but points out that some imperfections in the original may be apparent

Contents

Contributors

Professor Donald Harman Akenson, Queen's University, Ontario, Canada and University of Liverpool, England.

Gráinne Blair, University of Warwick, England.

Professor Joanna Bourke, Birkbeck College, London, England.

Eibhlín Breathnach, *formerly* University College, Dublin, Ireland.

Mary Clancy, National University of Ireland, Galway, Ireland.

Dr Caitríona Clear, National University of Ireland, Galway, Ireland.

Mary Cullen, National University of Ireland, Maynooth, Ireland.

Rosemary Cullen Owens, University College, Dublin, Ireland.

Professor Mary E. Daly, University College, Dublin, Ireland.

Professor Hasia R. Diner, New York University, United States.

Professor David Fitzpatrick, Trinity College, Dublin, Ireland.

Alan Hayes, National University of Ireland, Galway, Ireland.

Dr Mona Hearn, *formerly* Dublin Institute of Technology, Ireland.

Professor David Hempton, The Queen's University of Belfast, Northern Ireland.

Dr Myrtle Hill, The Queen's University of Belfast, Northern Ireland.

Professor Greta Jones, University of Ulster at Jordanstown, Northern Ireland.

Dr Sharon Lambert, University of Lancaster, England.

Professor J. J. Lee, University College, Cork, Ireland.

Dr Maria Luddy, University of Warwick, England.

Áine McCarthy, University College Dublin, Ireland.

Dr Trevor McClaughlin, Macquarie University, Sydney, Australia.

Dr Margaret MacCurtain, University College Dublin, Ireland.

Dr Dympna McLoughlin, National University of Ireland, Maynooth, Ireland.

Professor Cliona Murphy, California State University, Bakersfield, United States.

Dr Anne O'Dowd, National Museum of Ireland, Dublin, Ireland.

Dr Mary O'Dowd, The Queen's University of Belfast, Northern Ireland.

Professor Yvonne Scannell, Trinity College, Dublin, Ireland.

Dr Diane Urquhart, University of Liverpool, England.

Dr Maryann Valiulis, Trinity College, Dublin, Ireland.

Dr Margaret Ward, Bath Spa University College, England.

Acknowledgements

Every effort has been made to obtain permission to reprint all the extracts included. Persons entitled to fees for any extract reprinted here are invited to apply in writing to the editors. We are very grateful to all the contributors to this *Reader* who responded to our invitations promptly and with much enthusiasm.

In addition to the contributors and copyright holders we would also like to thank the following: Wolfhound Press, *The Irish Review*, *History Ireland*, *Labour History News*, The Institute of Irish Studies of The Queen's University of Belfast, Ink Links, Poolbeg Press, *The Irish Journal of Psychology*, *The Women's History Review*, Triangle Journals Limited, Irish Academic Press, Oxford University Press, *The Social History of Medicine*, Gill and Macmillan, Routledge, Galway University Press, *Saothar*, Cambridge University Press, *Irish Economic and Social History*, *Rural History*, Mercier Press, Arlen House, University of Massachusetts Press, P. D. Meany Co., Genealogical Society of Victoria, Johns Hopkins University Press.

Our thanks to all at Routledge for their patience throughout this project, but especially for their initial invitation to compile this *Reader*. The comments and suggestions proffered by our four anonymous readers not only helped clarify our thoughts regarding this project, but also threw light on rare sources.

Diane Urquhart and Alan Hayes thank all their colleagues in their respective institutions, The Queen's University of Belfast, University of Liverpool and National University of Ireland, Galway, for assistance and help. Diane also wishes to thank colleagues on the Women's History Project, and Alan would like to acknowledge the advice and support of Noel Coughlan, Pauline Nic Chonaonaigh and Kieran Hoare, James Hardiman Library, NUI, Galway during this project. Thanks also to Brendan Flynn, NUI, Galway for helpful critical reading. We would also like to express our thanks to Dr Eileen Black and the Trustees of the Ulster Museum, Belfast.

Introduction: Reclaiming Women's Past

■ Alan Hayes and Diane Urquhart

I hope the present Era will produce some women of sufficient talents to inspire the rest with a genuine love of Liberty and just sense of her value.

Mary Ann McCracken, 16 March 1797[1]

THIS IS A COLLECTION OF THIRTY-ONE key articles which together chronicle the history of women in Ireland in the nineteenth and twentieth centuries. This collection was born from the realisation that an immense amount of research and publication had been carried out in the field of Irish women's history over recent years. Some of this material was appearing in obscure scholarly journals and books with low print runs, which were difficult to obtain. Furthermore, from our own experiences of researching or teaching Irish women's history we were aware of the need for a core text. We were also aware of the strong public interest in women in Ireland's past. This interest was initiated over two decades ago with the publication of the pioneering collection, *Women in Irish Society: The Historical Dimension*, a book which went on to generate 10,000 sales and receive critical acclaim.[2] From that date onwards women's history in Ireland has experienced a steady growth, developing to the stage where it is now taught at an undergraduate level and seen as a key area for postgraduate and academic research. In 1997 it was also recognised by the government of the Republic of Ireland, which funded the first major survey into sources for the history of women in Ireland. This work is being conducted on a cross-border basis by the Women's History Project. There is also a thriving body of professional historians of women, the Women's History Association of Ireland, which encourages and furthers research and interdisciplinary co-operation in the field. Women's history has, therefore, not only experienced a steady growth, but also gained acceptance from the academic community. It now stands as a crucial area of historical enquiry.

Obviously the work contained herein is only a representation of the hundreds of pieces of work that have been produced in recent years. Our remit was to select articles that opened up whole new areas of enquiry for the history of Irish women living at home and abroad. We have also included those that prompted debate, caused controversy or moved the boundaries of what was considered worthy of historical attention. Here, these articles are brought together for the first time, in an edited and abridged format, highlighting some of the scholarly and innovative research that has been amassed over two decades. Our contributors are drawn not only from Northern Ireland and the Republic of Ireland, but also from Britain, America, Canada and Australia. There are also contributions from a number of male historians, which goes some way to refute the notion that women's history is a feminine occupation for a female audience.

It is anticipated that this *Reader* will act as a guide to all those who are interested in women's history. Indeed, we hope that it will stimulate the interest of active participants in the field on a number of levels: academics, postgraduate researchers and undergraduates. We hope that it will also inform and awaken interest amongst a more general readership — those who are keen to uncover the varied roles women have played in Ireland's past.

With these audiences in mind the *Reader* has been divided thematically into six sections: historiography, politics, health and sexuality, religion, emigration and work. However, the areas covered in this collection should not be seen in isolation from one another. Indeed artificial compartmentalisation of women's lives should be avoided as far as possible. Moreover there are many overlaps and similarities throughout the book. For instance, the area of work is overlaid with considerations of class, age, health and so on. Similarly the act of emigration, which touched so many women's lives in nineteenth- and twentieth-century Ireland, involved a complex interaction of factors. These were affected by the social standing of individuals, their place in the familial structure, and their marriage and employment prospects, amongst others.

The focus of this *Reader* is on the nineteenth and twentieth centuries. There are practical reasons for this, such as the relative scarcity of primary source and published material on the medieval and early modern period.[3] In addition to this, the nineteenth century witnessed a significant change in women's position in society. Women became involved in an array of public activities, ranging from philanthropy to the first reform campaigns, in which some women began to challenge their position of legislative and social inferiority. Moreover, women began to claim power and authority and to redefine these concepts, both consciously and unconsciously. This can be seen in areas as diverse as paid domestic service, religion, unpaid household work and family production. The twentieth century also saw manifold changes: a radicalisation of Irish politics with the associated rise of nationalism and unionism, the enfranchisement of women and the partition of Ireland, which created a gulf between the experiences of the north and south of the country. Women of all classes, religions and ages were affected by these and other developments. The middle decades of the century were defined by an increasing conservatism and the restriction of women's rights in the south of Ireland; these remained largely unchallenged until the advent of the civil rights and women's rights movements. Yet, until recently, the impact of these events in women's lives remained largely unremarked upon and unrecorded in the historical record.

The development of Irish women's history, with its roots in the rise of second-wave feminism in 1970s Ireland, asked the misleadingly simple question – what did women do in the past? In striving to answer this, a significant challenge to that which had previously been considered as historically important was posed. The dawning realisation that women were almost wholly absent from the historical record, bar the exception of a few isolated 'greats', and the subsequent search to reclaim the history of all women – both the 'great' and the 'ordinary' – has presented a potentially revolutionary challenge to the teaching, research and publishing of Irish history. The increasing number of historians, both female and male, undertaking gender-related research is to be warmly welcomed and will doubtless cause a revision of the historical record. While we look forward to this and the research which is still to come, we present here thirty-one seminal pieces which have been written on Irish women's history since the 1970s.

Notes

1   Mary McNeill, *The Life and Times of Mary Ann McCracken 1770–1866: A Belfast Panorama*, Dublin, 1960, reissued Belfast, 1988, p. 127.

2   This collection was edited by Margaret MacCurtain and Donnchadh Ó Corrain and was published by Arlen House, Dublin in 1978.

3   This is with the exception of, for example, Mary Condren, *The Serpent and the Goddess: Women, Religion and Power in Celtic Ireland*, San Francisco, 1989; Margaret MacCurtain and Mary O'Dowd (eds), *Women in Early Modern Ireland*, Dublin and Edinburgh, 1991; Lisa Bitel, *Land of Women: Tales of Sex and Gender from Early Ireland*, New York and London, 1996; and Christine Meek and Katharine Simms (eds), *'The Fragility of Her Sex'? Medieval Irishwomen in their European Context*, Dublin, 1996.

PART ONE

Historiography

THIS COLLECTION OPENS WITH a section on historiography, that is, the theory of the writing of history. With the development of second-wave feminism in 1970s' Ireland, some women began to ask what the women of past decades and past centuries had done. Striving to answer this question was a wholesale and radical challenge. Just what had women done in the past? Had women been written out of history and what was the best approach to unearth their varied and extensive histories?

In historical terms, therefore, the writing of women's history is certainly something of a new phenomenon, but women have been writing history for centuries. In spite of this, the work of women historians has only recently been reclaimed. Recovering the work of women historians over the course of the last two centuries reveals many of the ways in which they have been marginalised within the profession. However, history rarely stands still and present-day historians of women have widened their analytical approach to encompass that of gender. Indeed, using gender as a tool for historical enquiry raises important questions for the writing of women's history in Ireland. Certainly gender should be used as a category for analysis. In so doing the revolutionary potential of gender as a historical tool becomes readily apparent. It will be in cojoining work of this nature to what has been accepted as mainstream history that a new 'human' history will develop; looking at the experiences of women alongside those of men and examining the relationships between the sexes. Such an approach has been the cause of some controversy, raising the question of the validity of writing history from a particular point of view, be it political or feminist. Thus the issue of objectivity has been a cause for some concern. The question of whether you need to be a feminist or a woman to write women's history has also aroused debate. These considerations all need to be addressed – which only serves to further develop the methodology of the writing of Irish women's history.

Suggestions for further reading

Mary Cullen, 'Invisible women and their contribution to historical studies', *Stair: Journal of the Irish History Teachers' Association*, 1982.

Mary Cullen, 'Women's history in Ireland', in Karen Offen, Ruth Roach Pierson and Jane Rendall (eds), *Writing Women's History: International Perspectives*, Bloomington, 1991.

David Fitzpatrick, 'Women, gender and the writing of Irish history', *Irish Historical Studies*, 27, 127, 1991.

Maria Luddy, 'An agenda for women's history in Ireland, 1800–1900', *Irish Historical Studies*, 28, 109, 1992.

Margaret Ward, *The Missing Sex: Putting Women into Irish History*, Dublin, 1991.

Chapter 1

Mary O'Dowd

■   from FROM MORGAN TO MacCURTAIN: WOMEN
HISTORIANS IN IRELAND FROM THE 1790s TO THE
1990s, in Maryann Gialanella Valiulis and Mary O'Dowd (eds),
*Women and Irish History: Essays in Honour of Margaret
MacCurtain*, Dublin, 1997, pp. 38–58

[. . .]

PUBLICATION OF WRITING BY WOMEN began in England and on
the continent in the late seventeenth century and developed in Ireland in the
eighteenth century. Poetry, novels and drama were the most popular genres used
by women and writing about the past tended to be through historical verse or
novels. [. . .] The political upheavals of the late eighteenth century led to an increase
in publications by women and in Ireland this development coincided with the
Gaelic literary revival, which increased the popularity of research into the Irish
past. Antiquarianism and archaeology became a fashionable leisure occupation for
men and women. [. . .] A small number of Irish women also undertook serious
historical research. Charlotte Brooke, for example, learnt Irish and translated Gaelic
poetry dating from the medieval period. Her *Reliques of Irish Poetry* included historical introductions to the poems as well as transcripts of some of them in Irish
script.[1] Maria Edgeworth compiled antiquarian notes for the glossary to *Castle
Rackrent* and demonstrated her awareness of the research being published by the
Transactions of the Royal Irish Academy as well as an interest in Irish folklore.[2]

Another woman writer whose work was strongly influenced by the [eigh-
teenth-century] Gaelic revival was Sidney Owenson, Lady Morgan whose historical
novels drew on the research into the Irish past undertaken by antiquarians such as
Charles O'Conor, Francis Walker and Sylvester O'Halloran. In many ways, indeed,
Morgan's work served as an important popularising medium for communicating
the work of the male scholars.[3] [. . .]

Towards the end of her life, Morgan added another theme to the history of
women historians in Ireland. She initiated a major historical project on the history
of women. She planned to write a multi-volume history of women from biblical
times to the early nineteenth century but failing eyesight meant that only two
volumes appeared. *Woman and her Master* is notable, however, as both the first
history book and the first history of women to be published by an Irish woman.[4]

It took the form of a collection of short biographies, which was a common format elsewhere for writing about the lives of women. Similar collections of 'women worthies' had appeared in England and on the continent and, as in Morgan's case, they were often written by women whose main literary output was in the form of novels.[5] [. . .]

The first collection of lives of Irish women appeared in 1877.[6] Its author, Elizabeth Owens Blackburne, [. . .] had established her literary reputation through the writing of novels but, she explained in her preface, the 'silent patriotism' of her life had been to 'preserve the names and achievements of some of the more gifted daughters of Erin'.[7] [. . .]

By the second half of the nineteenth century biography was, therefore, not just established as a genre for writing about women in the past but was especially popular among women writers. At the same time, the writing of Irish history was developed as archives were opened to researchers; new sources were discovered and edited and historical and archaeological societies were founded.[8] Women's participation in these developments was on the whole a peripheral one. They continued the popularising tradition established by Morgan and Brooke but also took on auxiliary services editing documents and acting as (often unacknowledged) assistants and researchers for their husbands. It was also frequently the women in a family who took responsibility for the preservation of the posthumous memory and documentary record of their male relatives, a task which combined the work of the biographer with that of document editor.

[. . .] A number of women [. . .] continued what seems to have been the increasingly lucrative market of writing books for children. It was not, however, until the beginning of the twentieth century that the writing and publishing of history books by women for a more adult audience became more common and consequently more central to the professionalisation of Irish history writing.

Two developments converged to account for the growth of women's interest in history. The Gaelic literary revival created a new awareness of Irish literature and history, particularly in Irish society before the arrival of the English. Secondly, the improved facilities for the education of women in the late nineteenth century meant that a significant number of women participated in the literary movement, writing fiction and verse but also taking an interest in antiquarianism, archaeology and history, and in learning to write and speak Irish. They joined literary and historical societies and wrote and published on Irish history.[9] The admission of women into Irish universities from the 1880s onwards also led to women studying history at graduate level and acquiring positions within the academy.[10]

The writing of the women historians was central to the construction of the historical past on which the revival was based and of particular significance in this context was the work of Alice Stopford Green. In the first decades of the twentieth century Stopford Green wrote a series of books which supported the literary movement's emphasis on the civilised and cultured nature of Irish society before it was debased by English influence. [. . .] Stopford Green believed that she was bringing 'about a new study of Irish history', by which she meant the history of people rather than of politicians and making use of Gaelic literary material as historical sources.[11]

Reviewers accused Stopford Green of being too partisan, a view which has been echoed by many critics since.[12] Concentration on Stopford Green's nationalist bias overlooks, however, the new contribution which she made to the study of late medieval Irish society through her discovery of references to Irish merchants and trade in continental and English sources. It was not until the 1970s that her work in this area was extended and elaborated.[13] [. . .]

Consistent with her belief in the social role of history, Stopford Green was [. . .] concerned with the educational role of history. She encouraged the development of history as a school subject in England and was from its foundation in 1906 an active supporter of the Historical Association. She wrote for its journal, *History,* and served as its president from 1915 to 1918.[14] She also lectured and participated in discussions on the school history curriculum in England and wrote a series of booklets for use in Irish schools.[15] In addition, Stopford Green's work continued the role of the woman historian as populariser of the work of the more scholarly but less readable research of male scholars. [. . .]

Another woman scholar who combined, like Stopford Green, a concern to popularise the historical and literary research of the Gaelic literary revival with an interest in fostering high scholarly standards was Eleanor Hull. In 1926 Hull wrote *A History of Ireland and Her People* (London and Dublin) which was intended for a general rather than a specialised readership. She also, like other women scholars, wrote a school textbook and a series of books for children.[16] [. . .] Hull, like Green, was also involved in the institutional development of the academic study of Irish history and literature. She was one of the founders of the Irish Texts Society, which edited scholarly editions and translations of historical and literary sources in Irish. [. . .] Partly through Hull's sponsorship a number of other women Celtic scholars edited texts for the Irish Texts Society and served on its council.[17] Some later became involved in the institutional development of Celtic studies and established a tradition of women scholars working in this field.[18] [. . .]

Neither Stopford Green nor Hull attended university or held academic positions and in many ways their literary careers represent a transition period between the popularising and auxiliary role of women historians of the nineteenth century and the more scholarly and central position of women historians in the academy in the early years of the twentieth century. [. . .]

A remarkable phenomenon of the development of history as an academic subject in Irish universities was the success of the first generation of Irish women graduates in acquiring academic posts in history. The first professor of modern Irish history at University College, Dublin was Mary Hayden, appointed in 1911;[19] the first professor of history in University College, Galway was Mary Donovan O'Sullivan, appointed in 1914;[20] and in Trinity College, Dublin, Constantia Maxwell was among the first generation of women graduates in history. She graduated with a first class degree and after a year spent in Bedford College, London, she was appointed assistant to the professor of history in Trinity in 1908 and became the first woman member of staff in Trinity. Maxwell was subsequently created a lecturer, then a professor of economic history (becoming the first woman professor in the college) and in 1947 she was appointed to the Lecky chair of history.[21] In Queen's University, Belfast, Maud Violet Clarke, a medievalist, held the chair of history temporarily from 1916 to 1919 when the holder of the chair, F. M. Powicke was in the army.[22]

[. . .] Despite their different interests and backgrounds [. . .] the women history professors shared a common concern with teaching and in Maxwell's and Hayden's case in writing texts for use by students in schools and universities. All three were also concerned to communicate the results of academic research to a wide audience.[23] Thus it might be suggested that despite their positions in the academy the women history professors continued to fulfil the traditional role of the woman historian as synthesiser, populariser and educator of the young. [. . .] All three women professors appear to have also approved of the new developments in Irish history writing which took place in the 1930s. O'Sullivan supervised a large number of research students in Galway while Hayden was very supportive of one of the leaders of the new movement, R. W. Dudley Edwards.[24] [. . .]

Yet, although the women professors offered support for the new developments in Irish history writing in the 1930s, their absence from active involvement in the 'revolution in Irish history writing' is also striking. In the new movement dedicated to 'the scientific study of Irish history',[25] the historical writing of all three women history professors was out of fashion and not in keeping with its method or philosophy. Constantia Maxwell's history books were both readable and popular but her failure to use primary source material and her self-proclaimed admiration for the Anglo-Irish landed gentry of the eighteenth century left her open to criticism from the reviewers in *Irish Historical Studies,* the flagship of the new form of history writing.[26] In her many book reviews in *Irish Historical Studies* and elsewhere Mary Hayden refused to adhere to the new standards being set, and implicit in some of her reviews is her distaste for 'scientific' history.[27] Mary Donovan O'Sullivan's studies of the history of Galway were closer to the journal's methodology but her book, *Old Galway: The History of a Norman Colony in Ireland* (Cambridge, 1942) received a highly critical, and in many ways unfair assessment, from H. G. Richardson in *Irish Historical Studies.*[28] [. . .]

In 1939 T. W. Moody was appointed to the Erasmus Smith chair in history in Trinity College Dublin while in the same year Constantia Maxwell was awarded a personal chair in economic history in Trinity. Five years later R. Dudley Edwards replaced Mary Hayden as professor of modern Irish history in University College, Dublin. With the academic appointments of Edwards and Moody, history in Ireland, with special emphasis on Irish history, became firmly centred in the academy. It is tempting, therefore, to view the succession of Hayden by Edwards and the appointment of Moody to the established chair in Trinity as the replacement of the history women by the history men. Edwards and Moody dominated the Irish history world for the next forty years. As history became a prestigious subject in Irish universities, women's involvement in the subject declined.

But if the methodology of the women history professors was found lacking by the criteria set by *Irish Historical Studies,* their pedagogic concerns conformed to the stated aim of the new journal 'to be of service to the specialist, the teacher, and the general reader'. [. . .] A number of commentators have noted that the revolution in Irish history writing was slow to make an impact on public perceptions of Irish history or on its teaching in Irish schools[29] but it might also be noted that as a consequence Hayden and Noonan's, *A Short History of the Irish People* dominated the textbook market until the 1960s. It is intriguing to speculate if the book was in fact silently sanctioned by the two editors of *Irish Historical Studies* as a suitable textbook in Irish schools and universities and particularly by Edwards who had been a student of Hayden's. [. . .] As late as 1960, eighteen years after Hayden's death, *A Short History of the Irish People* was revised and edited by anonymous editors, although the substance of the volume was not changed. It remained recommended reading for history students in University College, Galway, University College, Dublin and Queen's University, Belfast until the 1960s.[30] Eleanor Hull's *A History of Ireland and her People* and Síle Ní Chinnéide's textbook in Irish, *Stair Euroip*, were also among the key texts recommended to Irish university students in the 1950s and 1960s, while Alice Stopford Green's work was listed as recommended reading by the Department of Education for school teachers during the same period.[31] Thus it might be argued that the revolution in Irish history writing tacitly reinforced the tradition of women historians as textbook writers.[32]

Within the universities, the experiences of women historians in the middle decades of the twentieth century was a rather mixed one. The 1940s witnessed an increase in the enrolment of women graduate students in history but the numbers declined sharply in the 1950s and 1960s. In 1954 there were no women students enrolled for research in Irish history in Irish universities and in 1964 only five women graduates were registered.[33] At the same time a small number of women continued to be appointed to teaching posts in history departments including Maureen MacGeehin (later Wall), Miriam McDonnell (later Daly) and Margaret MacCurtain, all of whom worked in University College, Dublin. [. . .] In Trinity, Jocelyn Otway Ruthven replaced Margaret Griffith as lecturer in medieval history in 1939 and in 1951–2 Moody had as his assistant Clara Crawford, a doctoral student in medieval history. Dorothy Clarke was appointed to the history department in Queen's University, Belfast in 1955.[34]

But with the exception of Otway Ruthven who was appointed Lecky professor in history in 1951, the academic status of women historians declined following the initial success of the first generation of women graduates. [. . .] As John A. Murphy has indicated in his history of University College, Cork, despite the formal admission of women students to Irish universities, academic life in early and mid-twentieth century remained a male club, from many parts of which women were still excluded. The National University of Ireland had a marriage ban on non-statutory women staff, which clearly had a detrimental effect on women's admission to the academy.[35] When Maureen MacGeehin married in the 1950s she was asked by the college authorities in University College, Dublin to resign from her teaching position, and although she continued to lecture in history (through a redefinition of the official title of her post), she was not formally recognised as a member of the academic staff until the early 1960s and then at the lowest grade.[36] In over thirty years of distinguished service at UCD, Margaret MacCurtain never advanced beyond the grade of college lecturer. [. . .]

From the early 1970s, the number of students enrolling in Irish universities dramatically increased and concurrently there was a rise in the number of women students undertaking graduate research in history at doctoral and masters' level. Since that time a succession of Irish women historians have completed Ph.D.s in

English and Irish universities. Trained in the methodology of *Irish Historical Studies,* the women graduates have an approach that is now virtually indistinguishable from that of their male peers. Less dramatic has been the growth in the numbers of full-time academic staff, and consequently women historians still form a tiny minority of staff employed in history departments in Irish universities, and for most, promotion within their profession has remained elusive.

Thus despite the initial academic success of the first generation of women history graduates, women's contribution to the revolution in Irish history has been limited. [. . .] Coincidentally or not, the advance of the scientific study of Irish history led to a decline in the status of women historians in the academy.

Notes

1 Charlotte Brooke, *Reliques of Irish Poetry,* Dublin, 1789. See also Clare O'Halloran, 'Irish re-creations of the Gaelic past: the challenge of MacPherson's Ossian', *Past and Present,* 124, 1989, pp. 86–9.

2 Maria Edgeworth, *Castle Rackrent,* Oxford University Press, 1995. See also Tom Dunne, *Maria Edgeworth and the Colonial Mind,* Cork, 1984; Marilyn Butler, *Maria Edgeworth, a Literary Biography,* Oxford, 1972, p. 365; W. J. McCormack, 'Maria Edgeworth (1768–1849)' in Seamus Deane (ed.), *Field Day Anthology of Irish Writing,* 3 vols, Derry, 1991, I, pp. 1011–13.

3 O'Halloran, 'Irish re-creations of the Gaelic past', pp. 91–2.

4 *Woman and her Master,* 2 vols, London, 1840.

5 Natalie Zemon Davis, 'Women's history in transition: the European case', *Feminist Studies,* 3, 1976, pp. 83–103; Kathryn Kish Sklar, 'American female historians in context, 1770–1930', *Feminist Studies,* 3, 1976, pp. 171–84; Bonnie G. Smith, 'The contribution of women to modern historiography in Great Britain, France, and the United States, 1750–1940', *American Historical Review,* 89, 1984, pp. 709–32.

6 Elizabeth Owens Blackburne, *Illustrious Irishwomen, Being Memoirs of Some of the Most Noted Irishwomen from the Earliest Ages to the Present Century,* 2 vols, London, 1877.

7 Ibid., I, p. vii. For biographical details of Blackburne see D. J. O'Donoghue, *The Poets of Ireland: A Biographical and Bibliographical Dictionary of Irish Writers of English Origin,* Dublin and London, 1912; *The New Ireland Review,* XXVII, 1907, p. 369.

8 R. W. Dudley Edwards and Mary O'Dowd, *Sources for Early Modern Ireland, 1534–1641,* Cambridge, 1985, pp. 185–201.

9 For a general account of the Gaelic literary revival see Seamus Deane, *A Short History of Irish Literature,* London, 1986, pp. 141–209.

10 Eibhlin Breathnach, 'Charting new waters: women's experience in higher education, 1879–1908', in Mary Cullen (ed.), *Girls Don't Do Honours: Irish Women in Education in the Nineteenth and Twentieth Centuries,* Dublin, 1987, pp. 55–76.

11 Alice Stopford Green to Oliver Wendell Holmes, 22 December [1919] (Alice Stopford Green Papers (National Library of Ireland, MS 11487(2); Alice Stopford Green's speech at commemoration ceremony for her husband in Oxford (loc. cit., MS 8714(1)).

12 Alice Stopford Green, *The Old Irish World,* Dublin, 1912, pp. 168–97 was a response to a critical review of *The Making of Ireland and its Undoing, 1200–1600,* London, 1908, by the historian Robert Dunlop. See also *The Irish Nation,* 26 December 1908–January 1909 (copy in Alice Stopford Green papers in National Library of Ireland); Roy Foster, 'History and the Irish question', *Transactions of the Royal Historical Society,* 5th series, 1988, reprinted in Ciaran Brady (ed.), *Interpreting Irish History: The Debate on Historical Revisionism,* Dublin, 1994, pp. 137–9.

13 See Steven Ellis, 'Nationalist historiography and the English and Gaelic worlds in the late middle ages', *IHS,* XXV, 1986–7, reprinted in Brady, *Interpreting Irish History,* p. 162, note 4 and p. 173, note 47 for an example of the way in which Stopford Green's work is criticised for its nationalist bias while still being considered a reliable source for its contribution to the economic and social history of late medieval Ireland.

14 *The Historical Association, 1906–1956* (published by the Historical Association, London, 1955), p. 22; Mrs J. R. Green, 'Irish national tradition', in *History,* new series, II (1917–1918), pp. 67–86.

15 See Alice Stopford Green Papers, National Library of Ireland, MS 10428 for the text of a lecture on how to teach history to girls which she delivered at Notting Hill High School, 18 November 1895. See loc. cit., MS 15126(2) for Green's correspondence with Bonaparte Wyse, Minister for Education in Northern Ireland on the proposed use of her books in schools in Northern Ireland.

16 *Pagan Ireland (Epochs of Irish history – 1)* (Dublin, 1904); *A Textbook of Irish Literature,* parts I, II, Dublin, 1906, 1908; *Cuchulainn, the Hound of Ulster,* London, 1909.

17 Eleanor Knott (ed.), *The Bardic Poems of Tadhg Dall Ó Huiginn,* 2 vols, Irish Texts Society, Dublin, 1922; Agnes O'Farrelly was also commissioned to edit a text on the flight of the earls, *7th Annual Report of the Irish Texts Society,* 1905, p. 4. Sophie Bryant was nominated to the council of the society by Hull, *8th Annual Report of the Irish Texts Society,* 1906, p. 8.

18 These include Maud Joynt, see obituary by Eleanor Knott, *Éigse,* vol. II (1940), pp. 226–9 (I am grateful to Briana Nic Dhiarmada for supplying me with a copy of this reference); Eleanor Knott, the first woman member of the Royal Irish Academy (see obituary by Daniel A. Binchy, *Ériu,* vol. XXVI, Dublin, 1975, pp. 182–5); Kathleen Mulchrone, Professor of Celtic in University College, Galway (see *The Catholic Bulletin,* 1938, pp. 615–17); Cecile O'Rahilly, Nessa Ní Shéaghdha (see obituary in the *Irish Times,* 9 June 1993) and many others.

19 Mary M. Macken, 'In memoriam: Mary T. Hayden', *Studies,* 31, 1942, pp. 369–71.

20 Obituary by G. A. Hayes-McCoy, *Analecta Hibernica,* 26, 1970, pp. xii–xiv.

21 Obituary in the *Irish Times,* 8 February 1952 and by F. S. L. Lyons, *Trinity,* 14, Michaelmas, 1962, p. 35. See also R. B. McDowell and D. A. Webb, *Trinity College, Dublin, 1592–1952,* Cambridge, 1982, p. 352.

22 B. Walker and A. McCreary, *Degrees of Excellence: The Story of Queen's Belfast 1845–1995,* Belfast, 1994, p. 77.

23 It is also worth noting that Maxwell and O'Sullivan are remembered by former students as enthusiastic and stimulating teachers while Hayden was noted as an outstanding public speaker (personal communications from Professor James Lydon and Dr R. B. McDowell; Mary M. Macken, 'In memoriam: Mary T. Hayden', *Studies,* 31, 1942, p. 370).

24 G. A. Hayes McCoy and James Lydon were two of O'Sullivan's most successful students. For others see lists of 'Research in Irish universities', *Irish Historical Studies,* I, 1938–1957. For Hayden's support of Dudley Edwards see Edith Mary Johnson, 'Managing an inheritance: Colonel J. C. Wedgwood, the *History of Parliament* and the lost history of the Irish parliament', *Proceedings of the Royal Irish Academy,* 89, section C, no. 7, 1989, p. 179. Hayden also wrote the preface to R. W. Dudley Edwards, *Church and State in Tudor Ireland,* Dublin, 1935, pp. vii–x. I am grateful to Dr R. B. McDowell for information on Maxwell's appreciation of Moody's activities.

25 Preface to *Irish Historical Studies,* I (1938–9), reprinted in Brady, *Interpreting Irish History,* p. 36.

26 See, for example, *Irish Historical Studies,* V, 1946–7, pp. 260–1; XI, 1958–9, pp. 248–9. A more favourable review of the revised edition of Maxwell's *Dublin under the Georges,* London, 1956, appeared in *IHS,* XI, 1958–9, p. 24.

27 See, for example, *IHS,* I, 1938–9, p. 87.

28 Ibid., IV, 1944–5, pp. 361–7. O'Sullivan's *Italian Merchant Bankers in Ireland in the Thirteenth Century,* Dublin, 1962, was treated more fairly by J. A. Otway Ruthven, *IHS,* XIV, 1964–5, pp. 265–7.

29 Brady (ed.), *Interpreting Irish History* pp. 23–4, 140–1.

30 *Calendar of University College Galway for 1968–1969,* Dublin, 1968, p. 94; personal communications from Dr Ciaran Brady and Dr Nini Rodgers.

31 See, for example, *Calendars of University College, Cork, 1948–55,* Cork, 1949–56; Department of Education, *Notes for Teachers: History,* Dublin, 1933, 1955, 1962.

32 The tradition continued into the second half of the twentieth century. Among the students of Dudley Edwards who have been involved in the writing of school textbooks are M. E. Collins, *Conquest and Colonisation,* Dublin, 1969; *Ireland, 1868–1966,* Dublin, 1993; Mary E. Daly, *Social and Economic History of Ireland since 1800,* Dublin, 1991; and Margaret MacCurtain, who edited the series *A History of Ireland,* 4 vols, Dublin, 1969. Maureen Wall was one of the founders of the Dublin Historical Association and wrote the first pamphlet of the association, *The Penal Laws,* which was primarily intended for a student and teacher readership. In 1966 Margaret MacCurtain was one of two historians who served on the Study Group on the Teaching of History in Irish Schools ('The teaching of history in Irish schools', *Administration,* 15, 1967, pp. 168–285).

33 *IHS,* IX, 1954–5, pp. 83–5; XIV, 1964–5, pp. 61–4.

34 *Dublin University Calendar 1938–39,* Dublin, 1939, p. 28; *Dublin University Calendar 1951–2,* Dublin, 1951, pp. 26–7; *Calendar of the Queen's University of Belfast, 1956–57,* Belfast, 1956, p. 38.

35 John A. Murphy, *The College, a History of Queen's/University College, Cork 1845–1995,* Cork, 1995, pp. 127–31, 286, 346.

36 I am grateful to Professor Donal McCartney for this information.

Chapter 2

Mary Cullen

■ from **HISTORY WOMEN AND HISTORY MEN:
THE POLITICS OF WOMEN'S HISTORY**, *History Ireland,*
2/2, summer 1994, pp. 31–6

C URRENT DEVELOPMENTS IN WOMEN'S HISTORY did not just
happen. They grew directly from the contemporary feminist movement. The
roots of feminism lie in the behaviour patterns societies have prescribed for women
and men. While these have differed over time and place, feminism has always
grown from women's perception that the sex roles prescribed by their own society
conflicted with their knowledge of themselves and with their development as
autonomous persons. [. . .]

The new wave of feminism which emerged in Western society around 1960
challenged the prevailing stereotype which insisted that every female, by virtue of
her sex, was individually fulfilled and made her best contribution to society solely
as a wife and mother, subordinating the development of other talents and leaving
responsibility for the organisation of society to males. The American Betty Friedan
called this model the 'feminine mystique', and women around the globe recognised it as corresponding to what they knew in their own cultures.

Feminist rejection of the feminine mystique was challenged by the assertion
that history showed that women had always been satisfied with this role. Since
history books seldom mentioned women at all, with the exception of a few
monarchs and revolutionaries whose lives and careers hardly conformed to the
mystique model, feminists turned to the historical evidence with the question,
'What *did* women do?' The answers which have come so far, and they are only
the beginning, raise wide-ranging challenges to establishment history.

As feminist enquiry focuses on different areas of knowledge, history included,
the first stage is seeing and saying that women are invisible in the knowledge
and theory of the particular discipline. Next comes the search for 'great' women,
individuals who have 'achieved' within the criteria by which men are judged to
have 'achieved'. From this the focus moves to the contribution of a wider range
of women to political, social and intellectual movements which underlie patterns
of continuity and change in societies. The fourth stage sees women as a group,
defined by their shared female sex, demanding the attention of historians. This

development has a radical potential to which this essay will return. The ultimate stage should be the writing of a new integrated history incorporating the historical experience of both sexes. [. . .]

Let us consider the implications of one early discovery by feminist historians: the women's emancipation movements of the nineteenth and early twentieth centuries and the causes that gave rise to them. While feminist movements were neither the central nor the most important phenomena in women's history, their existence allows us to bypass one regularly repeated explanation of the invisibility of women in the history books. Since women were not participants in public politics, historians, it was asserted, could hardly be blamed for not dealing with them. The women's emancipation movement, a highly visible and international political movement, refutes this explanation.

While laws, regulations and customs were not identical in all countries the position of women relative to men was fundamentally similar. In virtually every country in Western society, women were excluded from political life, whether by holding public office, or as members of parliaments, or as voters. They were barred from higher education and the professions. Titles and property passed to sons in preference to daughters. The home was seen as 'the woman's sphere', yet, to take a representative example, under English common law, in force in Ireland, when a woman married her legal identity merged into that of her husband. Her property, whether earned or inherited, passed under his control to dispose of as he pleased and the law gave him full authority over her and their children. Divorce was considerably more difficult for a wife to obtain than it was for a husband, and if a woman left her husband his duty to maintain her lapsed while his right to her property did not. In sex-related offences such as adultery, prostitution and illegitimate birth, the law treated women as the more guilty and punishable party.

In campaigns starting around the middle of the nineteenth century and continuing into the 1920s and 1930s, in country after country, feminists revolutionised the status of women by removing most of the legally imposed civil and political disabilities based on sex. By any standards it was a sizeable achievement even if with hindsight we know that the underlying stereotypes of 'natural' or 'correct' feminine and masculine behaviour were harder to shift. [. . .]

One aspect of this rediscovered history of the women's emancipation movement is its relevance to women's self-knowledge today, its restoration of part of their lost group memory. It tells us that we have not been paranoid in perceptions of oppression, and that the problem of sexism has older and deeper roots than many have realised. On the more positive side, the better sexism is understood, the better the chance of eliminating it. Further, the history of the women's emancipation movement establishes beyond argument that relations between the sexes, including relations of power, have not been unchanging throughout history and dispels the belief that women have always conformed happily to a 'natural' role of passivity and subordination. It places current feminism in context as part of a long historical process, rather than the historical aberration often suggested. Feminists today can start from the knowledge that women before them dissented from imposed patterns of behaviour and changed them. It frees them to build on what is already there instead of re-inventing the wheel in each new generation.

It also raises the question of why all this had to be rediscovered in the first place. Why had it ever been lost? Why has the historical reality that the structures of Irish society included a systematic limitation of women's autonomy and freedom of action, a limitation not applied to men, gone unrecorded in histories of Irish society? It is difficult to see why an organisation of society which gave men a monopoly of access to political and economic power, and excluded women from virtually every avenue of approach to these, should be something that historians have not seen as a significant or important aspect of Irish society. It is equally difficult to see how feminist organisation to abolish sweeping civil and political disabilities could be regarded as more sectional, more trivial or less significant than, for example, nationalism or the labour movement.

It appears that the answers are not to be found in the content of the historical record but in the minds of historians. If we dismiss a conspiracy theory of deliberate suppression, the explanation can only be that most historians have not seen women as important or 'significant' in the history of their societies. They have written history within a paradigm that sees men as the active agents in the patterns of continuity and change historians look for. This paradigm does not see women as an integral part of human society, but as peripheral and essentially outside history. Once the question 'What did women do?' was seriously asked, it became clear that this paradigm blinkered historians' vision and distorted findings and interpretations. [. . .]

With the revelation that there have been real political, social and economic differences consequent on being born a male or a female at a particular time or place, and that these differences have varied from one society or culture to another and changed over time, sex emerged as a category of historical analysis. This was not sex in the sense of biological determinism but in the way societies create sex roles to which individuals are socialised or coerced to conform. The word 'gender' was drawn into use to denote the social construction of sex.

Used with precision within specific historical contexts, gender is a valuable concept in historical research and interpretation. It focuses attention on the relationships between the sexes, how these are structured and maintained and how they change over time and place. It also directs attention to relationships *within* the sexes, those between different groups of women and between different groups of men. It enables the historian to apply the concept of sex as a social construction in research and interpretation. Historical specificity also makes it clear that gender does not stand on its own as the only important analysis. It interacts with other factors such as class, colour, nationality, ethnic origin, political affiliation, religion, age, marital and parental situation and many more, in locating individuals or groups in their historical context. Feminist historians argue that, while gender is not the only essential analysis, it is one of the essential analyses, and that, if it is excluded, the picture drawn by the historian will be to a greater or lesser extent distorted.

Thus defined and used, gender analysis forestalls reductionist interpretations that all women have shared the same history, or that women's history is simply a history of the oppression of all women by all men. Women have been oppressors both as individuals and as members of oppressing classes or nations. Men have been oppressed, by other men and by women, as well as being oppressors.

Women's history is far more than oppression and resistance to it, important as both these aspects are. [. . .]

History as it has been written has been less the history of men than the history of the activities of privileged groups of men who occupied positions of public power. It has seldom looked at men as a group, the subset of humanity defined by their male sex. Just as the history of women cannot be written without reference to gender relationships, neither can the history of men.

Women's history has made it no longer tenable to see the male role in society as the human norm, from which women were for some reason, whether 'biological' inferiority, slower cultural development or whatever, left behind in human evolution and so having to try to catch up with men and attain the male role. The interdependence of the gender roles of the sexes rules out this interpretation.

We do not yet know the extent of the re-evaluations to which this will lead. One will certainly focus attention on definitions of what is recognised as significant historical change and the respective contribution to it by individuals or groups in positions of public power and by individuals and groups far distant from such locations.

They are also likely to include reassessment of the contribution of the full-time male politicians, intellectuals, artists, soldiers, revolutionaries or whatever who have been all these full-time because of women's work. Male privilege, control of resources and freedom from daily family responsibility undermine theories which incorporate the idea of the 'naturalness' of male 'achievement' and which cite in support the relative paucity of similar female achievement. [. . .]

Instead of asking why women have dissented, it might be more useful in increasing our understanding of the past to ask why male élites have so consistently tried to keep control of wealth, education and political power as male monopolies, and to limit women's freedom of action by expanding their child-bearing capacity into a life-time career devoted exclusively to care of family and home at the expense of any serious participation in the affairs of society at large or sustained commitment to intellectual or artistic endeavour. Can the pronouncements by so many of the 'great masters' of Western philosophy on the intellectual and moral inferiority of women as compared to men continue to be dismissed as unimportant hiccups which do not affect the overall evaluation of their systems of thought? By whose instigation and in whose interests did the dualities and theories of opposites that have bedevilled Western thought about the sexes come into being? Why has male identity so often been built on being different to and having control over women? What impact have male sex-role stereotypes which see aggression and dominance as acceptable or desirable masculine characteristics had on the history of different societies? [. . .]

This leads on to the big question of how a more embracingly 'human' history will be written. Seeing relationships between the sexes as an integral part of the history of a society will be central. We can also hope that women's history will carry into all areas of research and interpretation its concern with the origin and operation of systems of power and control, as well as its openness to the complexities of human experience and to the danger of imposing absolutes and dichotomies, not only when dealing with women and men but throughout the search for the past.

Who then is going to write the new integrated history and when? One view is that first we need to build a sufficient base of publication in women's history to provide a firm foundation. Then, once a critical mass of knowledge and theory has been reached, the patriarchal paradigm at present in possession will collapse under the weight of the increasing mass of contrary evidence, and leave the way open for a new paradigm within which historians can rewrite history. [. . .]

Some recent developments suggest that vigilance may be needed to prevent the radical potential of women's history being diverted into a cul-de-sac. These include a tendency to misuse 'gender' as a synonym for 'women', a misuse which allows the essence of gender analysis, that sex is a social construct, to be bypassed and allows men as a group to again elude the historian's scrutiny. This can produce a descriptive social history, valuable in the information it gives, but which does not ask the 'hows' and 'whys' which push social, economic and political history into engagement with each other.

Particularly ironic is the emergence in the United States of 'gender history' as a rival to 'women's history' and claimed to be more universal and less biased. Since women's history led to the concept of gender history, it is hardly surprising that the sceptical see this new dichotomy as an attempt to neutralise the challenge of women's history by marginalising it as less than fully academically respectable.

Here I believe the politics of women's history come into play. Today's women's history, including the concept of gender, came from today's feminism, a movement which asserts women's autonomy and responsibility and challenges male and female sex-role stereotypes which limit these and which incorporate male dominance over women. The diversionary movements described above appear either to fail to understand the concept of sex as a social construct, or to fail to engage with it, and may be seen as elements of a counter-revolution. [. . .] It is arguable that historians who do not understand current feminism will have difficulty in accepting that women's history is 'real' history, and so a real part of human history, however well-intentioned they may believe themselves to be. [. . .]

It may be going too far to suggest that women's history and the new integrated human history can only be successfully written by feminists, whether they be women or men. However, I am convinced that, if the potential of women's history is to be realised, the historians concerned need to at least *understand* feminism today, whether or not they agree with its analysis. Unfortunately it appears that most historians, like most people generally, see feminism as essentially women wanting to be like men, and so as a 'women's issue' which need not involve men. Believing this is an effective defence against having to think about feminism seriously, and in particular about its challenge to men and male stereotypes.

If my argument has any validity, it follows that, in tandem with the work of research and publication, we need a debate about the nature of women's history and its methodologies and politics. The objective will be to put this debate on the agenda of historians of women and from there to move it on to the agenda of the wider community of historians.

Further reading

G. Bock, 'Women's history and gender history: aspects of an international debate', *Gender and History*, 1/1, spring 1989.

G. Bock, 'Challenging dichotomies: perspectives on women's history', in K. Offen, R. R. Pierson and J. Rendall (eds), *Writing Women's History: International Perspectives*, London, 1991.

J. W. Scott, *Gender and the Politics of History*, New York, 1988.

Chapter 3

Cliona Murphy

■ from WOMEN'S HISTORY, FEMINIST
HISTORY, OR GENDER HISTORY?, *The Irish Review,*
12, spring/summer 1992, pp. 21–6

T**HE CONTROVERSY REGARDING REVISIONISM** in Irish history
is ironic considering the narrowness of the history that has been at the centre
of the dispute – nationalist history. What has been perceived as revolutionary
in Irish historiography is merely taking a new angle on an old problem. In fact,
revisionism should be synonymous with the very nature of history itself. A much
broader example of revisionist history which has been taking place over the last
two decades and which has had an impact on the discipline as a whole internationally, has been the attempt to put women into history. While most of the initial
research, theory and publications have come out of the United States and Britain,
work has also been appearing in many other countries. Ireland has not been
left untouched and over the last decade there has been a silent revolution in Irish
historiography which is only now beginning to be appreciated. This is evident in
the appearance of monographs, journal articles and edited collections, as well as
the establishment of three organisations set up for research and communication
in women's history. There have been a number of women's history conferences
as well as women's history panels at other conferences. Articles are beginning
to appear in history journals such as *Irish Historical Studies* and *Irish Economic and
Social History*, which a few years ago would not have considered the area worthy
of attention.

The origins of women's history can be traced further back than the oft-quoted
American civil rights movement of the 1960s, back to the French *Annales* school
and the American school of New History in the 1920s and 1930s, both of which
advocated a broader view of history than the strictly national, political, military
and intellectual. These theorists and practitioners of history asked how there could
be a true history if it dismissed one sex entirely and studied only a tiny percentage
of the other. The development of women's history has gone through a series of
stages since the early 1970s, documented by such as Gerda Lerner, Joan Kelly and
Joan Scott (and a few articles recently appeared on its slow but steady expansion
in Ireland, written by Cullen, Luddy and Murphy, Ward and Fitzpatrick). It is

generally agreed that early women's historians attempted to show that women were important in history, by demonstrating their contributions and achievements. New sources were found and old sources were re-read from a different point of view. Women's history had then to broaden its scope in answer to criticisms that only élite women were being studied, and shifted its focus to include ordinary working-class and peasant women.

Thus there has been concern that the only women who received attention from Irish historians until recently were a handful of prominent nationalist women. While work continues to be done on them, it is less laudatory and more critical. Increased attention has been devoted to other women who were politically active in suffrage movements, labour movements and various political, agricultural, educational and philanthropical organisations. There has also been a concerted effort to look at more 'hidden' women like prostitutes, workhouse inmates, domestic servants, peasant women and nuns. [. . .]

The revisionist nature of women's history is evident in the theoretical debates which have accompanied its growth. Besides being concerned with the content, language and theory of history it also questions the validity of institutionalised themes, periodisation and the importance of certain events in the history of mankind. Joan Kelly's article 'Did women have a Renaissance?' provides a good example of how the solid 'truths' of traditional history have been shaken by this revisionist approach. Likewise in the introduction to *Women Surviving*, a collection of articles on women in Ireland in the nineteenth and twentieth centuries, the editors (inspired by Kelly) asked to what extent the traditional landmarks in nationalist history have mattered or had an impact on the lives of ordinary Irish women. History from the perspective of those previously left out (in this case a majority) takes on entirely new dimensions and emphases.

Besides asking questions about the structure of history, women's historians have extended their revisionist outlook to querying the actual teaching, practice and writing of the discipline. The literature is full of discussion on the writing of textbooks, the subject-matter of history courses, the staffing of history departments, the composition of journal editorial boards and book-prize panels and on what is considered a work of scholarly importance or a worthy dissertation topic. As one article in the *Journal of Women's History* has pointed out, whoever holds the power in these areas determines the type of history that is most widely accepted and propagated.

Questions and debate which have arisen among the practitioners of women's history also serve as a reminder that this is a history which is constantly undergoing revision within itself, as well as attempting to revise mainstream history. The question of whether women's historians are historians of women or feminist historians has become a central one. There are those who are convinced that feminist history must begin with a feminist ideology. This causes alienation and prompts great criticism from other historians, who argue that this is a 'history with a purpose', providing a philosophical, theoretical and historical background to the feminist movement. This criticism cannot be completely dismissed nor would some feminist historians want it to be. But it must be conceded that all of the history of women does not lead to the feminist movement as its culmination, and the imperatives of a present-day ideology should be avoided as far as possible when interpreting the past. Women's historians, on the other hand, argue that they are first historians, not feminists, and are, therefore, writing a more objective history. However, if revisionism has shown anything, it is that historians, despite their best efforts, can never completely release themselves from their own past, values or political orientation. Nevertheless, there should be a persistent effort to do so.

Another aspect of the whole debate is that women's history has been viewed as exclusively the preserve of women, with most male historians blissfully unaware of, uncaring about, and sometimes hostile to, the many sophisticated developments in its theory and their implications for mainstream history. Some historians still cling on to the comforting thought that it is merely the rhetoric of man-hating viragos and ignore the fact that there are significant questions being asked about the discipline that might enrich, or lead to a reinterpretation of their own areas. For example, a study of the relationship between the Irish Parliamentary Party and the Irish Women's Franchise League leads to a surprisingly different portrait of constitutional nationalists and their politics. The general feeling among critics is that women's history is an inferior type and best left to women. However, there are an increasing number of male historians writing in the area, like Richard Evans, Brian Harrison, or David Fitzpatrick in this country [Ireland]. Such contributions are inevitably subjected to criticism by feminist historians. In some cases the criticism is related to their gender and it is felt that, as a consequence, they lack the necessary insight to write women's history. This is reminiscent of the debates concerning whether Americans can write Irish history or whites write black history. Surely, if the answer is in the negative, all historians might as well put down their pens. For how can any of us, whatever our gender, nationality, class or religion, understand the actions of the people in the past, when none of us has been there? It is empathy with, rather than identity with, the subject-matter that makes the difference between a good insightful historian and a passionate propagandist.

Women's history in Ireland has its own unique set of problems. Since it is not as well established as it is in Britain and the United States, historians have to decide what to adopt from the experiences of women's historians abroad, and what in the Irish context will determine their subject-matter and influence their conclusions. Likewise, what priority should be given to nationality, colonial status, religion, class and gender when assessing Irish women's experience? How do all of these interact? To what extent should Irish women's history be comparative? Much of what is published so far is written in isolation from what has been done abroad and Irish women's historians lack a solid training in a wider women's history. This is through no fault of their own, since courses in women's history are only now gradually being introduced into Irish institutes of higher education (and most of these are on Irish women) and there is a dearth of qualified mentors to guide students of women's history. Underlying all of this is the not very nourishing political, social and academic climate which has little interest in providing institutional, intellectual or economic support for research in women's history.

The debate has broadened in the 1980s, outside of Ireland, and proponents of *gender* history have argued that a more comprehensive picture would be found in a study of both men and women interacting with each other in the past. While it remains difficult for women to be mainstreamed into a male-determined framework, is it not academically unsound to be creating a separate women's history?

Women, like men, did not exist alone in the past. Indeed one backlash to women's or feminist history has been Peter Stearns's history of men in the Western world: *Be A Man!* The valid argument has been made by Stearns and others that not only have women been left out of history but so also have most men. Traditional history has told us about men in their public lives, leaving us with little knowledge or insight into life experiences of men and the roles they were expected to play as boys, adolescents, fathers and husbands at different periods in history.

The advocacy of gender history is reflected in the setting up of institutes for gender studies and the establishment of gender history journals in the United States and Britain. Its proponents believe in using gender as a tool of analysis for looking at history – much like using class, nationality and religion. However, there need not necessarily be a separate gender history but rather a mentality which includes it as yet another category to examine the state of society, along with economic, nationalist, political, religious and other approaches. Many women's historians argue that it is too soon to even consider this and such a criticism was vehemently expressed when this writer made the suggestion at the 1991 American Conference for Irish Studies conference in Wisconsin. Some women's or feminist historians believe that many more monographs and specialist studies are necessary first, so that a knowledge base can be built up. It is argued that without years of ground-work and separate studies on women, they will again be neglected and perhaps lost in history and to history. Why, they ask, should they try to coax or convert the male (and indeed some female) historians with a compromise of gender history, when those very historians have expressed their lack of interest by scoffing and refusing to read or review books published in women's history? While there are grounds for their scepticism and certainly individual research projects must still continue, such separatist views will only intensify ghettoisation and do little to change the big picture. At the same time, there will be no gender or compre-hensive history until traditional historians are willing to integrate the findings of publications in women's history into their own research, courses and textbooks. There needs to be a meeting-ground between traditional or mainstream historians and feminist or women's historians to pool information and findings of new research and thus create a more valid history. There is a responsibility on both sides. Otherwise, we will forever be looking at distorted pictures of the past.

Bibliography

Bernice A. Carroll, 'The politics of "originality": women and the class system of the intellect', *Journal of Women's History*, 2/2, fall 1990, pp. 136–63.

Mary Cullen (ed.), *Girls Don't Do Honours: Irish Women in Education in the Nineteenth and Twentieth Centuries*, Dublin, 1987.

Mary Cullen, 'Women's history in Ireland', in Karen Offen, Ruth Roach Pierson and Jane Rendall (eds), *Writing Women's History: International Perspectives*, Indiana, 1991, pp. 429–42.

Richard Evans, *Comrades and Sisters: Feminism, Socialism and Pacifism in Europe 1870–1914*, Brighton, 1987.

David Fitzpatrick, 'The modernisation of the Irish female', in Patrick O'Flanagan, Paul Ferguson and Kevin Whelan (eds), *Rural Ireland: Modernisation and Change, 1600–1900*, Cork, 1987, pp. 162–80.

David Fitzpatrick, 'Women, gender and the writing of Irish history', *Irish Historical Studies*, XXVII, May 1991, pp. 267–73.

Brian Harrison, *Separate Spheres: Opposition to Women's Suffrage 1867–1928*, London, 1978.

Joan Kelly, *Women, Theory and History*, Chicago, 1984.

Gerda Lerner, *The Majority Finds its Past: Placing Women in History*, New York, Oxford, 1979.

Cliona Murphy, *The Women's Suffrage Movement and Irish Society in the Early Twentieth Century*, Hemel Hempstead, 1989.

Maria Luddy and Cliona Murphy, 'Cherchez la femme: the elusive woman in Irish history', in Maria Luddy and Cliona Murphy (eds), *Women Surviving: Studies in Irish Women's History in the Nineteenth and Twentieth Centuries*, Dublin, 1990, pp. 1–14.

Joan Scott, 'Gender: a useful category of historical analysis', *American Historical Review*, 91, 1986, pp. 1053–75.

Joan Scott, *Gender and the Politics of History*, New York, 1989.

Peter Stearns, *Be a Man! Males in Modern Society*, New York, 1979.

PART TWO

Politics

NOT HAVING FORMAL ACCESS to political power in the sense of possessing the vote and being able to stand for elective positions did not lead to political inertia amongst Irish women. Pre-1800 women were involved in food riots and canvassing for political candidates, amongst many other political activities. But as the nineteenth century progressed women's political involvements augmented to include single-issue campaigns that aimed to procure legislative change, such as the campaign to abolish the Contagious Diseases Acts, to obtain equal educational opportunities or procure votes for women. Protesting against dire economic conditions and striving to do work of a practical and philanthropic nature to assist those in need also spurred women to join political associations like the Ladies' Land League. Yet what is perhaps most striking is the diversity of the female political experience from the nineteenth century onwards. From exceptionally committed or talented individuals such as Isabella Tod, Anna Haslam and Anna Parnell to those women who organised petitions and deputations, lobbied politicians, wrote letters to the press or joined political associations, many women were active agents of change.

As women were gradually admitted to the formal avenues of politics – firstly to local government administration from 1896 onwards, and then as voters and candidates in parliamentary elections from 1918 – they continued to play a crucial political role. In addition to these legislative changes, the political climate of the late nineteenth and early twentieth centuries, where the struggles between nationalism and unionism came to dominate, led to the establishment of auxiliary women's political organisations. On the nationalist side of the political spectrum, Cumann na mBan (Irishwomen's Council) exercised an important and specifically female role in support of independence and the Irish Volunteers. Similarly the Ulster Women's Unionist Council, which quickly developed into the largest female political force in early twentieth-century Ireland, clearly believed their work to be a complement to that of male unionists. Significantly both women nationalists and unionists developed and promoted a female aspect to their respective political ideologies. Both, for instance, alerted women to the prospective benefits or dangers of life under a home-rule parliament, couching their messages in maternalistic and domestic phraseology.

Once women were admitted to parliament, few were willing to promote gender-related issues within the legislative system. This is true for both the parliaments of Northern and Southern Ireland. Perhaps the clearest example of this came in 1937 with the passage of De Valera's constitution, which confined women's political, economic and social roles within narrow parameters. Although some opposition was encountered in parliament, it was mainly left to women's groups to oppose the clauses which were seen to be restrictive. As the decades passed, further challenges to the constitution and to women's legal position were presented in the judiciary.

The study of women in Irish politics touches on many aspects of women's lives. Class, familial background, religion and individual capabilities all play a role in determining why women become politically active. Moreover, much is revealed about women's legislative position and the social mores defining codes of respectability for women. Ultimately then, the vibrant role which women have undertaken in voicing their political opinions and calling for legislative change clearly refutes any idea of political inactivity amongst the women of nineteenth- and twentieth-century Ireland.

Suggestions for further reading

Mary Cullen (ed.), *Girls Don't do Honours: Irish Women in Education in the Nineteenth and Twentieth Centuries*, Dublin, 1987.

Rosemary Cullen Owens, *Smashing Times: A History of the Irish Women's Suffrage Movement, 1889–1922*, Dublin, 1984.

Yvonne Galligan, Eilís Ward and Rick Wilford (eds), *Contesting Politics: Women in Ireland, North and South*, Boulder, 1999.

Beth McKillen, 'Irish feminism and national separatism, 1914–23', *Éire-Ireland*, 17/3–4, 1982.

Cliona Murphy, *The Women's Suffrage Movement and Irish Society in the Early Twentieth Century*, New York and London, 1989.

Anne V. O'Connor, 'Influences affecting girls' secondary education in Ireland, 1860–1910', *Archivium Hibernicum*, 141, 1986.

Louise Ryan, 'The Irish Citizen, 1912–20', *Saothar*, 17, 1992.

Janet K. TeBrake, 'Irish peasant women in revolt: the Land League years', *Irish Historical Studies*, 27/109, 1992.

Hilda Tweedy, *A Link in the Chain: The Story of the Irish Housewives' Association, 1942–92*, Dublin, 1992.

Diane Urquhart, *Women in Ulster Politics, 1890–1940: A History Not Yet Told*, Dublin, 2000.

Margaret Ward, *Unmanageable Revolutionaries; Women and Irish Nationalism*, Dingle and London, 1983, reprinted with a new preface, London, 1995.

Chapter 4

Maria Luddy

■ from **WOMEN AND POLITICS IN NINETEENTH-CENTURY IRELAND**, in Maryann Gialanella Valiulis and Mary O'Dowd (eds), *Women and Irish History: Essays in Honour of Margaret MacCurtain*, Dublin, 1997, pp. 89–108

IT IS GENERALLY ASSUMED that nineteenth-century Irish politics were a function of public life, a male activity in which women played little if any role. Political historians pay scant attention to the role of women in political life, seeing it as either peripheral, or of small consequence.[1] Women, of course, were not voters,[2] nor did they have access to high political office in the nineteenth century. Although individual women such as Isabella Tod and Anna Haslam can be regarded as politicians, for most of the nineteenth century Irish women were excluded from formal male political culture. The ideology of 'separate spheres', the world of work and politics advocated for men and the world of domesticity advocated for women, played some part in limiting their political aspirations. [. . .]

In this paper I would like to extend the boundaries of what we consider to be political by looking at a range of informal and formal political activity engaged in by Irish women in the last century. [. . .] They were involved in indirect and direct action at local and national level. They also played a role in political parties and pressure groups, such as anti-slavery and temperance societies. For some women, formal political activity culminated in the suffrage campaign, while for others it involved more nationalistic aims. The political aspirations of women activists were not necessarily for the benefit of other women. Arguments about gender difference abounded in the nineteenth century and these played a role in shaping women's political involvement. Particular constructions of gender difference arose in the arguments which informed women's political activities. Women were not a homogenous mass and their politics differed according to their class. Women's role in politics in nineteenth-century Ireland was diverse and involved women from all social classes. Women as well as men expressed political opinions, played a part in political rituals, and created a role for themselves in public political life so that their political presence had become commonplace by the end of the nineteenth century. [. . .]

Looking at women's informal political activity reveals that they were exercising political power long before they won the franchise. It is clear, for example, that some wives and daughters could exert influence over the male members of their families, Daniel O'Connell's wife, Mary, being a case in point.[3] [. . .]

Agrarian disturbances were a feature of Irish life from the 1760s. [. . .] In 1843 for example, Bridget Maher was arrested and tried for attempting to burn down the house of one Thomas Coughlan as part of a Ribbon conspiracy. [. . .] Women's involvement in violent activities during the tithe war of the 1830s is also recorded. For example, in 1833 two tithe proctors were murdered in County Cork, with a number of women being involved in the murder, which was particularly brutal.[4] [. . . M]any of the agrarian outrages which occurred in pre-famine Ireland were carried out by groups of individuals with the official or unofficial sanction of their local community. In the majority of instances, such disturbances reflected resistance to imposed economic changes by communities whose structures of economic interdependence encouraged group action. Such activities were generally conservative and sought to preserve the status quo concerning the group's particular economic arrangements.[5] [. . .] Though most of the violent activity was carried through by men, women were not barred from such activity. [. . .]

Election mobs, as K. Theodore Hoppen has shown, offered those without a formal political voice a variety of roles within the world of politics.[6] He has shown that women could achieve local political influence. For example, a Miss Forrest of the Gort Hotel in County Galway was described in 1872 as the MP Sir William Gregory's 'right hand man'.[7] Anne Brien was a Dungarvan mob leader in 1868; the Claddagh fishwives constituted guards of honour for Michael Morris in Galway in 1872; and there is ample evidence that numbers of women negotiated their husbands' election bribes.[8] [. . .]

Women's enthusiasm at election time often attracted commentary from public officials, particularly when they became involved in riots. Women were noted, in the pre- and post-famine periods, for taking a prominent part in such disorders. Perhaps poorer women found the riots one way of asserting their needs in a society which allowed them no formal political voice. [. . .] Women were observed with banners and placards supporting or denouncing particular candidates, and were also to be found in large numbers at political demonstrations. For example, a demonstration for the release of Fenian prisoners took place in Drogheda in 1868 and it was noted that 'women had their bonnets trimmed in green, or their hair bound in the national colour. From their necks flowed thin stripes of the green silk, in almost every instance some portion of their dress was rendered conspicuous by the introduction of the prevailing colour.'[9] Women were thus making a visible public display of political activism. Disenfranchised women were as adept as disenfranchised men at utilising whatever power they had, through rioting, accepting bribes, demonstrating and becoming involved in violent activities to affect the political climate of the period. They expressed allegiance to causes, such as Fenianism, through these public displays. They heckled and rioted at election times and in the process contributed to the vibrancy of political life. Such women were not involved in any way in developing a feminist agenda of action. But, in terms of the assertion of a female presence and its display in demonstrations and riots, these women offered more of a challenge to assumptions about the female role, and female behaviour, than did the first women voters of the twentieth century. As Hoppen notes, such activity also offered women far more political opportunities than the suffrage campaign ever would.

Apart from being involved in riots and mobs at elections, women were also prominent in the food riots which occurred throughout the century. During the Great Famine in particular, such action was necessary to stave off starvation. [. . .] Rising unemployment and increasing food prices led to hundreds of men, women and children venting their anger on local landlords and relief committees. A large crowd of men, women and children, for example, marched into Macroom in County Cork in September 1846, striking terror into the townspeople and shop-keepers.[10] [. . .] Similar rioting was to occur at other times of crisis. [. . .]

When associated with nationalist uprisings of the last century, such as those involving the Young Irelanders, or the Fenians, women are generally seen in symbolic terms and rarely acknowledged as playing an active role in the practical or theoretical formulations of these organisations. The structure of many of these organisations was laden with culturally constructed concepts of gender, which in turn helped to define clear gender specific roles. [. . .] Women were not ignored in these organisations but they were kept in a subordinate role. Within the Young Ireland movement, women such as Ellen Mary Downing, Mary Eva Kelly, Jane Francesca Elgee and others played a role in helping to create a sense of national identity. Whilst helping to create this identity, the writers were also consciously or unconsciously appealing to specific gender constructions. Ellen Downing, for example, writing in 1848, appealed to Irish women, as consumers, to support Irish industry. 'I have striven,' she noted, 'with my weak endeavours to work for Ireland, because she is my country and 'twas right to love and serve her. Won't you begin too, and let us all work together? [. . .] and if all of us would unite, it would be a great step towards nationhood.'[11] This attempt at politicising women's purchasing power was reminiscent of campaigns urged by members of anti-slavery organisations in Ireland and dates back to the late eighteenth century. Boycotting British goods was not just a symbolic act; it was also an attempt to encourage native industry.

Women played a role, not only in creating a sense of national identity through their writings, but also through the practical support which they gave to these organisations. Women, for example, carried despatches between the local leaders of the Fenian movement in the 1860s.[12] In October 1865, a group of women formed the Ladies' Committee to aid the families of imprisoned Fenians and that work continued until 1872, when a general amnesty was announced for the prisoners.[13] The organisational pattern of men's and women's leadership roles was not equal in these nationalist societies. Equality between men and women was rarely advocated. Where women's groups were affiliated to male groups, they tended to be placed in an hierarchical relationship to the male society. We need to look no further than the Land League and the Ladies' Land League to see this in action.[14] Many women accepted subordination and the attendant roles they were expected to play as natural, but others such as Anna Parnell created modified positions of authority for themselves.

The Ladies' Land League was established in New York in October 1880 for the purpose of collecting money for the Land League. On 31 January 1881, Anna

Parnell presided over the first official meeting of the Ladies' Land League in Dublin. From that time until its formal dissolution on 10 August 1882, the women of the League raised funds, oversaw the housing of evicted tenants and took a very visible role in the public and political life of the country. [. . .] It does appear that leadership within branches was confined to the middle classes, but it is also clear that peasant women played a part in protests organised by the League. [. . .] Women who involved themselves in the Ladies' Land League had to act against prevailing ideas of women's place. The famous pronouncement of Archbishop McCabe, telling the clergy in his diocese not to admit these women to sodalities, placed Irish women in subordination to the Church and advocated their removal from politics.[15] [. . .]

Public discussion on women's role in the Ladies' Land League asserted that the rightful place for women was in the home, and that their involvement was a temporary measure, resulting from extraordinary circumstances. It appears that the women of the Ladies' Land League were predominantly Catholic. Catholic women were more active in nationalist organisations than in societies or groups which organised and campaigned for social change, a fact which may be linked with their relative inactivity in philanthropic organisations. They appear to have been more willing to become politically involved through nationalism than through social activism. [. . .]

The patriarchal structure of society led naturally to women's subordination and to their exclusion from the body politic. Women in nineteenth-century Ireland were denied a legal and political identity. Single women and widows (*femme sole*) had full legal capacity, but married women were legally dependent on their husbands (*femme covert*). The control of women's property through the idea of 'coverture' and the increasing implementation of primogeniture in post-famine society significantly affected women's economic and political claims. The state, through legislation, reinforced traditional gender roles for men and women and thus prevented equality. From 1857 women lobbied parliament in an attempt to alter the property laws, but change was slow in coming. Discrimination in the area of property rights led women to campaign, not only for changes in these laws, but also for the right to make political claims based on property qualifications. This formed the basis of their claim to the vote and thus political equality with men.

Protestant middle-class women created a political identity for themselves in the nineteenth century based on ideas of civic duty, just as peasant women had created their political identity through ideas of communal rights. Political organisation by middle-class women was more formal and structured than that of peasant women. Philanthropic activity provided middle-class women with an enhanced public role in society and a number of women philanthropists entered the public world of politics through their charitable work. [. . .]

Some of the earliest formations of [gender] difference can be discerned in the anti-slavery societies which were organised by Irish women from at least the 1830s.[16] The information available on anti-slavery societies is quite scant, but the committees of those societies for which we have information were composed almost entirely of women.[17] [. . .I]t appears, from some of the available membership lists, that the majority of members were Quakers, and Quaker women were to the fore in campaigning for women's rights in Ireland during the nineteenth century.

The primary objective of these anti-slavery societies was to raise the consciousness of the Irish people to the horrors of slavery. To this end, some societies annually distributed thousands of copies of a leaflet entitled 'Address to emigrants' to emigrant offices in Dublin, Belfast, Cork and Derry. The dubious effect of such a paper blitz was noted in an annual report of 1860, when the committee was obliged to 'regret to acknowledge that hitherto our Irish emigrants have done small credit to the land of their birth and have generally thrown their influence into the pro-slavery side.'[18] They also invited speakers from America to address the Irish public on the issues of slavery. An anti-slavery petition presented to Queen Victoria in 1838 was signed by 75,000 Irish women.[19]

[. . .] The debates concerning women's roles and status in Ireland were not formulated in a vacuum and were affected, amongst other things, by debates occurring in the English women's movement. The immediate connecting point for some of the views being expressed was the National Association for the Promotion of Social Science. When Isabella Tod, the pioneer of most feminist organisations of nineteenth-century Ireland, first entered public life at the age of 31, it was under the auspices of the National Association for the Promotion of Social Science, which held its annual meeting of 1867 in Belfast. [. . .] It was this association, Tod later wrote, which gave her her first experience 'of direct political effort for a social purpose, and [I] was also first led by it to speak in public.'[20] From this meeting, Tod undertook the formation of the first consciously feminist group in nineteenth-century Ireland when she organised a small committee to press for changes in the married women's property laws. Shortly afterwards Tod also instituted committees to actively campaign for improvements in the educational opportunities, at both secondary and university levels, available to women.[21] These societies and committees were consciously political. [. . .]

The demand for suffrage was the principal means whereby women fought for political involvement on the same terms as men in the late nineteenth and early twentieth centuries. A sizeable majority of those women who began the suffrage campaign in Ireland had activist roots in various philanthropic organisations. Tod, for example, established the first suffrage society in the north of Ireland in 1872, and Haslam organised a similar society in Dublin in 1876. The demand for enfranchisement in nineteenth-century Ireland was grounded in one principle — equal treatment of men and women. These Irish suffragists also believed that reform was achievable only in stages. The methods used were 'genteel'. Drawing-room meetings, petitions, letters and the like, were the means preferred to lobby politicians or win public favour. [. . .] The suffrage issue in nineteenth-century Ireland received little widespread support. Membership of the two suffrage organisations remained small. [. . .] A number of issues prevented the suffrage cause from achieving wider support. There was little public interest in suffrage. The Land War had overtaken the country in the 1880s, and the Ladies' Land League had caused controversy over women's public role. Suffragists of the nineteenth century expected the democratic procedures of petitioning and lobbying to advance their cause. They did not recognise the extent to which party divisions would hamper the passage of the requisite legislation. Suffragists generally did not ally themselves to any one party. However, the introduction of the Home Rule Bills forced some Irish women activists to associate themselves with either the Liberal Unionist or Conservative camps.

The introduction of Gladstone's first Home Rule Bill in 1886 had a profound impact on a number of women in Ireland. In Belfast, Isabella Tod reacted with horror to the bill, seeing in it the seeds of the destruction of all her work. Tod, on the announcement of the bill, organised a Liberal Women's Unionist Association. [. . .] Anna Haslam, also a staunch unionist, established a branch of the Women's Liberal Unionist Association in Dublin. [. . .] In 1893, a memorial addressed to Queen Victoria opposing Home Rule had 103,000 female signatures. Another petition sent at the same time from Ulster women had 145,000 signatures.[22] If there was a mass movement of women in nineteenth-century Ireland, it was to be found amongst unionist rather than nationalist or suffrage women.

Unionist women were extremely adept at organising themselves, a fact that has been little recognised by historians. This involved lobbying, mass letter-writing, petitions to Queen and parliament, public speeches, with Tod even taking to the election campaign trail in England to support the Liberal Unionist candidate and suffrage supporter, Leonard Courtney.[23] By the 1890s women were certainly expressing strong political preferences as to how they expected their country to be governed. [. . .] That Irish women were as affected by the Home Rule issue as English women is clear from the petitions they organised. Some Irish women found expression for their political convictions in the Conservative Party, through involvement in the Primrose League. The League, organised in England in 1883, had a number of branches in Ireland, and women appear to have played a significant role within these. In Cork, for example, Lady Mary Aldworth was convenor of the Mitchelstown branch of the organisation, while her sister-in-law held the same position in Bandon.[24] [. . .]

There were other organisations and societies which claimed the allegiance of women during the period of the suffrage campaign. By the end of the nineteenth century vigorous campaigning, mainly by women involved in the suffrage issue, secured a place for women in local government. Women began to seek admittance to workhouses as visitors soon after the establishment of the poor law system in the 1830s. It is difficult to gauge the extent of philanthropic women's involvement in these institutions. It was not until 1880 that the North Dublin Union Board of Guardians allowed Catholic and Protestant women to 'visit the sick of their own persuasion'.[25] [. . .] By 1899, the government officially recognised that women did play an important role as visitors to the workhouse. In that year, the Local Government Board requested that all workhouses which boarded out children should form ladies' committees to oversee the boarding-out system, and by 1900 there were fifteen such committees in existence.[26] Women played a key role in the Irish Workhouse Association (1897) and the Philanthropic Reform Association (1896), two of the few charitable organisations in which men and women had an equal share in management. Both organisations lobbied to bring about changes in the workhouse system. [. . .] It was not, however, until 1896 that a bill was passed which allowed women with certain property qualifications to serve as poor law guardians. [. . .]

Women, through the 1898 Local Government Act, also won the right to vote and sit on district councils, but it was not until 1911 that Irish women could become county councillors. Haslam was to write in 1898 that the passing of the act represented 'the most significant political revolution that has taken place in the history of Irish women'.[27] [. . .]

Local politics in nineteenth-century Ireland provided the only continuous and effective channel through which nationalist and unionist politicians could exert practical power. Local government thus constituted a key forum for the development of political ideology and was a primary means of distributing power amongst political elites. [. . .] The Local Government Act of 1898 established elected county councils to conduct county administration, rural and urban district councils, and poor law boards. It represented a major alteration in local administrative structures and, at county level in particular, heralded a wholesale transfer of power to the Catholic majority, excluding, of course, the Ulster counties. The eligibility of women to stand as councillors and their impact in the council chamber has gone unremarked by historians.

This brief survey of women's political involvement shows the diversity and range of activity by women which crossed class boundaries. [. . .] Clearly women's political involvement was substantial. That historians of Irish politics need to accept the participation of women as a significant aspect of political life seems beyond doubt. Once their contribution is incorporated, a more complete picture of Irish political history will emerge.

Notes

1   See the comments by Mary E. Daly, 'Women and labour: margins to mainstream?', *Saothar*, 19, 1994, p. 70.

2   Some women had the municipal franchise in the townships of Blackrock and Dun Laoghaire, as a result of special charters. Women in Belfast acquired the municipal franchise in 1887. [. . .]

3   For accounts of women's involvement in parliamentary politics through canvassing and petitions see Mary O'Dowd, 'Women and politics, *c.* 1500–1850', *Field Day Anthology of Irish Writing*, 4 (forthcoming). [. . .]

4   See reports of the case in *The Constitution or Cork Advertiser*, 28 March, 24 August 1833.

5   [. . .] James Donnelly Jr., 'The Rightboy movement 1785–8', *Studia Hibernica*, 17/18, 1977–8, pp. 120–202. [. . .]

6   K. Theodore Hoppen, *Elections, Politics and Society in Ireland 1832–1885*, Oxford, 1984, pp. 406–8.

7   Galway county election petition, H.C. 1872 (241–1), xlviii, 539, cited in Hoppen, *Elections*, p. 406.

8   *Waterford Mail*, 18 September 1868: *Report from the Select Committee on the Newry Borough Election Petition*, H.C. 1833 (76), x, 612, cited in Hoppen, *Elections*, p. 406.

9   *The Banner of Ulster*, 24 August 1869.

10   James S. Donnelly Jr., *Landlord and Tenant in Nineteenth-Century Ireland*, London, 1973, p. 89.

11   Anonymous typescript, 'Women of Young Ireland' (National Library of Ireland, MS 10906). [. . .]

12   Report of a lecture by James Reidy on 'The influence of the Irish woman', *The Gaelic American*, 24 March 1906.

13   *The Irishman*, 28 October 1865.

14   Jane McL. Côté, *Fanny and Anna Parnell: Ireland's Patriot Sisters*, Dublin, 1991, pp. 130–219.

15   *Freeman's Journal*, 12 March 1881.

16   For more information on these societies see Maria Luddy, *Women and Philanthropy in Nineteenth-Century Ireland*, Cambridge, 1995, pp. 64–6. [. . .]

17   For information on these societies see Report of the Hibernian Ladies' Negroes' Friend Society, 1833; Catherine Elizabeth Alma, *An Appeal from the Dublin Ladies' Association*, Dublin, 1837. [. . .]

18   Annual Report, Dublin Ladies' Anti-Slavery Society, 1860, p. 5.

19   Richard S. Harrison, 'Irish Quaker perspectives on the anti-slavery movement', *The Journal of the Friends' Historical Society*, 56/2, 1991, p. 115.

20   *Englishwoman's Review*, 15 January 1897, pp. 58–63.

21   For more information on Tod see Maria Luddy, 'Isabella M. S. Tod, 1836–1896', in Mary Cullen and Maria Luddy (eds), *Women, Power and Consciousness in Nineteenth-Century Ireland: Eight Biographical Studies*, Dublin, 1995, pp. 197–230.

22   Anon., 'Irish women and home rule', *The Englishwomen's Review*, 16 October 1893.

23   Luddy, 'Isabella Tod', p. 222. See also *Londonderry Sentinel*, 21 March 1893.

24   Ian d'Alton, 'Keeping faith: an evocation of the Cork Protestant character, 1820–1920', in Patrick O'Flanagan and Cornelius Buttimer (eds), *Cork: History and Society*, Dublin, 1993, p. 770.

25   Cited in *The Englishwoman's Review*, 15 April 1880, pp. 172–3.

26   Laura Stephens, 'Irish workhouses', in J. P. Smyth (ed.), *Social Service Handbook*, Dublin, 1901, p. 79.

27   Anna Haslam, 'Irishwomen and the Local Government Act', *The Englishwoman's Review*, 239, 15 October 1898.

Chapter 5

Rosemary Cullen Owens

■ from **VOTES FOR WOMEN**, *Labour History News*, 9, summer 1993, pp. 15–19

[. . .]

DURING THE NINETEENTH CENTURY a series of movements emerged in England and Ireland aimed at improving the social, economic and political status of women. Similar movements emerged throughout Europe and the USA. Demands for better educational and employment opportunities for single, middle-class women usually provided a springboard for a series of further demands, including property and child-custody rights for married women, female representation on public boards and local authorities, the right to vote in local elections, and ultimately the right to the parliamentary vote. [. . .]

Two important factors contributed to the emergence of a vocal women's campaign during the nineteenth century: the consolidation of a strong middle class, allied to the gradual democratisation of local and national government. The franchise reform acts of 1832, 1868 and 1884 significantly shifted the power structure within the UK from the wealthy landowning and aristocratic classes, to 'newly rich' industrialist and professional groups. Despite the added enfranchisement of many urban and rural workers towards the end of the century, the parliamentary vote retained two major disabilities: it was still property based, and excluded all women. It was the 1832 Reform Act which had specifically introduced sex discrimination into electoral qualifications, with the use of the words 'male persons'. So the campaign for women's suffrage must be viewed against a backdrop of ever-widening male eligibility for the vote, with no recognition of equal rights for women with similar qualifications.

There were strong Irish connections with the early development of the campaign for women's suffrage. In 1825 William Thompson from Cork, socialist and pioneer of the co-operative movement, and Anna Wheeler, daughter of a Protestant cleric and a godchild of Henry Grattan, co-authored the first publication explicitly demanding women's franchise, pointing out that 'all women and particularly women living with men in marriage [. . .] having been reduced by the want of political rights to a stage of helplessness and slavery [. . .] are more in need of political rights than any other portion of human beings'.

This was written in a context where a women's property became her husband's on marriage, and she had custody rights over her children only until the age of seven years – a situation that remained legal until the 1870s. In 1866 John Stuart Mill presented the first petition seeking female suffrage to the House of Commons. Twenty-five Irish women were among the signatories, including Anna Haslam from Youghal, Co. Cork. The following year Mill attempted an amendment to the new Representation of the People Act, suggesting the word 'man' be replaced by the word 'person'. The amendment was defeated, but ensured the first Commons debate on the issue of female suffrage.

In 1876 Anna Haslam and her husband, Thomas, formed the first Irish suffrage society – the Dublin Women's Suffrage Association. Thomas Haslam had, in 1874, published the first Irish suffrage journal, the *Women's Advocate*. Anna and her husband were active in all aspects of the early women's movement, leading Frank Sheehy Skeffington to describe them in 1912 as 'the pioneers of feminism in Ireland'. Like its founders, most early members of the new association were Quakers. Both men and women could become members, and as the association expanded outside Dublin, its name was changed to the Irish Women's Suffrage and Local Government Association (IWSLGA). The IWSLGA was strictly non-militant in its methods and sought to influence public opinion by use of petitions, meetings and letters to the press. It agitated for reform of all the various legal and social measures discrimi-nating against women, paying particular emphasis to improved educational opportunities for women. The society also devoted much time and effort to agita-tion for married women's property rights, and the repeal of the Contagious Diseases Acts, which regulated prostitution.

[. . .T]he IWSLGA initially sought the extension of poor-law guardianship and the local government vote to qualified women. Under the poor-law system, extended to Ireland in 1838, Irish women rate-payers could elect poor-law guardians on the same terms as men but, unlike their English sisters, could not serve as poor law guardians. Similarly, Irish women householders (with localised exceptions) were not entitled to the municipal franchise enjoyed by their English counterparts. The IWSLGA argued that attainment of these lesser franchises was essential if women were, [. . .] to gain experience in public affairs, while simul-taneously proving the value of their contribution. Following an 1883 act which declared canvassing and election work would no longer be salaried, women suddenly found themselves very much in demand as unpaid party workers! In the next couple of years women's auxiliaries of the main political parties were formed, but it soon became clear that it was women's usefulness, rather than acceptance of their equality, that prompted this development. By including women in party work and using them as canvassers during elections, such organisations temporarily diverted attention away from suffrage demands. Significantly between 1886 and 1892 the issue was not discussed once in the House of Commons. The IWSLGA was not idle; its annual reports note that twenty-seven petitions in 1886 and seven-teen in 1890 had been sent to the House of Commons. When attempts were made to include women in the 1884 suffrage extension, Prime Minister Gladstone rejected such an amendment on the grounds that the proposed law was as much as could be safely carried. Increasingly the issue of women's suffrage came to be viewed in the context of party politics, a development which continued into the militant stage of the campaign.

In 1896 a bill was passed which allowed Irish women fulfilling certain property qualifications to serve as poor law guardians. There was some criticism of the bill in both houses, one MP declaring his opposition to bisexualism in public life. [. . .] Two years later the Local Government (Ireland) Act 1898, granted Irish women with certain property qualifications the local government vote, despite the fears of some MPs. One warned that if women ever got into parliament the end of the country was nigh, and another stated his objections to petticoat government, declaring the vast majority of women recognised they were not fit to govern in that house and did not wish to do so. In the spring of 1889 eighty-five women were elected as poor-law guardians, thirty-one of these were also elected as rural district councillors and a further four were elected as urban district councillors. So after twenty-two years of activity the IWSLGA had both reason to be pleased and grounds for optimism. The organisation pointed out that not just those elected, but also the new female electorate had participated in a new significant political experience. Like male home rulers, women would later point to their competency in local government as justification for greater responsibility. Events would show, however, that women could not become complacent about their new-won political rights. In 1903 attempts to have women poor-law guardians co-opted rather than elected, 'to relieve them from the worry and turmoil of a popular election', reinforced the belief of suffragists that women must obtain the parliamentary vote to ensure maintenance of existing rights. The IWSLGA now set its aim on attaining that goal.

With the new century came a generation of women activists, many of whom had benefited from the work of pioneers such as Anna Haslam, particularly in education, where a series of significant gains had been made from the 1870s. Under the provisions of the Intermediate Education Act 1878, and the Royal University Act 1879, boys and girls competed on equal terms, although still educated separately. To this end a number of girls' colleges were established, specifically to prepare girls for such competition. In the early years of this century, Trinity College, Dublin, the National University of Ireland, Dublin and Queen's University, Belfast, opened their doors to women. These important developments resulted in a new body of educated articulate young women impatient for change. Initially many of these joined the existing IWSLGA. A number travelled to London to take part in militant suffrage demonstrations, some of whom were subsequently imprisoned for their actions. Impatience with the conservative methods of the IWSLGA, admiration for the militant tactics of Emmeline Pankhurst's Women's Social and Political Union (WPSU), and recognition of the need for a distinctly independent Irish suffrage society, led Hanna Sheehy Skeffington and a group of her friends to form a new militant suffrage society: the Irish Women's Franchise League (IWFL), in Dublin in 1908. The new society was avowedly militant but strictly non-party. It aimed to obtain the parliamentary vote for Irish women on the same terms as men had it, or might have it in the future. This latter point was particularly relevant in an Ireland immersed in talk of home rule. One of its founders, Margaret Cousins, explained:

> We were as keen as men on the freedom of Ireland, but we saw the men clamouring for amendments which suited their own interests, and made no recognition of the existence of women as fellow citizens. We women were convinced that anything which improved the status of women would improve, not hinder, the coming of real national self-government.

The IWFL was not the only sign of renewed interest and vigour on the issue of women's suffrage. Between 1908 and 1912 a number of other smaller suffrage societies were established throughout the country to cater for particular regional, religious or political groups. To co-ordinate the work of these groups Louie Bennett and Helen Chenevix, in 1911, formed the Irish Women's Suffrage Federation (IWSF). Societies from Belfast, Galway, Birr, Derry, Lisburn, Cork and Waterford were among fifteen societies which affiliated to the Federation. It was non-party and non-militant, although some members were occasionally involved in militancy. Louie Bennett (later to be prominent in the Irish Women Workers' Union) formed the Irish Women's Reform League (IWRL) as a Dublin-based branch of the Federation. In addition to seeking votes for women, the IWRL focused attention on the social and economic position of women workers. These various suffrage societies, while catering for women of diverse social, political and religious background, were united in their aim of votes for women on the same terms as men, differing principally on their choice of tactics. While the militant IWFL admired the tactics and courage of the WSPU, they were determined not to allow their association to be run by any other than Irish women, claiming they were quite capable of running their own affairs, and knew the Irish situation and psychology best.

In 1912 an Irish suffrage paper was produced by Frank Sheehy Skeffington and James Cousins. The *Irish Citizen* was designed to cater for all suffragists in Ireland, militant and non-militant. Circulated throughout the thirty-two counties, the paper acted as an important link between the various suffrage societies in Ireland. Its editorials and articles kept readers informed of current national developments on the issue of women's suffrage, as well as covering broader aspects of feminism and the struggle for women's rights. The paper was published weekly from 1912 until Sheehy Skeffington's shooting in 1916. Thereafter it was published monthly until 1920, with Hanna Sheehy Skeffington and Louie Bennett its main editors.

From 1910 onwards there were a number of attempts to introduce a women's suffrage bill in the House of Commons. The British Liberal Prime Minister, Herbert Asquith, was known to be keenly anti-suffragist. The Irish parliamentary party held the balance of power, and despite the commitment of some Irish MPs to the principle of female suffrage, fears of endangering imminent home-rule legislation were sufficiently strong that the party united behind Redmond in defeating all such bills. When Redmond organised a national convention in Dublin, April 1912, to consider the Home Rule Bill, women were excluded from the meeting. A mass meeting of Irish women was held in the Mansion House, Dublin, to demand the inclusion of women's suffrage in the Home Rule Bill. Women trade unionists and nationalists joined suffrage campaigners from all over Ireland in this demonstration of solidarity. Among those on the platform were Constance Markiewicz,

Dr Kathleen Lynn, Jenny Wyse Power, Delia Larkin, Helen Chenevix, and Professor Mary Hayden. When resolutions from this meeting to Irish and English politicians were ignored, the IWFL decided to initiate militant action. [. . .]

In June 1912, Hanna Sheehy Skeffington and seven other IWFL members were arrested and imprisoned for breaking windows in government offices in Dublin. From this time up to the outbreak of war in 1914, there would be thirty-five convictions of women for suffrage militancy in Ireland. Twenty-two of these incidents took place in Dublin, the remainder in Belfast and Lisburn. Twelve women went on hunger strike while in prison. Hanna Sheehy Skeffington later wrote, 'Hunger strike was then a new weapon – had we but known we were the pioneers in a long line'. Forcible feeding of suffrage prisoners was not automatically introduced, as in England. In fact, the only suffrage prisoners forcibly fed in Ireland were two English women members of the WPSU who had demonstrated against Asquith during his visit to Dublin in 1912 promoting his Home Rule Bill. [. . .] Their actions unleashed the most virulent public demonstrations against any group of women thought to be suffragette. A meeting of the IWFL being held close to Liberty Hall at the same time as Asquith's Theatre Royal meeting had to be abandoned on police advice, the women receiving a police escort to their tram. Numerous incidents of mob violence and threats against women occurred, moving the *Irish Independent* to report that, 'Every woman respectably dressed went in danger of being singled out by the mob as a suffragette, and a state of panic prevailed.' The paper reported cases where women's clothes were almost torn from them before police could intervene. Constance Markievicz had to take shelter in Liberty Hall from a booing crowd, and the home of Jenny Wyse Power was surrounded by hostile crowds. For some weeks after, all suffrage meetings were attended by booing and egg-throwing crowds. All the main papers joined in condemning such activities, the *Leader* taking its own inimitable line, when it argued, 'These people however eccentric they may be [. . .] should not be treated to physical violence'. Hanna Sheehy Skeffington later recounted how suffrage campaigners brought public opinion to their side:

> Women speakers who could hold their own, who could lift their voices in the Fifteen Acres, meeting heckling on their own ground, being good-humoured and capable of keeping their temper under bombardments of rotten eggs, over-ripe tomatoes, bags of flour, stinking chemicals, gradually earned respect and due attention.

At this time of low morale among suffragists, as a mark of solidarity for the women, James Connolly travelled from Belfast to Dublin to speak at the IWFL's weekly meeting, an action long and greatly appreciated by the women. Also members of his union provided protection at suffrage meetings during this troubled time. Pressure of public opinion, newspaper editorials and articles, combined with police activity and arrests eventually brought an end to this violent episode. [. . .] Forcible feeding had been widely used for suffrage prisoners in England, and was much criticised. To solve the problem of hunger-striking prisoners a new act was introduced in April, 1913 – quickly nicknamed the 'Cat and Mouse Act'. This act allowed for the temporary release of prisoners on hunger strike until they were fit to be recommitted. Their period of release did not count as part of their sentence, and so most of the women so reimprisoned immediately resumed their hunger strike, [and] the act soon became the subject of much criticism. In Ireland the act was only partially enforced: women were released under the act when their health was considered in danger, but were not reimprisoned. [. . .]

The outbreak of war in 1914, and the separatist spirit leading to the rising of 1916, split the ranks of suffrage campaigners. Sharp differences arose whether national freedom or individual freedom should take priority, the formation of Cumann na mBan in support of the Volunteers being particularly divisive. Similarly, the pacifist commitment of many suffragists caused bitter division between the groups on the outbreak of war in August 1914 and later with the struggle for Irish independence. A rising spirit of militarism left women such as Louie Bennett much disquieted, not reassured by MacDonagh's promise that it would not be used against their own people. Women's groups played a large role in the movement against conscription in 1918. Despite such divisions, most Irish suffrage societies remained active during and after the war, in sharp contrast to England, where all suffrage activities ceased in August 1914.

When the Representation of the People Act was passed in January 1918, Irish politicians tried to postpone its implementation in Ireland. Both Unionists and members of the Irish Parliamentary Party feared the effect of an increased electorate in the next general election, justifiably as events proved. While criticising the 'odious age restriction' the *Irish Citizen* welcomed the fact that the sex barrier in politics had at last been broken. Proof of this fact was soon to hand, with women suddenly in demand as speakers on party platforms. No longer would the parliamentary party advertise meetings with notices which stated 'Public admitted – ladies excluded'. The Labour Party was the first to nominate a woman candidate for the 1918 General Election – Louie Bennett – although she declined to stand. Constance Markiewicz and Winifred Carney were the only women candidates in the December election, the *Irish Citizen* commenting, 'it looks as if Irishmen (even Republicans) need teaching in this matter'. With her election Markiewicz became the first woman MP elected to Westminster, although she never took her seat. While pleased with this historic achievement Irish suffrage campaigners were not blind to its limitations, the IWFL noting prophetically:

> Under the new dispensation the majority sex in Ireland has secured one representative. This is the measure of our boasted sex equality. The lesson the election teaches is that reaction has not died out with the Irish Party – and the IWFL which has been so faithful to feminist ideals, must continue to fight and expose reaction in the future as in the past.

Unfortunately there were to be many such lessons learnt over the following decades. While short-term gains were evident during the revolutionary period, in the long term, attainment of the vote did not affect the role of women in Irish society. Adult suffrage had been included in the 1916 proclamation, and in the spirit of the proclamation was included in the Irish Free State constitution of 1922.

Under the provisions of this act, all citizens of twenty-one years were enfranchised. This was to be the last piece of progressive legislation affecting women for some fifty years. [. . .]

Chapter 6

Eibhlin Breathnach

■ from **WOMEN AND HIGHER EDUCATION
IN IRELAND (1879–1914)**, *The Crane Bag*, 4, 1980,
pp. 47–54

[. . .]

A NOTABLE TREND IN POST-FAMINE Ireland was the growth of the number of single women in the [female] population, rising from 43.3 per cent in 1861 to 48.26 per cent in 1911.[1] Many factors accounted for this trend: the changing pattern of farming, the relentless inroads caused by emigration, the demands of a dowry which often limited the option of marriage to one daughter in a family, and the rising marriage age. [. . .] For the middle- and upper-middle-class urban woman, convention dictated that work and career were no part of her life even for those who failed to marry or enter a convent, in which case the family was expected to provide support.

The education offered to middle-class girls in schools and by governesses alike reflected society's expectations as to their future. It consisted of English, history, geography, arithmetic, French (sometimes Italian and German), music, religious instruction and needlework. The object was to equip girls with accomplishments considered suitable for young ladies. The spirit was unmistakably aristocratic, the useful was spurned in preference for the ornamental. The fact that fate might not necessarily confer security in the shape of a husband or comfortable legacy was ignored. Yet profligacy, bankruptcy, illness, an untimely death could with frightening ease throw a woman back on her own resources. Circumscribed by notions of respectability and limited by an inadequate education, only bleak alternatives presented themselves: 'to be a governess, to stitch or to die'.[2]

The plea for better education arose from an awareness of the 'plight of [. . .] unemployed women [. . .] fading with ennui, or starving, dying or living in degradation worse than death'.[3] The first steps were taken in England with the founding of the Queen's Institute in London in 1841, which offered a course of general education to governesses in an effort to improve their status. Through the meeting of the Social Science Congress in Dublin in 1861 and Belfast in 1866, these ideas spread and were enthusiastically taken up by a small group of middle- and upper-class Protestant men and women. The Queen's Institute was founded in Dublin in 1861[4] and the Ladies Institute in Belfast in 1866.[5] Conditions in Ireland proved to be different than those in London and consequently the emphasis lay in providing practical training in order to open up new avenues of employment for the indigent lady. One of the most successful ventures was the Telegraph Class of the Queen's Institute, which became officially recognised as the Post Office Training School for Female Telegraphers in 1873.[6]

[. . .] A more advanced line of thinking which argued for systematic education of girls as a worthy end in itself found expression in the founding of colleges such as Bedford College in London and the inauguration of the High School movement for girls.[7] [. . .] In Belfast, Mrs Byers, among the pioneers of the education movement, founded the High School for Girls, better known by its later title, Victoria College, to give girls an education similar to that bestowed on their brothers.[8] Richard Chenevix Trench, the Church of Ireland Archbishop of Dublin, disseminated the new ideas in Dublin. Under his influence, Mrs Jellicoe (one of the governesses of the Queen's Institute) abandoned her idea of setting up a training school for governesses in favour of the more far-reaching goal of establishing a college, Alexandra College, for 'the higher education of girls' in 1866.[9] [. . .]

English influences continued to be of crucial importance to the developments in Ireland. Its apogee was reached with the passing of the Intermediate Education Act, 1878 and the Royal University Act in 1879 which, while effecting fundamental changes in Irish education in general, caused a revolution in female education. Girls' schools, for the first time in Ireland, could compete on equal terms with boys in a public exam and thereby earn much needed financial remuneration. [. . .]

Alexandra and Victoria College began to prepare girls for the Intermediate exams in the company of a few convent schools, mainly those under the Dominican and Loreto orders. The prejudice against girls [Catholic and Protestant] presenting themselves for public exams on equal terms with boys was not easily dispelled. Mrs Byers (Victoria College), commented in evidence to the Endowed Schools Commission in 1886 that 'there is a prejudice – an undefined prejudice against sending girls to the Intermediate exam'.[10] As late as 1895, the Bishop of Limerick in his prize-day speech in Laurel Hill boasted, 'we have no girl graduates here, nor even Intermediate students but we are working away on old Catholic rules and principles and I am not aware that we lose anything thereby'.[11]

The notion of women competing for university degrees encountered much greater opposition. [. . .] Hence, the first nine women graduates in 1884 excited much attention and curiosity. Mary Hayden, herself a second-year student of the Royal University wrote an account of their graduation in her diary: 'the long procession of hooded and gowned male graduates [. . .] the girls coming last. As soon as they appeared at the door, there was a burst of applause . . .'[12] [. . .] Those most closely connected with the women's institutes and the more progressive schools, realising the great need to protect the new position of women's education in the uncertain and often hostile climate in which it had to struggle to develop, came together in Belfast and Dublin in 1883 and set up the Central Association of Schoolmistresses and other Ladies interested in Education (hereafter called CAISM). The new association was formed 'with the object of promoting the Higher Education of Women in Ireland, of affording the means of communication and co-operation between Schoolmistresses and other Ladies interested in Education, and of watching over the interests of girls, especially with regard to Intermediate education and the Royal University'.[13] [. . .]

The problems facing women students were considerable. Few women had the benefit of a good secondary education and all were handicapped by the fact that the existing university colleges were for male students only. Alexandra College set up classes, the Royal College of Surgeons admitted women and gradually other possibilities opened up. Victoria College in Belfast started university classes and, petitioned by the Belfast Ladies Academy, Queen's College Belfast admitted women to its arts classes in 1882;[14] Queen's College Cork followed in 1885[15] and Queen's College Galway in 1888.[16] From the beginning there was a marked preference among women for classes attached to girls' secondary schools; parents seemed to prefer the security of the more sheltered environment and, since the Queen's Colleges offered no tutorial classes, it avoided the need to pay a separate set of fees for this type of teaching.

Women students faced the greatest difficulties in Dublin. The reorganised Catholic University, renamed University College, had been entrusted to the Jesuit Order by the hierarchy. The President, Fr. William Delany SJ, was very conservative in outlook and when asked to admit women to the Fellows lectures, in 1882, refused brusquely.[17] An appeal by the CAISM to the Senate of the Royal University asking them to ensure women undergraduates had access to the university (i.e. Fellows) teaching met with a similar albeit more sympathetic refusal.[18] As a result Alexandra College developed a university department attended by Protestants and those Catholics who were willing to face a Protestant environment.

Fr. Delany's disapproval of mixed education was shared by Dr Salmon, Provost of Trinity College. Trinity had played a leading role in the development of women's education during the 1860s and 1870s by providing special exams for women and through the involvement of the staff and college authorities in the governing and teaching in Alexandra College. The appointment of Dr Salmon as Provost in 1888 halted any extension of benefits to women. The new provost was ultra-conservative and given his considerable authority in the college was in a position to block any change to which he was opposed.

The CAISM chose the occasion of the college tercentenary to request that the much vaunted benefits which Trinity claimed to have conferred on the nation, be extended to the female sex. A memorial signed by 10,500 'Irish-women of the educated classes' was presented to the Board of the College along with three other supporting memorials, two from the Trinity staff and one from prominent clergymen, academics and businessmen.[19] Using the considerable power at its disposal, the Board fought off the attempt to have women admitted as students. The meagre concessions granted after three years of protracted negotiations reveal the deep irrational hostility which the question provoked. Women, under the regulations of 1895, were allowed to sit moderatorship exams but no teaching was made available nor was any prospect of being awarded a degree.[20] [. . .]

Two orders, the Loreto and Dominican orders, had shown particular interest in becoming involved in the provision of higher education. In 1893, the Dominican

St Mary's College and High School for Girls opened. Shortly afterwards, Mother Michael Corcoran set up Loreto College in Stephen's Green and ordered the head-mistresses of all Loreto schools to send their university students to the new college.[21] [. . .]

Renewed interest in the university question resulted in the establishment of two commissions at the turn of the century; the Robertson Commission, 1901–3, was set up with the brief to examine the workings of the Royal University, and the Fry Commission, 1906–7, was appointed to conduct a similar investigation of the affairs of Trinity College. The announcement of the Robertson Commission galvanised the CAISM into action. A request that a woman be appointed as a member of the commission was, despite the English precedent of the Taunton Commission, rejected.[22] Undaunted, the association set about ascertaining the views of their members on the future of women's higher education as well as trying to establish a common front with the Catholic colleges as to the recommendations to be urged upon the commissioners. The replies to the questionnaires to the members led to the establishment of a new association, the Irish Association of Women Graduates and Candidate Graduates (hereafter called the IAWG) to represent the particular viewpoint of women graduates.[23] [. . .]

The report of the Robertson Commission came down strongly on the side of the progressive views expressed by the women's association. Praising the statement of the IAWG as the 'best', the commissioners welcomed this concurrence of views; 'we think', they wrote,

> that women and men should attend the same lectures and pass examinations in the same Colleges and obtain degrees on the same conditions [. . .] the existing women's colleges might easily be converted into residence halls in connection with the University of Dublin or within the constituent colleges in Dublin and Belfast under the reorganised Royal University.[24]

The unanimity of the commissioners' views was confined to the question of women and, in the absence of any agreement as to the future of the general university question, the report was shelved. The recommendation made in the report as regards women was possible because of the unexpected decision of Trinity College to admit women to their lectures and degrees in arts and medicine. Dr Salmon, even more conservative in his views with the passage of time, was still Provost but no longer had undisputed control over the decisions of the Board. [. . .]

The Board's resolution was put into effect in a very literal manner; women were admitted to lectures and degrees but were deliberately and carefully excluded from the corporate aspects of college life. Stringent rules regulating the behaviour of the women undergraduates were drawn up among which was the rule requiring them to be off the college grounds by 6 p.m.[25] Even the allocation of the rooms, just inside the entrance arch, nos. 5 and 6 emphasised their peripheral position. The junior fellows and professors had specifically asked the Board not to extend the privileges of rooms and commons to the college newcomers.[26] The social activities of the women undergraduates were organised along lines parallel with the male clubs and societies, a development totally accepted, as were the rules and regulations, by the women undergraduates and the two women's organisations. In this way the male character of the college was preserved intact, sanctioned by the unexpected collusion of both conservatives and progressives. [. . .]

In 1908 the Irish Universities Act was passed. This established two universities, the National University with three named constituent colleges, Queen's College Cork, Queen's College Galway and University College Dublin, and The Queen's University of Belfast. [. . .] In sharp contrast to the meagre concessions granted in Trinity, women were admitted not only to the teaching and examinations of the new [National] university on an equal footing with men, but were also eligible to hold office on the governing bodies of the constituent colleges as well as being entitled to become members of the Senate. [. . .]

In retrospect, the campaign to win equality of treatment for women in higher education seems to lack the excitement of the parallel suffragette movement. There were no riotous marches, axe throwing, imprisonment with the threat of forcible feeding; instead endless committee meetings, writing memoranda and constant public representation of the female point of view. Yet the seeming ordinariness of this should not obscure its significance. Pursuing public campaigns and representing cases at government commissions were activities hitherto confined to men even where women's interests were involved, a practice which was abandoned when women proved to be equally proficient and adept at advancing their own cause. The aims of the education movement were deliberately set within the social parameters of the day. The goal of wife and motherhood remained unassailed and great importance was attached to reassuring a suspicious public that no social revolution was intended. Yet all these verbal assertions could not hide the significant breaches made by women in the social order. The status of the woman graduate teacher improved, though their financial remuneration continued to lag behind that of their male colleagues — and a brave few ventured into male preserves of medicine and law. A new respectability was conferred on the idea of women working, though prejudice against married women working remained undisturbed. But while career opportunities remained limited, the success of women in university examinations challenged in a fundamental way their allotted position in the patriarchy. [. . .]

The impact of the women graduates was necessarily limited, the number obtaining degrees were small and were all from the middle class. The majority pursued arts, an area considered particularly suited to the female caste of mind. Teaching remained the haven of women in search of employment; while a small number became doctors, the professions remained almost inaccessible, and the rewards commensurate with the highest academic performance eluded women; the doors of the Civil Service remained tightly closed and those of law and medicine were merely breached by a foothold. Yet that foothold, secured by the admission of women on equal terms with men to the three Irish universities, provided a springboard for a later generation of activists, of which the early women were worthy progenitors.

Notes

1   General Report of Census of Ireland 1861, Dublin 1864, vxl; 1911, Athlone 1913, xxvi.
2   N. J. Gossan, *A Plea for Ladies*, Dublin, 1875, p. 16.
3   'Womanhood and its mission', *Dublin University Magazine*, LIII, no. ccxvii, May 1859, p. 699.
4   *Irish Times*, 20 August 1861.
5   *Northern Whig*, 10 August 1866.
6   9th Annual Report of Queen's Institute for Training and Employment of Educated Women, Dublin 1871, p. 11.
7   Josephine Kamm, *Hope Deferred*, London, 1956, p. 261.
8   Report of the Commissioners on University Education in Ireland, 1901–3, iii, p. 60.
9   Isabell Forbes, '1866 and 1906, a memory', *Alexandra College Magazine*, June 1906, p. 4.
10 Education Endowments (Ireland) Commission, Annual Report 1885–6. 257 [C 4903] HC 1886, xxvi.
11 *Freeman's Journal*, 14 July 1895.
12 Diary of Mary T. Hayden, 22 October 1884, National Library, Ms. 16,641.
13 Minutes of the Central Association of Irish Schoolmistresses and other Ladies interested in Education, 28 January 1882 (Mss. in possession of Muriel Jago, Hyde Pk Gdns, Blackrock, Co. Dublin).
14 Council Minutes of Queen's College Belfast, 13, 23 January; 14 March; 10, 19 April, 1883.
15 Report of the President of Queen's College Cork, for the session 1887–8, H.C. 1888 [C 54841] xl, 45.
16 Report of the President of the Queen's College, Galway, for the session 1888–9, [C 5776] xxi.
17 Fr. Thomas Morrissey, SJ, 'Some Jesuit contributions to Irish education' (unpublished thesis for Ph.D. in UCC, p. 568).
18 RUI Senate, 2 February 1883, ii, p. 5.
19 Statement of the Proceedings of the Movement for Admission of Women to Trinity College, Preface by W. G. Brooke, Dublin, 1895.
20 Minutes of the Board of Trinity College Dublin, 24, 29 June 1894, TCD v mun/16.
21 Sion Hill Annals, October 1893, Dominican Archives, Eccles St, p. 191.
22 Central Association of Schoolmistresses and other Ladies interested in Education, Annual Report, 1901, p. 5.
23 *University College: A Page of Irish History*, Dublin, 1930, pp. 463–4. The records of the Irish Association of Women Graduates were destroyed during the 1950s.
24 Report of the Commissioners on University Education in Ireland, 1901–3, i–iii.
25 Companion to Register 1905, TCD v mun 6/4 p. 81.
26 TCD Board minutes, 20 Febuary 1904, TCD v mun 5/18 p. 61.

Chapter 7

Diane Urquhart

■   from 'THE FEMALE OF THE SPECIES IS MORE
DEADLIER THAN THE MALE'? THE ULSTER
WOMEN'S UNIONIST COUNCIL, 1911–40, in Janice
Holmes and Diane Urquhart (eds), *Coming into the Light: the
Work, Politics and Religion of Women in Ulster, 1840–1940*,
Belfast, 1994, pp. 93–123

[. . .]

IN THE PERIOD 1890–1914 British women became involved in party
political work, not for feminist reasons, but for pragmatic ones. The Corrupt
and Illegal Practices Act of 1883, which forbade the payment of political canvassers,
and the extension of the electoral franchise in 1884, encouraged party organisers
to reconsider their electoral strategies. The emergence of women's political associations from the late nineteenth century[1] should therefore be identified with this
background of deviating party systems, and the genesis of an organisational network
which harnessed the energies of party workers, who increasingly were female.
Intrinsically women became a source of voluntary and unpaid political labour. After
1900 women became more politically prominent, volunteering in their thousands
within a relatively short period of time.[2] Although women were excluded from
the main political parties until the extension of the franchise to their sex in 1918,
women's auxiliary associations made their contribution an integral factor in the
political process before this date. The UWUC [Ulster Women's Unionist Council]
can be placed within this context. In the north of Ireland women had been sporad-
ically involved in the nineteenth-century protests against the implementation of
home rule[3] in 1886[4] and in 1893.[5] The institution of a formal body of women
unionists was induced by a heightened sense of crisis following the removal of the
House of Lords power of veto by the Parliament Act of 1911.[6] [. . .]

The inaugural meeting of the organisation was held in Belfast in January 1911,
initiating:

> the beginning of real and solid work and a thorough organising of the
> women of Ulster . . . to begin work at once, to canvass voters, to trace
> removals, and to endeavour to bring every single voter to the poll
> during elections, so that every seat in Ulster shall be won for the Union

. . . the women of Ulster will be in no way behind the men in striving
for so noble a cause.[7]

The UWUC co-operated with the men's Ulster Unionist Council[8] (UUC) in
promoting religious, economic, constitutional and imperial arguments against home
rule. The women were sufficiently politically astute to realise that their 'Council
should urge the Ulster case against Home Rule mainly on social and economic
grounds, by which the charge of Ulster bigotry will be avoided'.[9] [. . .]

The organisation also highlighted a 'women's dimension' to home rule. In
1911 they voiced their opposition to any home-rule bill for Ireland:

> as they know that the civil and religious liberty of the women of Ireland
> and the security of their homes can only be guaranteed under the
> Legislative Union of Great Britain and Ireland.[10]

Indeed, the home, the traditional sphere where a woman's influence was socially
acceptable, featured prominently in the iconography of women's unionism.
Moreover, women's political action was portrayed as an extension of their maternal
and protective responsibilities:

> If our homes are not sacred from the priest under the existing laws,
> what can we expect from a priest-governed Ireland . . . let each woman
> in Ulster do a woman's part to stem the tide of Home Rule . . . the
> Union . . . meant everything to them – their civil and religious liberty,
> their homes and children . . . once the Union was severed there could
> be no outlook in Ulster but strife and bitterness . . . Home was a
> woman's first consideration . . . in the event of Home Rule being
> granted, the sanctity and happiness of home life in Ulster would be
> permanently destroyed.[11]

The council accentuated the point that women and their dependants would ultimately suffer most under home rule, 'for when bad times came and work was scarce
women and children were more severely affected than the men'.[12]

The UWUC rapidly developed into a strong, dynamic and democratic body.
The membership figures bear witness to the fact that the council was not only
popular, but was needed to co-ordinate the activities of unionist women. During
the first month of the council's existence over 4,000 women had joined the West
Belfast branch and by March 1911 women's unionist associations affiliated to the
council had been formed throughout Belfast, Londonderry, Antrim, Armagh,
Tyrone, Fermanagh and Monaghan.[13] Within a year of its establishment the minutes
of the organisation record membership of 40,000–50,000. No further overall
membership figures are available in the council's records, but newspaper coverage
dating from 1913 quotes figures of between 115,000 and 200,000.[14] Membership
of the council was mainly upper and middle class, especially amongst its leaders.
Analysis of presidents clearly reveal the UWUC's social composition: second
Duchess of Abercorn was president 1911–13, succeeded by sixth Marchioness of
Londonderry 1913–19, third Duchess of Abercorn 1919–21, and Lady Cecil Craig

(later Viscountess Craigavon) 1923–42. Similarly, in the period 1911–39 only one of ten vice-presidents was untitled. In Ulster, the rest of Ireland and throughout Britain, women of these classes possessed the time and economic freedom to participate in public life. However, within the council there were no membership restrictions on the basis of social classification. Undoubtedly some working-class women were involved; for instance, it has been alleged that 80 per cent of the West Belfast association of the council were mill workers and shop girls.[15]

The council's appointment of a male organising secretary[16] in 1911 provides the only indicator of any sense of insecurity with regards to their single sex composition. The organisation seemingly experienced no initial learning phase when they were unsure of policy or direction, as four months after the establishment of the council six of its members were in England canvassing electoral support for a unionist candidate and by May 1911 the council's executive sent women speakers around Ireland studying the Irish question at first hand. In their canvassing work the council co-operated with women's unionist associations in England and Scotland, the Primrose League and the Women's Amalgamated Tariff Reform Association. Addressing the political meetings of these organisations, the UWUC focused solely on the Union, as all other questions were believed to be of secondary importance. [. . .]

Unionist leaders were conscious of the importance of maintaining unity and discipline within their ranks to present a favourable public image of Ulster unionism to the English electorate. Consistent attempts were made to demonstrate that unionists were a respectable community with valid reasons for resisting home rule. Illustrative of this was a scheme for the establishment of an Ulster covenant, exemplifying unionist solidarity, self-discipline and determination. As women were barred from signing the male unionists' covenant, the UWUC organised their own declaration with the primary aim of associating unionist women with 'the men of Ulster in their uncompromising opposition to the Home Rule Bill'.[17] The date of 28 September 1912 was proclaimed Ulster Day for the collection of signatures for both the declaration and covenant. The fact that 218,206[18] men signed the covenant, compared to 234,046[19] female signatures on the declaration construes the comparative strength of women's unionism.

The council was also accountable for sending thousands of leaflets and newspapers relating unionist anti-home-rule contentions to Britain, America and the Dominions. The UWUC aimed to enlighten Britain's populace, not only of the impact home rule would have on Ulster, but also to publicise, what unionists believed to be, the 'true' character of Irish nationalists, who:

> were not the kind of half angels which Mr. Redmond had described.
> . . . The Nationalists painted the future of Ireland in glowing colours,
> but the Protestants of the country did not come into the picture [. . .]
> it was a masterpiece of impressionist painting, as the further one stood
> away from it the better it looked.[20]

The didactic element of the women's work was extensive and unrelenting. Working through their philosophy of 'Prevention is better than cure'[21] the council established a literary subcommittee to co-ordinate their huge propagandist workload.[22] By September 1913, 10,000 leaflets and newspapers were being sent weekly to Britain under the auspices of the women's council[23] and by March 1914 literature was forwarded to 14,902 electors in 65 constituencies.[24] Moreover, local associations of the council were coupled with English women's unionist organisations, and by 1912, twenty-one of their thirty-two branches, representing 66 per cent of the UWUC, were involved in this work.[25] Many women unionists were sent from Ulster to work in England and Scotland[26] and by March 1913 nineteen women were permanently based in Britain working as Unionist missionaries.[27] Indeed by the end of this year, 'it was reckoned that not less than 100,000 electors heard the Unionist case from the lips of earnest Ulsterwomen'.[28] [. . .]

Although unionists attempted to focus solely on home rule, the issue of women's suffrage infringed on their concerns during the third home rule crisis. Consistently the UWUC:

> kept the one question of the Union before them pre-eminently. On other questions – [like] women's suffrage . . . they might have and hold different opinions – but on the one question of the Union they had no room for differences – the Union was their one rallying point, and held them together with a force that no varying opinion on lesser subjects would interfere with.[29]

However, it seems that the existence of the council had a positive, though indirect and unintentional, impact on the question of women's enfranchisement. By bringing women into the political arena and initiating extensive political work, the women's council provided a visible illustration of how women could be civically responsible. There were suffragists within the ranks of the women's council,[30] but unionists who also campaigned for the vote increasingly had to develop different political facades and prioritise their own political convictions. However, the women's council was unable to totally evade this issue, as suffragette militancy focusing on unionist-owned property began in Ulster in 1913. [. . .]

Their reluctance to discuss the question of women's enfranchisement continued, as in March 1914, the council's president, Theresa Londonderry requested that the organisation 'took no action [. . .] in connection with the recent deputation of Suffragettes to Sir Edward Carson, as it was considered advisable not to re-open the matter'.[31] The women's council made no further comment on suffrage, concentrating instead on their consequential political work. [. . .]

The whole unionist political campaign was officially suspended for the duration of the war.[32] However, when circumstance rendered inaction dangerous to the unionist cause, the women's council did embark on political work. The organisational machinery of the UWUC remained operative, although their priorities altered. With the outbreak of war the council initially believed that it was their 'duty to see that the families and dependents [of men in military service] are cared for, and that any want and suffering which may result shall be minimised as much as possible'.[33] To fulfil this aim the women's council became engaged in extensive charity work, co-operating with organisations like the Soldiers' and Sailors' Families Association. [. . .]

In the post-war period the political work of the women's council was fully revived, and they expanded their areas of interest. Preceding the establishment of the Northern Ireland Parliament, unionists accepted six-county exclusion for Ulster and not nine counties as originally intended. Partition had vexed the UWUC even during the war. For instance, Lady Dufferin expressed the organisation's anxieties, writing to Lady Theresa Londonderry in July 1916:

> Our women are naturally much upset by the turn things have taken, and are longing to be up and doing [. . .] of course we all feel heart-broken over the proposed partition of Ulster, and are still hoping some better solution of our difficulties may come out of the melting pot.[34]
> [. . .]

Sentiments expressed by Lady Cecil Craig in April 1919 summarise the unionist women's view of partition, as they, 'all agreed that they would rather remain under the Union, but if that was not possible they had to do the best they could.'[35] Partition was debated at a UWUC meeting in March 1920, where the 'majority of the meeting was of the opinion that Ulster should remain intact and abide by the covenant'.[36] The council sent delegates to the UUC meeting held to decide policy on the geographical definition of Ulster but the women's council imposed no restrictions on their representatives, leaving them 'free to vote as their consciences direct them'.[37] Ultimately the UWUC sanctioned six-county exclusion, although there was some internal criticism and resignations did occur within their ranks.[38] [. . .]

War may have forced a reconsideration of women's capabilities, but it failed to permanently alter the entrenched belief that women were responsible for the home life of the nation. [. . .] The council was not immune from this ideological climate. For example their concerns over security were tainted by domestic and maternalistic ideals:

> To the women security meant even more than it did to the men. If they had secure and happy homes in which to rear their children they would bring up a race of men who would rally to the aid of their country in its hour of danger . . . It was the men who won the war but it was the women who would win the peace.[39]

These sentiments were clearly expressed in the papers that the UWUC produced inter-war. Their first paper, entitled *Ulsterwoman, a Journal for Union and Progress*, was published from July 1919 until August 1920, whilst its successor, *Northern Ireland, Home and Politics, a Journal for Women*, was produced from October 1925 until June 1927. [. . .] Although Carson wrote an article in the first edition of [. . . *Ulsterwoman*] paying tribute to the work of female unionists, his tone of condescension was apparent, as he gave his 'heartiest wishes [. . .] to this little journal'.[40] *Ulsterwoman's* contents were somewhat contradictory. Articles discussing women's position in trade unions appear alongside others enshrining the inter-war ideal of a woman's place being firmly in the home, with domestic management, gardening and other areas being seen as suitable for women's attention. [. . .]

The UWUC deferred politics throughout the Second World War to concentrate on war work. This suspension was more determined than it had been two decades previously, when the perception of political crisis had lingered over their war efforts. However, as in the previous conflict, women's war work afforded no guarantee of change. Indeed Edith Londonderry commented in her autobiography, 'It is not unjust to say that women as a whole had a very poor time in these [. . .] years'.[41] The Second World War produced an even stronger ideology of maternalism, fuelled by pronatalist interests and eugenic concerns about the quality and quantity of the race absent in its predecessor. Only a slight blurring of sexual divisions occurred, leaving attitudes largely unchanged. Although the period 1911 to 1940 saw dramatic legislative and socio-economic changes come into being in Britain, and by the late 1950s women possessed full property, political and judicial rights, there was no progressive erosion of what were deemed to be feminine and masculine spheres. [. . .]

However, the UWUC instilled many women with a sense of freedom and independence which was forbidden to them in other spheres. This was especially significant for their middle-class members, who were more firmly entrenched in the domestic world than their upper- or working-class sisters. Although the council must be viewed as a women's organisation largely under male control, the UWUC contributed to the strength of popular unionism. Further, the women's council proved to be more flexible in the inter-war years than many of its counterparts, continuing to introduce women to unionism and to political activity. [. . .]

Notes

1   The Conservative women's organisation, the Primrose League, was established in 1883, the Women's Liberal Federation dates from 1886 and the Women's Labour League was operative from 1906. For further information see Jane Rendall, *Equal or Different: Women's Politics, 1800–1914*, Oxford, 1987.

2   For example, the Primrose League was the largest and most widespread organisation of its time, having half a million members by 1887 (Martin Pugh, *The Tories and the People, 1880–1935*, Oxford, 1985, p. 25).

3   Information on the specifics of women's involvement is scant, but women appear to have been actively involved in unionist mass demonstrations.

4   The first Home Rule Bill was introduced by W. E. Gladstone in April 1886. This legislation proposed the establishment of an Irish legislature with restricted functions, but was defeated in the House of Commons in June 1886.

5   This bill was introduced by Gladstone in January 1893 and only passed its third reading in the Commons with the repeated use of closure. It was subsequently rejected by the House of Lords in September 1893.

6   This was introduced by the Liberal government of H. H. Asquith and removed the House of Lords' ability to defeat a bill outright, replacing this with a power to veto for two years. From a Unionist perspective this meant that the future passage of any home rule bill could only be delayed.

7   *Belfast News-Letter*, 24 January 1911.

8   Hereafter UUC.

9   UWUC executive committee minutes (hereafter ECM), PRONI, D. 1098/1/1, 30 January 1911.

10   Ibid., 16 June 1911.

11   Minute book of Lurgan Women's Unionist Association (hereafter WUA), PRONI, D. 3790/4, 13 May 1911.

12   Minute book of Dunmurry and District branch of Lisburn WUA, PRONI, D. 1460/11, 31 January 1912.

13   The establishment of local branches of the council were not always welcomed. For example Catholic shop owners in Portaferry, Co. Down, threatened boycott in response to a branch of the women's council being formed in their vicinity in 1914. However, a successful branch was set up in spite of this. Mrs Kerr to Lady Theresa Londonderry, PRONI, D. 2846/1/8/1–78, 1914.

14   *Belfast News-Letter*, 22 September 1913, *Darlington and Stockton Times*, 22 November 1913. Although a margin of exaggeration is to be expected, it seems likely that previous assessments of the UWUC's membership have been very conservative.

15   Roland McNeill, *Ulster's Stand for Union*, London, 1922, p. 38.

16   John M. Hamill was organising secretary of the women's council, 1911–29. He was the only male member of the council in the period 1911–40, and all successors to this office were female.

17   UWUC ECM, PRONI, D. 1098/1/1, 16 January 1913.

18   A. T. Q. Stewart, *The Ulster Crisis: Resistance to Home Rule, 1912–14*, London, 1967, fig. p. 65.

19   UWUC ECM, PRONI, D. 1098/1/1, 16 January 1913.

20   Dunmurry and District branch of Lisburn WUA, PRONI, D. 1460/11, 31 January 1912.

21   McNeill, *Ulster's Stand*, p. 166.

22   This subcommittee was responsible for issuing leaflets and newspapers and for organising women unionist speakers.

23   *Belfast News-Letter*, 22 September 1913.

24   UWUC ECM, PRONI, D. 1098/1/2, 14 May 1914.

25   Dunmurry and District branch of Lisburn WUA, PRONI, D. 1460/11, 1913.

26   The majority of these workers were unmarried. [. . .]

27   *Northern Whig*, 29 March 1913.

28   UWUC ECM, PRONI, D. 1098/1/1, 17 February 1914.

29   *Belfast News-Letter*, 12 January 1912.

30   For example, Lady Edith Londonderry, vice-president of the UWUC 1919–59, was a vocal supporter of the non-militant campaign for women's enfranchisement and published several articles on suffrage.

31   UWUC advisory committee min., PRONI, D. 2688/1/6, 10 March 1914.

32   Ironically preparations the unionists had made to resist home rule by military force were quickly adapted to meet the wider imperial, instead of the Ulster, crisis, as UVF Nursing and Driving Corps were utilised during the war.

33   UWUC min., PRONI, D. 1098/1/3, 18 August 1914.

34   Lady Hariot Dufferin to Lady Theresa Londonderry, PRONI, D. 2846/1/8/38, 6 July 1916.

35   *Northern Whig*, 7 April 1919.

36   UWUC min., PRONI, D. 1098/1/3, 9 March 1920.

37   Ibid.

38   Especially from women unionists in the three 'excluded' counties of Monaghan, Cavan and Donegal.
39   *Northern Whig*, 20 May 1921.
40   *Ulsterwoman: A Journal for Union and Progress*, 12 July 1919.
41   Edith, Marchioness of Londonderry, *Retrospect,* London, 1938, p. 140.

Chapter 8

Margaret Ward

■ from MARGINALITY AND MILITANCY:
CUMANN NA MBAN, 1914–36, in Austen Morgan
and Bob Purdie (eds), *Ireland: Divided Nation, Divided Class*,
London, 1980, pp. 96–110

[. . .]

THE LADIES' LAND LEAGUE, the first popular women's political organisation, came into being in 1881 after the imprisonment of much of the Land League's male leadership at a time when it was politically necessary to buttress harassed tenantry with traditional female welfare activity.

This 'marginal' political involvement of women as a group, usually on a temporary basis and always in contexts determined by a male political leadership, has historically been responsible for women's uncompromising idealism. This has taken the form of a 'militancy' based more on political principles than an experienced appreciation of political practice. This 'militancy' has been determined by the character of women's entry into political action. An initial lack of sophistication has been crystallised by an exclusion from political decision-making during the period of their mobilisation.

This, in essence, has been the history of Cumann na mBan, a women's organisation which existed to provide revolutionary men with support facilities from the time of the militarisation of part of the nationalist movement in 1913 through the national revolution and into the stable years of the Free State. [. . .] An examination of the prominent members and many of the rank and file suggests that women's activism was related to at least one, but more usually two, of the following factors: economic independence, single status, supportive nationalist family background. Of the ten executive members of the provisional committee in 1914,[1] the married women's husbands were active in the nationalist movement; most of the single women had professions and some also had strongly nationalist family backgrounds; one woman was the widow of a Fenian, owned a shop and had been politically active since the days of the Ladies' Land League. In 1918, the executive (apart from Countess Markievicz, who was prominent in the Rising) comprised women who had either sons or husbands killed in 1916. There were also twenty executive delegates from Dublin and the provinces, fourteen of whom were single and many of whom had strong family connections with nationalism. Most were very young, either in their late teens or early twenties and often had relatively secure jobs – as nurses, teachers, secretaries, shop-assistants – or were supported by their families, sometimes working in the family business with brothers who were in the Irish Volunteers. For example, one girl's parents owned a pub which was used as a meeting place and arms dump.

The task of building up the organisation required a great deal of time and energy, with a few paid organisers travelling round the countryside giving lectures and establishing new branches. One Convention report described the work as 'so strenuous and laborious' that one woman's health was seriously impaired and she had to end her work. [. . .] Ideological pressures, in particular from the Catholic Church, as well as material ones, made it extremely difficult for women to break away from the traditional maternal role. [. . .]

The year 1913 was a time of constitutional flux in Ireland. A Home Rule Bill was going through Parliament, the Unionists were arming to resist it and the Irish Volunteers were formed to counter the Ulster Volunteer Force. The republican paper *Irish Freedom* assured women that 'there is nothing unwomanly in active patriotism' and recognised that a girl working for 'unpatriotic employers' could not be expected to take part openly in political work.[2] However, at the inaugural meeting of the Irish Volunteers in late 1913 it was made clear that women were to be excluded from full participation. [. . .]

Nationalist women refused to tackle the Volunteers on the question [of exclusion], believing that the fight for freedom was all-important, that there could be 'no free women in an enslaved nation' and that women could only be emancipated when the national fight was won. They refused to demand the inclusion of women's enfranchisement in the Home Rule Bill, because such a demand would admit Britain's right to govern the country, although male nationalists had been asking Britain for home rule for years.

Cumann na mBan was formed in April 1914 with the objects of advancing the cause of Irish liberty and assisting the arming and equipping of Irishmen for the defence of Ireland. In her inaugural address, Agnes O'Farrelly encapsulated the subordinate role of the movement: 'Each rifle we put in their hand will represent to us a bolt fastened behind the door of some Irish home to keep out the hostile stranger. Each cartridge will be a watchdog to fight for the sanctity of the hearth.'[3]

The women's assistance left the men with more time to mould their organisation into a military body. Cumann na mBan, however, was allowed no say on policies or expenditure, since it was not represented on the Volunteer executive. The two organisations remained formally distinct and, although Cumann na mBan claimed that this independence gave it substantial autonomy, in reality all it was ever able to do was to devise tasks which followed guidelines set out by the Volunteers. Some of the harshest criticism of Cumann na mBan came from its president, Countess Markievicz, but unfortunately she never used her considerable energies to change the situation, preferring to work with the Irish Citizen Army: 'Today the women attached to national movements are there chiefly to collect funds for the men to spend. These Ladies Auxiliaries demoralise women, set them up in separate camps, and deprive them of all initiative and independence.'[4]

Cumann na mBan was caught in a double bind: if nationalist women refused to work for the Volunteer movement until they were guaranteed equal status (as the Irish Women's Franchise League tried to persuade them to do), they felt they would isolate themselves in the emerging new nation, returning to the political oblivion that had swamped active women since Parnell dissolved the Ladies' Land League in 1882; if they sacrificed their own interests and worked hard for independence, some saw clearly that this renunciation would defeat whatever chance women stood of being accepted as partners – women's self-sacrifice would ensure that their needs remained unrecognised and therefore unsatisfied.

The first major challenge Cumann na mBan faced was the 1916 Rising. What stands out was the women's determination to participate. Most accounts mention their work in nursing, cooking and delivering messages, but omit to state that it was only through sheer persistence that they managed to enter the pages of history at all. With MacNeill's countermanding order, the first day of the Rising was a day of chaos for everyone: for the women it was also a day of looking for outposts, asking to be allowed to join and, sometimes, of being turned away and advised to go home. It was evening before two members of Cumann na mBan managed to reach the GPO headquarters and inform Pearse, Connolly and Clarke of the difficulties being experienced. A hurried Cumann na mBan mobilisation order was then sent out and reluctant commandants were forced to accept female help. But no women were allowed into Boland's Mill – de Valera remained adamant that a women's place was in the home. [. . .]

Women's participation in 1916 established an image of the women's role within the nationalist movement which closely resembled that of an ideal housekeeper, able to cook appetising meals out of unsavoury ingredients. For some women it was the high point of their existence; for others, in particular the younger women who were to join Cumann na mBan in the next few years, it was an indication of the limitations of their organisation. They proved determined advocates of total militarisation, of Cumann na mBan becoming a female version of the Volunteer movement. The main internal debate over the next few years centred on this question.

After the Rising Cumann na mBan grew rapidly (from 100 branches in 1917 to 600 in 1918)[5] and was re-organised on a quasi-military basis so that each company of Volunteers had a squad of Cumann na mBan women attached to it. New branches of Cumann na mBan could only be formed where there was a company of Volunteers.[6] The 1918 Convention decided that all funds collected were to be devoted to 'the arming and equipping of the men *and women* of Ireland'. During the Black and Tan War, particularly when fighting occurred in the countryside, women did much more than bind wounds; they were engaged in intelligence work, in transporting arms, supplying safe houses and continuing civilian work, especially in connection with the functioning of local government and Dáil Éireann courts. The 1918 Convention decision appears to have been a compromise between two opposing factions – a compromise which did not resolve the problem of the opposed conceptions of the organisation. It led to increasing antagonisms between the women and the men; some of the men felt that, as the women were supposed to be only a support group, the men had the right to interfere in the women's internal affairs (for example, in the appointment of Cumann na mBan officers). After further debate it was agreed that, with regards to military operations *only*, the women would take orders from the local Volunteer officer.[7]

Towards the end of 1921 the debate was renewed with vigour. Cumann na mBan had now been militarily active for five of its seven years' existence and some believed that these were years in which they had been unable to realise their full potential because of the constraints imposed upon them. At the 1921 Convention a proposal called for Cumann na mBan to be run on strictly military lines, with Dublin having a commandant. This was defeated and another resolution calling for the establishment of a regular military staff under the directorship of a chief officer was recommended to the executive, where it seems to have remained. At no stage were the women critical of their exclusion from the Volunteers; the only alternative ever considered was the creation of a female equivalent, not a merger of forces where the women would have had a measure of direct control. Other women placed less emphasis on military activity and more on political education, calling for the setting up of study circles and of the production of a newspaper. These suggestions were not pursued; those who favoured continuation along established lines remained the majority and the dissidents appear to have been reconciled – at least for the time being.[8]

Women over thirty had been given the vote in 1918. During the Dáil Treaty debates in 1921–2 Mrs O'Callaghan proposed that all men and women over the age of twenty-one be enfranchised. Griffith protested that this was a device to 'torpedo the Treaty'. The motion was lost by thirty-eight votes to forty-seven.[9] This meant that some of the most militant nationalists – women between the ages of twenty-one and thirty and men who had turned twenty-one since the compilation of the last register in late 1918 – were unable to vote in the 1922 election. The Dáil had voted to accept the Treaty in January 1922; Cumann na mBan voted against at a Convention on 5 February by 419 to 63, the first organisation to publicly support rejection. [. . .]

With the beginning of the Civil War a number of women unconnected with Cumann na mBan organised a delegation to the leaders of both sides. Maud Gonne stated: 'We claimed, as women, on whom the misery of the civil war would fall, that we had a right to be heard.'[10] The Free State Government refused to negotiate the truce they requested. Cumann na mBan had immediately come out on active service, carrying dispatches and supplies to the Four Courts – headquarters of the anti-Treaty forces – and later joining the fighting in the other garrisons. They also bore the brunt of the political struggle: providing military escorts at republican funerals, circulating *Éire*, the republican newspaper, and generally doing everything that required a degree of visibility; it was felt too dangerous for the men to show themselves in public. Their contribution did not pass unnoticed by the government; O'Higgins, Minister of Justice, referred contemptuously to 'hysterical young women who ought to be playing five-fingered exercises or helping their mothers with the brasses'.[11] However, his conception of the kind of sheltered life women should be leading did not prevent him jailing 400 of them. [. . .]

Loyal and willing they were; equal comrades-in-arms they were not. When rumours of peace started, Cumann na mBan wrote to [assistant IRA Chief-of-Staff Ernie] O'Malley, demanding that in the event of the army executive opening peace negotiations, they should be represented. O'Malley passed this request to Liam Lynch, Chief-of-Staff, but nothing came of it.[12] De Valera's address to the 'Legion of the Rearguard' – his admission of defeat – failed to mention the women's contribution.

Although the Free State Government kept the promise that Griffith had made during the Treaty debates, giving women over twenty-one the vote (in 1923), women made very few other gains in the new state. Cumann na mBan remained one of the most vocal and intransigent supporters of republicanism. It attempted to revive a boycott of British goods and initiated anti-juror campaigns in order to prevent jurors from convicting republicans for anti-government activities (the government's response was to introduce military tribunals in 1931). As well as publicity-seeking stunts, an educational drive was launched: the study of economics was recommended so that 'members will understand and be able to explain to others, that a social system suited to the needs of the country can be set up in place of the present system founded on capitalism'.[13] The 1933 Convention pledged Cumann na mBan to 'organise and train the women of Ireland to put into effect the ideals and obligations contained in the (1916) Proclamation'.[14] This committed them to social and economic views which the previous Cumann na mBan consti-tution had left undefined; that document had merely pledged them to maintain the republic established in 1919, which had become an increasingly unrealistic task. As a result of this decision, three members (including Mary MacSwiney) left to form Mná na Poblachta (Republican Women), a narrowly nationalistic organisa-tion totally devoid of social politics.

The attempt to find a political basis for resistance to the Free State continued. In 1931, executive members of Cumann na mBan joined Saor Éire (Free Ireland), whose aim was the creation of an independent revolutionary leadership amongst the working class and small farmers and the overthrowing of both Irish capitalism and British imperialism in Ireland. However, in October 1931, the Free State Government banned twelve organisations, including Saor Éire, the IRA and Cumann na mBan; members of Cumann na mBan were among those imprisoned for membership of 'illegal organisations'. Saor Éire, denounced by the Catholic hierarchy for being 'frankly communistic', rapidly collapsed.

With the formation of the left-wing Republican Congress in 1934, further effort was made to develop economic and social policies for the republican move-ment. Cumann na mBan was briefly associated with the Congress group. They withdrew because they felt that the main aim of the Congress was not the ending of capitalism but the destruction of the IRA. (It has also been claimed that there was pressure from the IRA.) [. . .]

[A Congress leader, Peadar] O'Donnell articulated the *raison d'être* of Cumann na mBan: the principles of the IRA were beyond dispute; Cumann na mBan was its auxiliary organisation; the problem arose when the IRA failed to act upon these principles, thereby denying the women opportunity for action. Although Cumann na mBan was often considerably more militant than its male counterpart, this militancy was, at least in part, an expression of their ambiguous status as a sepa-rate women's organisation, formed to assist the men in their work for national independence. This subordination also meant that they felt they had to prove them-selves as political equals and, in order to achieve this, their activities had to centre on nationalist and male-defined goals. Consequently, any interest in women's issues was suppressed. In 1932, Nora Connolly had attacked Irish women for having returned without protest to their domestic role and she warned that progressive and revolutionary women were again content to be 'drudges', without a voice in the council of the revolutionary movement.[15] [. . .]

Although Cumann na mBan berated itself for being 'too retiring, too shy' and urged members to have 'the courage to lead public opinion', this advice was not combined with any concrete suggestions. After the withdrawal from the Republican Congress, Cumann na mBan remained condemned to follow the fluctuations of IRA fortunes. As republican momentum ebbed and de Valera's political star rose, Cumann na mBan faded from the scene, having failed to enrol new members to take the burden from the shoulders of those who had carried it for over twenty years. Irish society was becoming increasingly conservative: the Conditions of Employment Act of 1936 directly attacked the rights of working women and although the Irish Women Workers' Union initiated a campaign against it, Cumann na mBan failed to become involved in the fight; they were also unable to mobilise against the 1937 Constitution. [. . .] By the 1940s it had, for all practical purposes, ceased to exist.[16] [. . .]

Notes

1   Mrs Agnes Eoin MacNeill, Mrs Wyse Power, Madam O'Rahilly, Mrs Tuohy, Mrs Agnes O'Farrelly, Nurse McCoy, Miss Bloxhan, Miss Gavan Duffy, Mrs Padraic Colum and Miss Margaret Dobbs.
2   *Irish Freedom*, November 1913. Article by 'Countrywoman'.
3   *Irish Volunteer*, 18 April 1914.
4   *Irish Citizen*, 23 October 1915. Report of speech delivered to the Irish Women's Franchise League on 12 October.
5   Reports of Cumann na mBan conventions and leaflets, National Library of Ireland (NLI).
6   Lil Conlon, *Cumann na mBan and the Women of Ireland*, Kilkenny, 1969, p. 121.
7   1918 Convention of Cumann na mBan, Report, NLI.
8   1921 Convention of Cumann na mBan, Report, NLI.
9   Dáil Éireann Minutes of Proceedings, 2 March 1922, pp. 197–214.
10 *Éire: The Irish Nation* (newspaper of anti-Treaty forces), letter from Maud Gonne, 22 September 1923.
11 *Éire*, 17 February 1923.
12 Desmond Greaves, *Liam Mellows and the Irish Revolution*, London, 1971, p. 372.
13 *An Phoblacht*, 23 September 1933. Report of speech made by a Cumann na mBan organiser.
14 *An Phoblacht*, 25 November 1933. Report of Convention.
15 *An Phoblacht*, 25 June 1932.
16 Reports and meetings against Conditions of Employment Bill, 15 June and 13 July 1935, *Republican Congress*. On opposition to the 1937 Constitution, see *Prison Bars*, July 1937.

Chapter 9

Mary Clancy

■ from **ASPECTS OF WOMEN'S CONTRIBUTION TO THE OIREACHTAS DEBATE IN THE IRISH FREE STATE, 1922–37**, in Maria Luddy and Cliona Murphy (eds), *Women Surviving: Studies in Irish Women's History in the 19th and 20th Centuries*, Dublin, 1989, pp. 206–32

[. . .]

A MARKED CONTRAST BETWEEN the contribution in the Dáil and that in the Seanad was to distinguish the participation of the eleven women who entered the Houses of the Oireachtas between 1922 and 1937. [. . .] In general, the level of debate among women in the Seanad was marked by a confidence which was superior at all times to that of the women in the Dáil. Deputies, it would appear, participated in public life more for symbolic reasons deriving from family connections than from any motivation arising from their own political ambitions.[1] Their outstanding contribution to the Dáil lay in their solid enduring support for the political parties to which they belonged. Both Deputy Bridget Redmond (Cumann na nGaedheal) and Deputy Mary Reynolds (Cumann na nGaedheal) were elected following the death of husbands who were Dáil deputies. The brothers of Margaret Collins-O'Driscoll (Cumann na nGaedheal) and Margaret Pearse (Fianna Fáil) were widely revered as symbolic nationalist figureheads by the political parties which they represented.[2] Mary Reynolds and Margaret Pearse, who were elected in 1932 and 1933 respectively, did not speak on any issue in this period, while Bridget Redmond occasionally commented on local Waterford questions.[3] Deputy Redmond spoke against the 1937 Constitution, but only at the insistence of women's organisations, and was absent for much of the debate. While Margaret Collins-O'Driscoll and Helena Concannon (Fianna Fáil) contributed on a more regular (though by no means impressive) basis, neither initiated any legislation in respect of women, or played any significant role during debates on such legislation. Both deputies, however, endorsed women's responsibilities towards maternal and domestic duties. [. . .] When the more difficult problems of female sweated labour, infant mortality or infanticide were raised in the Dáil, such issues were ignored by both women.

Given such enthusiasm for the private and domestic life, surprisingly little mention was made of their role as public representatives during Dáil debates.

Collins-O'Driscoll reminded the House, in 1925, that she was not elected to the Dáil 'on the question of sex' but sought to serve 'the interests of the community at large'.[4] Regarding her Dáil behaviour as exemplary 'by never missing a day's parliament attendance and rarely a division,' Helena Concannon felt privileged to represent Eamon de Valera 'in a back-bench way'.[5] Any advantage accruing to Cumann na nGaedheal and Fianna Fáil from their parliamentary attendance would appear to be sufficient motivation for the women Dáil deputies between 1922 and 1937. Since questions of equal rights were not supported by the deputies in question, this could serve as an appropriate reminder that women public representatives are not necessarily progressive merely by virtue of gender, but that factors such as conservative political orientation, religion and class must also be taken into consideration.

[. . .] In contrast to the Dáil emphasis on women's domestic function, the concept of women's rights enjoyed considerable sympathy in the Seanad, despite some variation in the nature of individual contributions. Little part, for instance, was played by Senator Ellen Odette, Countess of Desart, in any debate concerning women. Indeed, it was noted in her obituary, in 1933, that she had 'played an energetic part' in opposing women's suffrage, in the belief that 'women should not compete against men at work or play.'[6] [. . .] Alice Stopford Green spoke only on matters of history and culture and did not contribute to any debate concerning women.[7] Senator Eileen Costello insisted that women's rights were a necessary part of equal citizenship, while Senator Kathleen Clarke was motivated by the concept of equality which was promised in the 1916 Proclamation.[8] Although Senator Kathleen Browne spoke regularly and at length (particularly on agriculture), her contribution to debates on women's issues remained brief.[9] [. . .]

Of all the women elected to the Seanad between 1922 and 1937, Jenny Wyse Power was to emerge as the most persistent and determined champion of equal rights for women. [. . .] When dealing with issues such as homeless children, infant mortality and the poor, her contribution is significant, in that the voice of Jenny Wyse Power was regularly the only one arguing on behalf of such groups in the Seanad.

[. . .] It was within the sphere of social legislation that the response of the women legislators proved the most problematic and varied. Claims that the moral standards of the new state were not as intact as in the past informed the opinion of many, irrespective of gender. In general, social issues were overlooked by the women deputies, while the intervention of women senators varied according to the nature of the issue in question. Divorce reform, contraception and prostitution tended to be ignored, whereas the provision of financial assistance for widows, children, and unmarried mothers and the protection of women from sexual assault, were resolutely pursued. [. . .]

State policy regulating birth control during the 1920s and 1930s derived from the Censorship of Publications Bill, 1928 and the Criminal Law Amendment Bill, 1934. Based on the recommendations of the Evil Literature Committee, 1926, the Censorship Bill aimed to ban birth-control publications as well as 'indecent literature'.[10] The government's enthusiastic welcome for the bill, along with a notable reluctance to discuss the section on contraception, was likewise reflected by Deputy Margaret Collins-O'Driscoll.[11] [. . .] The overwhelming Dáil support to ban birth-control literature, along with a reluctance to speak publicly on matters of sexual morality, no doubt tended to negate the need for much discussion on the contraception section.

Underlying the censorship debate, however, was a significant desire to extend control over aspects of women's lives in general. Not least was the disapproval shared by a number of deputies regarding the reading material enjoyed by girls and women. [. . .] Of more significance was the proposal to ban the reporting of rape and sexual assault cases. [. . . T]he issue of contraception did not receive much attention either during the Seanad debate.[12] [. . .] It is to be noted, however, that extra-parliamentary discussion of the bill was undertaken by the Irish Women Citizens and Local Government Association.[13]

The implications, on the other hand, of the Criminal Law Amendment Bill, 1934, were to prove contradictory for women.[14] The raising of the age of consent from sixteen to seventeen in respect of carnal knowledge or attempted carnal knowledge, and from thirteen to fifteen years in respect of indecent assault was an important reform. This section of the bill, indeed, was to attract the most attention from women senators, women's societies, social workers and clergy. [. . .] Secondly, the bill proposed to control prostitution through the imposition of heavier fines and increased powers for the police. [. . .] Finally, Section 17 of the Criminal Law Amendment Bill banned the sale or importation of contraceptives.[15] However, this outright banning of contraception, which represented a severe curtailment for women in the sphere of reproductive rights, failed to attract much debate within the House. Given the overall reluctance to discuss matters such as contraception in public debate, the non-intervention of the women deputies – Concannon, Pearse and Redmond – was not remarkable. However, their lack of interest in the raising of the age of consent would appear to indicate a more general resistance to the discussion of social issues.

[. . . I]n 1929, the introduction of the Illegitimate Children (Affiliation Orders) Bill, had also attracted the attention of certain women senators. The principal significance of this measure lay in the autonomy and control it extended to unmarried mothers over the running of their own lives and the lives of their children. It was possible to bring an action for seduction, but as the law stood, the woman's predicament was evaluated in terms of injury to her father or of services lost to an employer. While the bill did not propose to discontinue such actions, it enabled proceedings to be brought 'by the women in her own name for the support of an illegitimate child'.[16] The demand for an *in camera* clause, and the publication of the father's name, were the issues which tended to dominate the Oireachtas debate. Indeed, more time was spent discussing the implications of the bill for men, than in discussing the situation of unmarried mothers and their dependants. The image which was reinforced throughout the debate was that of the falsely charged, blackmailed, innocent man as against the 'hardened sinner' who sought endless affiliation orders. In the Seanad, however, Jenny Wyse Power argued persuasively on behalf of unmarried mothers, denying the danger of blackmail and emphasising their fear of a court appearance. In this she was supported by Senator Kathleen Browne, who agreed that women would have difficulty facing a public court.[17] [. . . T]he *in camera* amendment was accepted, and the bill was passed in June, 1930.

[. . .] While restraint, therefore, distinguished the performance of elected women in the sphere of reproductive rights and sexual morality, it was in the sphere of equal rights that the women representatives made their most impressive and sustained contributions. In particular, the legislative control and regulation of women's employment was resisted by the women senators during the 1920s and 1930s. In 1925, the Civil Service Regulation (Amendment) Bill, represented an attempt by the Cumann na nGaedheal Government to statutorily prohibit women from entering certain areas of the Civil Service solely on the grounds of sex. [. . .] The introduction of the bill indicated a pronounced disregard for existing legislation, notably the 1919 Sex Disqualification Act and Article 3 of the 1922 Free State Constitution, both of which sought to safeguard equality of opportunity regardless of sex. It was not a popular bill, however, and even though it was accepted by the Dáil, it was the subject of much criticism. Yet, this measure, which had serious implications for the position of women in the workforce, was to receive its main support in the Dáil from deputy Margaret Collins-O'Driscoll. Having been canvassed 'by very influential members of my sex to vote against this Bill,' the deputy added that she 'failed to see how it infringed upon women's rights under the Constitution.'[18] [. . .]

In the Seanad, the Civil Service Regulation (Amendment) Bill met with firm opposition from a number of determined speakers. Senator Eileen Costello attacked the bill as 'morally wrong' and 'monstrously unfair'. For the senator, the fundamental issue was that 'women are still to be subject to the obligations of citizenship, but their privileges are to be curtailed and restricted'.[19] Apart from some isolated support for the bill, the remainder of the second stage was dominated by the contribution of Senator Jenny Wyse Power who remained convinced that the proposed legislation was not in the interests of women workers. [. . .] She regretted that such a bill had come 'from the men who were associated in the fight (for freedom) with women when sex and money were not considerations.'[20] [. . .] In a debate which tended to be dominated by critics of the measure, the contribution of Senators Costello and Wyse Power proved critical in bringing about the bill's defeat. Seanad hostility to the measure was but one aspect of a wider campaign, which was also supported by the Irish Women Citizens and Local Government Association, and its success must be viewed as an important achievement for equal-rights feminists in the mid-1920s.

The restriction of women's industrial employment was one of the objectives of the Conditions of Employment Bill, 1935. It was agreed [. . .] by most deputies, that certain forms of work were unsuitable for women. It would appear, however, that opposition to women's industrial employment derived from a more fundamental fear that women industrial workers, encouraged by recent mechanisation, would pose a serious threat to male industrial workers. [. . .] Although the bill [. . .] was generally accepted among workers as well as employers, opposition was 'still being expressed by representations of women workers' organisations'.[21] [. . .] Firm support for the bill was evident, however, throughout the Oireachtas debate [. . .]

Significantly, however, once more, efforts to restrict women's work and keep them out of certain trades met with strong resistance from the women members of the Seanad [. . . which] represented the most radical demand of the debate in either House of the Oireachtas. [. . .] In response to the accusation that 'the feminists have run riot' over the Conditions of Employment Bill, Kathleen Clarke stated that, although she was 'sympathetic to the feminist movement', her opposition to Section 16 of the bill was based on nationalist grounds, and specifically on the 1916 Proclamation which granted equal rights to all citizens. [. . .] The response to legislation which sought to restrict employment solely on the basis of gender, as attempted by Cumann na nGaedheal in 1925, and Fianna Fáil in 1935, was characterised, therefore, by opposition from certain women senators. Such legislation was not directed at one class. While the Civil Service Regulation Amendment Bill, 1925, affected the employment of educated, middle-class women, the Conditions of Employment Bill, 1935, on the other hand, sought to regulate the employment of working-class women. It is to be noted that by 1937, the Irish Free State was placed on a black list at Geneva for its conduct in respect of women workers.[22]

[. . .] It was during the discussion of jury service, however, that the Free State legislature was presented with the first significant opportunity of discussing the public role of women. The right to sit on juries had been granted under the Sex Disqualification Act, 1919. [. . .] The proposal to exempt women altogether from jury service, as intended in the Juries Bill, 1927, was to prove controversial [. . .] The measure faced some resistance in the Dáil, but once more Margaret Collins-O'Driscoll – the sole woman deputy at this stage – did not take any part in the debate apart from voting with the government in Dáil divisions.[23]

In the Seanad, one of the most forceful arguments put forward on the second stage was that of Senator Wyse Power, whose protest was 'entirely influenced by the fact that if this Bill becomes law the civic spirit that is developing in women will be arrested'.[24] [. . .] For Senator Eileen Costello, the ideal position was that of 1919, when women were granted equality under the Sex Disqualification Act. [. . .] Women, she believed, needed to be educated into responsible citizenship, since 'they have not realised their power as yet'.[25] [. . .] In the Seanad, [. . .] opposition to the measure was so strong that it succeeded in bringing about a significant change in form, if not substance, of the bill's provisions. Women were to be included in Part II of the Schedule along with other exempted classes, while it was to be left open to women to have their names entered on the jury lists on application. [. . .] This departure from the rights granted in the Sex Disqualification Act, 1919, and Article 3 of the 1922 Constitution, must be regarded as a serious set-back for Irishwomen, but one which was, significantly, if unavailingly, opposed by feminists both inside and outside the Oireachtas. [. . .]

Controversy surrounded discussion of the place of women also during the debate on the 1937 Constitution. Although only undertaken by a limited number of deputies, Dáil opposition to the clauses affecting the status of women was persistent and enjoyed some success. Deletion of Articles 40, 41, and 45 – as demanded by women's organisations – was never suggested, however, in the Dáil.[26] Modification, on the other hand, of Article 45 – which initially sought to enshrine 'the inadequate strength of women' – was noteworthy in view of de Valera's insistence on the inclusion of that concept. Critics also determinedly opposed the President's omission of 'without distinction of sex' which was contained in Article 3 of the 1922 Constitution. [. . .] Opponents, [. . .] viewed its omission as an attempt to destroy 'the constitutional bulwark of women's rights', in the event of discriminatory ordinary legislation.[27] Although de Valera remained resolute in his claim that the phrase was superfluous, his subsequent decision to include it (in Article 16), represented an important achievement for critics both inside and outside the Dáil.

Notes

1   Published sources are inadequate at present [1989], but brief biographical details may be obtained in Vincent Brown (ed.), *Magill Book of Irish Politics*, Dublin, 1981; J. D. Hickey and S. E. Doherty, *A Dictionary of Irish History Since 1800*, Dublin, 1980; *Missing Pieces, Women in Irish History*, Dublin, 1983.

2   See also Ruth Dudley-Edwards, *Patrick Pearse: The Triumph of Failure*, London, 1977.

3   Deputy Reynolds was subsequently to enjoy a long Dáil career from 1937 to 1961.

4   *Dáil Debates*, vol. 13, 18 November, 1925, pp. 514–15.

5   Ibid., vol. 53, 5 July 1934, pp. 1498–502.

6   Obituary, *Irish Times*, 30 June 1933.

7   See also R. B. McDowell, *Alice Stopford Green: A Passionate Historian*, Dublin, 1967; L. O'Broin, *Protestant Nationalists in Revolutionary Ireland*, Dublin, 1985.

8   Eileen Costello was a local government representative, and a member of the Governing Body of UCG from 1923 to 1934. A supporter of Cumann na nGaedheal, and later the Army Comrades Association, she was primarily concerned with the promotion of the Irish language. Kathleen Clarke (1879–1972) was the widow of Tom Clarke, who was executed for his part in the 1916 Rising. In 1922 she became an Alderman on Dublin Corporation and in 1939 the first woman Lord Mayor of Dublin.

9   Kathleen Browne was a tillage farmer from County Wexford, a Peace Commissioner and committee member of the County Council, and Agricultural and Co-Operative Societies.

10   Apart from those directly involved with the book industry, those who submitted evidence to the Evil Literature Committee included the Catholic Truth Society of Ireland, the Irish Vigilance Association, the Boys' Brigade and the Irish Christian Brothers.

11   [. . .] *Dáil Debates*, vol. 26, 18 October 1928, pp. 594–611.

12   *Seanad Debates*, vol. 12, 11 April 1929, pp. 55–75. [. . .]

13   Attention was drawn to the IWCLGA campaign by Deputy Craig, an Independent University representative. *Dáil Debates*, vol. 26, 18 October 1929, p. 656. [. . .]

14   The impetus behind the bill's introduction was the Committee of Enquiry into the Criminal Law Amendment Acts, led by Mr William Carrigan, KC. [. . .] The Carrigan Committee report was never published but its details were reported in the *Irish Press*, 4 March 1932.

15   *Dáil Debates*, vol. 53, 28 June 1934, pp. 1246–51.

16   Ibid., vol. 32, 30 October 1929, pp. 519–21.

17   *Seanad Debates*, vol. 13, 19 March 1930, pp. 693–711.

18   *Dáil Debates*, vol. 13, 18 November 1925, pp. 514–15.

19   *Seanad Debates*, vol. 6, 17 December 1925, pp. 245–6.

20   Ibid., vol. 6, 17 December 1925, pp. 258–9. [. . .] The bill was held up for twelve months after being thrown out by the Seanad.

21   Ibid., vol. 20, 27 November 1935, p. 1221.

22   This was stated by Dr Mary Hayden (National Council of Women) during the anti-Constitution campaign in 1937. *Irish Times*, 22 June 1937.

23   [. . .] *Dáil Debates*, vol. 18, 15 February 1927, pp. 481–2.

24   *Seanad Debates*, vol. 8, 30 March 1927, p. 682.

25   Ibid., 8 April 1972, p. 808.

26   The Seanad had been abolished in 1936. [. . .]

27   Critics in the Dáil included deputies Costello, Lavery, McGilligan, O'Sullivan, Alton, Rice and Rowlette.

Chapter 10

Yvonne Scannell

■ from **THE CONSTITUTION AND THE ROLE OF WOMEN**, in Brian Farrell (ed.), *De Valera's Constitution and Ours*, Dublin, 1988, pp. 123–36

WOMEN HAD NO PART IN FRAMING Bunreacht na hÉireann. Not one woman took part in drafting it. Of the 152 TDs who had an opportunity to comment on the draft, only three were women. These three, known sorrowfully as the 'Silent Sisters', made no meaningful contribution whatever to the debate on the draft. Outside the Dáil, a number of women's organisations protested in vain against certain articles – so much so that de Valera admitted knowing that he had a 'bad reputation with women'.[1]

Why, therefore, did some women object to de Valera's Constitution? There are, after all, at least six articles that can be used, directly or indirectly, to vindicate women's rights. The answer to this question lies in the assumptions made in the Constitution – and by de Valera in piloting it through the Dáil – concerning the legal rights, the role and the status of women in Irish society.

It is clear from reading the Dáil debates that de Valera was no feminist. Neither, however, was he consciously anti-women. His views on women's rights reflected those of most people in Irish society at the time. They certainly accorded with those of nearly all of the deputies who spoke in the Dáil.[2] [. . .]

The Constitution expressly states that women are entitled to vote, to become TDs, and to become citizens on the same basis as men.[3] These rights had been granted under the 1922 Constitution.[4] There was nothing revolutionary about re-enacting them in 1937. But if de Valera was prepared to give women full political rights, that was as far as he would go. He deleted the words 'without distinction of sex' from the draft of Article 40.1, which now reads:

> All citizens shall, as human persons, be held equal before the law.
> This shall not be held to mean that the State shall not in its enactments have due regard to differences of capacity, physical and moral, and of social function.

The words 'without distinction of sex' were deleted because de Valera considered them 'altogether unnecessary'.[5] It is clear, however, from reading his justification for the deletion that he intended equal rights for women to be confined, initially at least, to the political sphere. Three times in his short justification he speaks, not of women's rights but of women's *political rights*.[6] The subtle qualification went unnoticed by his opponents.

The article in the Constitution that attracted the fiercest opposition from women at the time was Article 41.2. This article reads:

1° In particular the State recognises that by her life within the home, woman gives to the State a support without which the common good cannot be achieved.

2° The State shall therefore, endeavour to ensure that *mothers* shall not be obliged by economic necessity to engage in labour to the neglect of their duties in the home. [Emphasis added.]

There are two ways of looking at this article. The first is to take de Valera at his word and to regard the first paragraph as a tribute to the work that is done by women in the home as mothers.[7] The second paragraph, if it is to be regarded as anything other than a paternalistic declaration, can be read as a constitutional guarantee that no *mother* is to be *forced* by economic necessity to work outside the home to the neglect of her duties there. [. . .]

The second way of looking at Article 41.2 is different. To some, it is grossly offensive to the dignity and freedoms of womanhood. It speaks of woman's life within the home (not just her work there), implying that the natural vocation of woman (the generic is used, so it means *all* women) is in the home. It is the grossest form of sexual stereotyping. [. . .]

Despite the protests about Article 41.2, de Valera refused to delete it. His reasons for refusing show that his vision of the role of woman in Irish society was that of a full-time wife and mother in an indissoluble marriage, having 'a preference for home duties' and 'natural duties' as a mother.[8] [. . .] De Valera's defence of Article 41.2 can be rationalised by an attitude of romantic paternalism which, as a famous American judge has said, 'in practical effect puts women, not on a pedestal, but in a cage'.[9]

Constitutional history shows that it is the second and less positive interpretation of Article 41.2 that de Valera's successors in office have almost invariably adopted. Lawyers for the State tried to rely on Article 41.2 to justify tax discriminations against married women in the Murphy case,[10] and social welfare discriminations against women in the recent Hyland case.[11] They successfully relied on it to justify social welfare discriminations against deserted husbands obliged to assume full-time child care duties in *Dennehy* v. *Minister for Social Welfare*.[12]

The Oireachtas in its legislation continued to assume that the normal vocation of women was in marriage, motherhood and the home. In particular, the social welfare system until very recently was founded on the philosophy that women are dependent on men and that society must only support them when this dependence (for one reason or another) ceases. The women of 1937 were right to fear that the State would give Article 41.2 the most restrictive interpretation of their rights.

Consistent with his vision of women's role, de Valera, to his credit, did provide (in Article 42) that the right to educate children was to rest primarily with parents. This was to prove a significant enhancement of the rights of mothers, because at common law the right to the custody of legitimate children, even small children, automatically belonged to the father unless he was demonstrably unfit.[13]

Other direct and indirect references to women's rights are contained in Article 45. This article contains directive principles of social policy for the guidance of the Oireachtas, 'ideals, aims and objectives'[14] to be achieved when, and if, the Oireachtas thinks fit. Women's rights implied in this article are not fundamental rights: they are rights that may be granted to them by their political representatives.

Article 45 deals, *inter alia*, with certain social and economic rights for women. It obliges the State to strive 'to promote the welfare of the whole people by securing and protecting as effectively as it may a social order in which justice and charity shall inform all the institutions of the national life'. It specifically and particularly obliges the State to direct its policy towards securing that 'men and women equally' have 'the right to an adequate means of livelihood'. In the article, the State pledges to safeguard with special care the economic interests of the weaker sections of the community and, where necessary, to contribute to the support of the infirm, the widow, the orphan and the aged. [. . .] Lastly, Article 45 states that the State will endeavour to ensure that the strength and health of workers, men and women, and of children, shall not be abused, and that citizens shall not be forced by economic necessity to enter avocations unsuited to their sex, age or strength.

De Valera intended Article 45 to be a 'constant reminder to the legislature of the direction in which it should work'.[15] These then were the provisions dealing with women in de Valera's Constitution. Taken at face value, women were guaranteed equality before the law, tempered with regard to differences of capacity. [. . .]

For almost thirty years after the Constitution was adopted, the position of women in Irish society hardly changed at all. The common law relegation of women to domesticity and powerlessness continued. Laws based on the premise that women's rights were inferior to those of men survived in, and indeed even appeared on, the statute books. Despite the constitutional adulation of marriage and motherhood, the legislature preferred to keep women in the home by foul rather than fair means. Contraception was effectively illegal.[16] The economically powerless homemaker was denied access to free legal aid. No financial aid was available as of right to unmarried mothers, deserted wives or prisoners' wives, even when they were fulfilling their 'duties' in the home. The battered wife and mother could not exclude her violent husband from the home (which was almost invariably his) except by resort to the most cumbersome procedures. If she fled the home, her husband had a right to damages from anyone who enticed her away, or who harboured her or committed adultery with her. The married woman by her work in the home might give the State 'a support without which the common good cannot be achieved', but until the Succession Act, 1965, came into force in 1967, her husband could legally disinherit her and leave her homeless in his will. [. . .]

In *De Burca and Anderson* v. *Attorney General*[17] it was recognised that 'some preferential treatment of women citizens seems to be contemplated by the Constitution,' and it was noted that Article 41.2 'makes special provision for the economic protection of mothers who have home duties.' [. . .] Although Mrs Tilson succeeded in asserting the equal rights of a mother to custody of her children in 1951, it took the Oireachtas a further thirteen years to enshrine this right in the Guardianship of Infants Act, 1964.

Work outside the home for married women was regarded as a selfish distraction from home duties. The Civil Service Regulation Act, 1956, provided that women employed in the Civil Service, other than those employed in certain excluded non-pensionable posts, were required to resign on marriage. The Civil Service Commissioners Act, 1956, enabled the commissioners, in making regulations in relation to a competition for a Civil Service position, to require that a female candidate be unmarried or a widow. The Local Government Act, 1941, enabled the Minister for Local Government to declare as a qualification for a specified office that any woman holding that office be unmarried or a widow. A small number of married women were employed in the Civil Service and local authorities until these discriminations were abolished, but they were employed in positions where recruitment difficulties were experienced and in temporary (non-pensionable) capacities or on a fee-paid basis.[18]

Women working in many other jobs had no legal redress when obliged to resign on marriage. Women were not entitled to unemployment allowances, because it was assumed that some man would provide for them. The income of a married woman was deemed to be her husband's for tax purposes.[19] Women were grossly underrepresented in politics and in public life despite having equal political rights with men since the foundation of the state. [. . .]

In 1970 the government appointed a Commission for the Status of Women. The report of this commission (on which women and men were equally represented) contained forty-nine eminently reasonable recommendations for improving women's rights in a number of areas.[20] The government was in no rush to implement them. [. . .] Nevertheless, in spite of legislative inertia and political indifference to the injustices women suffered, the laws began to change.

From about 1970, three main factors combined to bring about a considerable improvement in the position of women in Irish society. The first was the flowering of judicial review. People began to seek redress in the courts for grievances that the Oireachtas had chosen to ignore.[21] The courts by their interpretation of the Constitution created an awareness of the citizen's constitutional rights and of the role the courts could play in protecting and vindicating these rights. [. . .]

The second factor that influenced improvements in the legal status of women was the re-emergence of the feminist movement in the late sixties and early seventies. [. . .] In 1970 the Irish Women's Liberation Movement was launched. The founders included a number of journalists who were to disseminate its message to the media. A manifesto, *Chains or Change*, was agreed and delivered to the people of Ireland on the 'Late Late Show' of 6 March 1971. It contained five demands: equal pay, equality before the law, equal education, contraception, and justice for deserted wives, unmarried mothers and widows. It sent shock waves through Irish society. Women's issues became news on radio and television. The *Irish Press*, the

Irish Times and the *Irish Independent*, in response to the chord that the movement struck, all started feminist 'women's pages'.

The unlikely coalition of economically socialist and conservative women that had formed the movement was not to last. It splintered; but many of the women in it went on to found, or become prominent in, a number of pressure groups for women's rights. From 1970 to 1980 the number of women's organisations in Ireland increased from seventeen to over fifty-five. [. . .] The women's movement was significant in bringing to public attention the extent to which women, and particularly women in their capacities as wives and mothers, were discriminated against.

The third factor, which was to provide the main impetus for the achievement of equal economic rights for women, was Ireland's accession to the European Economic Community in 1973. Article 119 of the Treaty of Rome obliges member states to ensure and subsequently maintain the application of the principle that men and women should receive equal pay for equal work. [. . .] This law is now part of our Constitution, and rights granted under it may not be challenged as unconstitutional.

In the 1970s, individual Irish women began to challenge the constitutionality of laws that discriminated against them. In this brave and expensive endeavour they frequently employed a young woman barrister, Senator Mary Robinson, who was counsel in most of the constitutional cases where women's rights were vindicated.

In 1970 the High Court, in *Murtagh Properties* v. *Clery*, declared that women had a right to earn a livelihood under Article 40.3 and that sex discriminations in employment recruitment policies were unconstitutional.[22] In 1973 the Supreme Court, again relying on Article 40.3, upheld the right to marital privacy and the right of married women to use contraceptives, in the McGee case.[23] Shortly afterwards, in *De Burca and Anderson* v. *Attorney General*, the Supreme Court declared the Juries Act, 1927, unconstitutional under Article 38.5 in so far as it provided that women were exempt from jury service but entitled to serve on application.[24] Until 1973, only three women had ever served on juries. At common law, women were regarded as unqualified for jury service by reason of the doctrine of *propter defectum sexus*. Some of the discriminations against married women in the income tax code were held to violate Article 41, which protects the institution of marriage. [. . .]

Although the courts were prepared to strike down laws that discriminated against women, they were sometimes reluctant and always cautious when doing this.[25] [. . .] [It] proved impossible to persuade the courts to strike down sex discriminations under the equal rights clause in Article 40.1. In all of [the cases decided], the plaintiffs' rights were held to derive from other articles in the Constitution. The courts preferred to limit the scope of Article 40.1 (All citizens shall, as human persons, be held equal before the law) by reading the words 'as human persons' as a restriction on the potential of the article, although individual judges did rely on it to disapprove of sex discriminations.[26] [in *Murphy v. Attorney General* . . .]

While the courts in their interpretation of the Constitution were prepared, when given the opportunity, to respond fairly positively in favour of women's rights, the same cannot be said of the legislature. There has admittedly been a great deal of legislation on family law and equal rights for women since 1970, but apart from the Succession Act, 1965, it is difficult to identify any major piece of legislation relevant to the rights of women that was not forced on our representatives by the courts, the women's movement or the EC.

In the 1970s, after vigorous and sustained campaigns by women's groups such as AIM, 'Cherish', and 'Adapt', legislation was passed entitling unmarried mothers, deserted wives and prisoners' wives to social welfare allowances.[27] Contraception facilities were made available, to some at least after *McGee v. Attorney General*.[28] Improved arrangements were made for the recovery of maintenance from errant husbands.[29] Better provision was made for the exclusion of violent spouses from the family home.[30] Married women were given the right to prevent the sale of the family home without their consent.[31]

In the 1980s, the oppressive court actions for criminal conversation, enticement, and harbouring a spouse – actions based on the notion that a woman was the property of her husband – were abolished.[32] Married women were given the right to a separate domicile from their husbands.[33] Discriminations against the children of unmarried mothers were removed.[34] A restricted right to free legal aid in family law cases was conceded after Josie Airey's courageous journey to assert it in the European Court of Human Rights.[35] Eventually, in *O'G v. Attorney General*,[36] the High Court invalidated a sex discrimination for being in violation of Article 40.1 by declaring section 5 of the Adoption Act, 1974 (which prevented widowers, but not widows, from adopting in certain circumstances), unconstitutional because it was 'founded on an idea of difference in capacity between men and women which has no foundation in fact'. And on 12 February 1988, in *McA. v. McA.*,[37] the High Court held that the dependent domicile rule, 'like all other appendages of female servitude', did not survive the enactment of the Constitution.

If the Oireachtas could be persuaded by the courts and the women's movement to improve the laws applicable to women as wives and mothers, nothing less than the European Economic Community could persuade it to give women equal economic rights, and in consequence to fulfil the objectives of Article 45. Imaginative tactics were employed by legislators, trade unions and employers to deny or delay women's rights to equal pay, equal opportunities, equal taxation and equal social welfare benefits. [. . .] Women campaigning for equal taxation were contemptuously dismissed by George Colley, the Minister for Finance, as 'well-heeled and articulate', as if they had no right to speak about the injustices they were subjected to, or to be well-heeled. The spectre of undeserving women holding down 'men's jobs', or of married women selfishly depriving young and single people of their right to work, was constantly raised. [. . .]

In 1983 a reactionary backlash against the achievements of the women's movement here and abroad was instrumental in persuading the legislature to countenance what may prove to be a constitutional erosion of women's rights.[38] In that year, legislative fools rushed in where angels feared to tread and commended to the people the Eighth Amendment of the Constitution. This so-called 'pro-life' amendment of Article 40.3 ensures that the right to life of an Irish mother is in no way superior to, or deserving of more respect than, the right to life of the unborn. [. . .][39]

De Valera's Constitution was not consciously designed to advance the cause of women's rights. Nevertheless, the judges have shown that it has the capacity to do just that. Under it, Irish women now have many rights unavailable to, and even superior to, those of their English and indeed their American sisters. [. . .] Ironically, then, the Constitution, though rooted in a patronising and stereotyped view of womanhood, may yet justify the claim that it is truly ours.

Notes

1 *Dáil Debates*, vols 67–8, col. 63.
2 The exceptions were John A. Costello, Professor John M. O'Sullivan and Cecil Lavery, all members of the opposition. Helena Concannon, the only woman TD who made a contribution, displayed great confidence in the *bona fides* of her leader.
3 Articles 16.1.1, 16.1.2 and 9.1.3, respectively. The Proclamation of the Irish Republic, 1916, specifically called on 'Irishmen and Irishwomen', and promised the franchise to men and women.
4 Constitution of the Irish Free State, articles 3, 14, 15.
5 *Dáil Debates*, vols 67–8, col. 64.
6 Ibid., cols 64–5.
7 Ibid., col. 67. 'Is it not a tribute to the work that is done by women in the home as mothers?', asked de Valera.
8 Ibid., col. 68.
9 Justice Brennan of the US Supreme Court, in *Frontiero* v. *Richardson*, 411 US 677, 93 S. Ct 1764. [. . .]
10 *Murphy* v. *Attorney General*, [1982] IR 241.
11 *Hyland* v. *Minister for Social Welfare*, High Court, unreported, 18 January 1988.
12 *Dennehy* v. *Minister for Social Welfare*, High Court, unreported, 26 July 1984.
13 The common law rule of paternal supremacy was replaced by the right of both parents jointly to educate and to have custody of their children in Re Tilson, [1951] IR 1.
14 *Dáil Debates*, vols 67–8, col. 69.
15 Ibid., col. 71.
16 The Criminal Law (Amendment) Act, 1935, made it a criminal offence for any person to sell or to import for sale any contraceptive.
17 In *De Burca* v. *Anderson*, [1976] IR 385, Chief Justice O'Higgins said that 'some preferential treatment of women citizens seems to be contemplated by the Constitution' [. . .]
18 See Commission on the Status of Women: Report to the Minister for Finance, Dublin: Stationery Office 1972 (Prl. 2760), 110.
19 Income Tax Act, 1967, section 192.
20 Commission on the Status of Women: Report to the Minister for Finance.
21 Between 1937 and 1970, a period of thirty-three years, there were only thirteen major constitutional challenges to post-1937 statutes. Between 1971 and 1987, a period of sixteen years, there were forty-five major challenges. See T. A. Finlay, *The Constitution: Fifty Years On*, Dublin 1988, p. 12.
22 [1972] IR 330.
23 *McGee* v. *Attorney General*, [1974] IR 284.
24 [1976] IR 38.

25 See Yvonne Scannell, 'Changing times for women's rights', in Eilean Ni Chuilleanain (ed.), *Irish Women: Image and Achievement*, Dublin, 1985, pp. 64–5.

26 Justice Walsh, in *De Burca and Anderson* v. *Attorney General*, [1976] IR 385, said that in his view 'it was not open to the State to discriminate in its enactments between persons who are subject to its laws solely on the grounds of the sex of those persons'. Justice Hamilton, in *Murphy* v. *Attorney General*, [1982] IR 241, held that section 192 of the Income Tax Act, 1967, violated Article 40.1, because 'it discriminated invidiously against married couples and the husband in particular'.

27 Social Welfare Act, 1970 (deserted wives' allowances), Social Welfare Act, 1973 (unmarried mothers' allowances), Social Welfare (No. 2) Act, 1974 (prisoners' wives' allowances).

28 Health (Family Planning) Act, 1979. See also the Health (Family Planning) (Amendment) Act, 1986.

29 Family Law (Maintenance of Spouses and Children) Act, 1976, and Maintenance Orders Act, 1974.

30 Family Law (Maintenance of Spouses and Children) Act, 1976, and Family Law (Protection of Spouses and Children) Act, 1981.

31 Family Home Protection Act, 1976.

32 Family Law Act, 1981.

33 Domicile and Recognition of Foreign Divorces Act, 1986.

34 Status of Children Act, 1987.

35 After the judgement in *Airey* v. *Ireland*, [1979] 2 European Human Rights Reports 305, the government established a non-statutory scheme of legal aid and advice, to be administered through law centres. The scheme is very defective. See Alan Shatter, *Family Law in the Republic of Ireland*, 3rd edn, Dublin, 1986, pp. 60–70.

36 [1985] ILRM 61.

37 High Court, unreported, 12 February 1988.

38 In *Attorney General (Society for the Protection of the Unborn Child (Ireland) Ltd.)* v. *Open Door Counselling Ltd,* [1987] ILRM 477, Justice Hamilton, President of the High Court, relied on this amendment to deny Irish women the right to information on abortion facilities available outside the jurisdiction. On appeal to the Supreme Court, this decision was upheld; the process of erosion may have begun.

39 The author's objections, as a lawyer, to this amendment relate to the very grave legal and ethical difficulties it presents for people (including the sick mother) involved in decision-making when pregnancy threatens a woman's life.

PART THREE

Health and Sexuality

I T IS WIDELY RECOGNISED that pre-famine Ireland was a country characterised by early marriage patterns and high marital fertility. This was significantly changed by the economic shock of famine which transformed the country into one of later marriage, with an exceptionally high level of celibacy and still high marital fertility. The Great Famine of 1845–9 resulted in widespread death and emigration, which appears to have affected women in different ways to men. Indeed, in some areas it seems that women were more likely than men to survive the ravages of famine. However, given the regional variations in famine suffering, women's survival rate was prone to fluctuate and the overall pattern of survival on a gendered basis is currently unclear.

Similarly, much has still to be uncovered about, arguably, the most private aspects of women's lives: sexuality and health. That Irish women's sexuality has, until recently, not been an area of historical enquiry is perhaps unsurprising. The dominant Catholic ideology of the newly established Irish Free State in the 1920s and 1930s in a sense desexualised women to such an extent that even sex within marriage was considered too risqué for public an often even for private discussion. One consequence of this taboo was that little historical attention was directed towards unearthing the sexual activities of Irish women. There was, however, a multiplicity of sexual alliances common in nineteenth-century Ireland. Sexual activity was affected by marital status, social and economic position, conditioning mores with their strictly defined codes of respectability, and the ostracisation that would be directed at those who failed to conform in terms of chastity and virtue. Hence the once one-dimensional view of women in nineteenth-century Ireland as wives and mothers, free from the stigmas of illegitimacy, pre-marital sex, infanticide and prostitution now gives way to a more complex representation of women.

Another hidden aspect of Irish women's lives is that of prostitution. Prostitutes were the very women who subverted the prevalent social mores demanding chastity and virtue. The experience of the prostitute was something of a twilight world of paid sex. Steps were taken by moral reformers, both lay and religious, to reform the so-called 'fallen' women of nineteenth- and twentieth-century Ireland whose very existence was believed to threaten the moral fabric of society. But the perceived threat posed by prostitutes ran deeper than this, as they were also seen as a physical danger in terms of the spread of disease. Prostitution continued to arouse controversy throughout the nineteenth and twentieth centuries. Equally controversial was the dissemination of birth-control advice and devices. Although steps were taken in the 1930s to make controlling fertility more accessible for women in Belfast, with the establishment of the first birth-control clinic in Ireland, the project was not an unqualified success. Indeed, the clinic actually closed its doors for the last time in 1947.

Mental illness and experiences in institutions are other controversial aspects of Irish women's health. Perhaps what is most striking about this area are the reasons for which women were labelled as 'mad'. Many were women who refused or were unable to conform to the prevalent gender ideology of the time, others were suffering from physical ailments, often associated with menstruation and miscarriage. Even too fervent a religious devotion could be interpreted as a symptom of mental imbalance. But common to all aspects of women's health and sexuality was the fact that so much in this area was unremarked upon for so long.

Suggestions for further reading

Linda Ballard, '"Just whatever they had handy": aspects of childbirth and early child care in Northern Ireland, prior to 1948', *Ulster Folklife*, 31, 1985.

Caitríona Clear, 'The decline of breast-feeding in twentieth-century Ireland', in Alan Hayes and Diane Urquhart (eds), *Female Experiences: Essays in Irish Women's History*, Dublin, 2000.

Margaret Kelleher, *The Feminisation of Famine: Expressions of the Inexpressible?*, Cork, 1997.

June Levine and Lyn Madden, *Lyn: A Story of Prostitution*, Dublin, 1987.

Pádraig Ó Héalaí, 'Pregnancy and childbirth in Blasket Island tradition', *Women's Studies Review*, 5, 1997.

Louise Ryan, 'The massacre of innocence: infanticide in the Irish Free State', *Irish Studies Review*, 14, 1996.

Elizabeth Steiner-Scott, '"To bounce a boot off her now and then . . .": domestic violence in post-Famine Ireland', in Maryann Gialanella Valiulis and Mary O'Dowd (eds), *Women and Irish History: Essays in Honour of Margaret MacCurtain*, Dublin, 1997.

Oonagh Walsh, 'A lightness of mind': gender and insanity in nineteenth-century Ireland', in Margaret Kelleher and James H. Murphy (eds), *Gender Perspectives in Nineteenth-Century Ireland: Public and Private Spheres*, Dublin, 1997.

Women's Committee of the National Union of Public Employees, *Women's Voices: An Oral History of Northern Irish Women's Health (1900–1990)*, Dublin, 1992.

Chapter 11

Dympna McLoughlin

■ from **WOMEN AND SEXUALITY IN NINETEENTH-CENTURY IRELAND**, *The Irish Journal of Psychology*, 15/2–3, 1994, pp. 266–75

As in Europe generally, there was a spectacular range of sexual relationships in nineteenth-century Ireland, thus challenging the stereotype of a country of exceptional chastity and prudery. Economic factors played a pivotal role in Irish women's sexual expression. Women of property had to be very circumspect in their behaviour. Women of different classes and circumstances could behave differently in entering short- or long-term liaisons, with men of their own or indeed higher social class. These women essentially drew up their own sexual contracts. However, by the late nineteenth century, there was less and less tolerance of sexual diversity and of women initiating their own destiny. This period (1880s onward) witnessed the triumph of respectability. Henceforth, there was only one acceptable life path for women – marriage and motherhood – and a diminishing tolerance for any type of sexual diversity. [. . .]

There were essentially three main characteristics of a respectable woman, regardless of class. The first was that she have an overwhelming desire to marry, remain faithful in a lifelong union, and remain subordinate and publicly dependent in that relationship. Second, the woman's natural sphere was the domestic, where she engaged in reproductive and not productive tasks. Mothering became newly defined and confined and the widespread practice of wet-nursing became severely curtailed. Third, and most significantly, women's sexuality was totally contained in marriage. This was not true for men and there was public leeway for male 'indiscretions'. Since women were believed to have no sexual desire they were compensated with a superior 'moral nature' and a heightened sense of right and wrong in sexual matters.[1] This belief made women into a moral army; not only were they responsible for their own shortcomings, they were also responsible for the shortcomings of their menfolk. Failings of women (especially of a sexual nature) were viewed as much more serious than the same failing in a man. There was a belief that a man could be easily led astray by a beguiling woman and since men had little powers of resistance (since they were creatures driven by desire), they could do little else but succumb. Thus the justification of the double standard was laid on biology, obscuring the strong economic factors which influenced the sexual behaviour of nineteenth-century Irishwomen.

[. . . Ireland was widely believed to be] a country with low nuptiality, high marital fertility, minimal illegitimacy, large scale emigration, and celibacy. Lending further credibility to this view were the testaments of nineteenth-century travellers such as Dickens and Kohl. Their assertions of a country filled with virtuous virgins, widespread abstinence and chastity gladdened the hearts of nationalists and clerics alike in the twentieth century. [. . .] It is naïve to accept that this tightly ordained structure of delayed inheritance, a dowry for one daughter and the easy disposal of the rest of the family through permanent celibacy, or the seeking after a religious vocation, operated without aberration or discord. Scepticism about the low illegitimacy rate and, by implication, the absence of sexual activity outside marriage, must be challenged in the Irish context considering the following range of factors.

1   In all countries a high level of marital fertility was accompanied by a similar level of extra-marital fertility. [. . .] Was the constant articulation of the purity of Irishwomen a warning to them rather than an accurate reflection of reality?

2   In Ireland there was a thriving trade in prostitution not only in the cities but also in the garrison towns. [. . .] The passing of the Contagious Diseases Acts in Ireland in 1864, 1866 and 1869 and their implementation in Dublin, Cork, Cobh and the Curragh and the subsequent campaign for their repeal, reveals not only a double standard of sexual morality, but a widespread public awareness of prostitution and the sale of sex.

3   Alongside the observations of the exceptional chastity of the Irish were parallel statements of shock at the ribaldry and sexual explicitness of games meant for the amusement of mourners at wakes. [. . .] Whilst accepting the many testimonies to the enduring and intimate nature of these sexual frolics at wakes, some may argue that this was an occasional and symbolic form of (simulated? actual?) sexual release. Looking to another source, Irish folklore, one will find that this was not the case. Matters of a sexual nature were not sanitised out of the folk memory. Women who were impatient with shy lovers administered love potions to them which 'set the man mad and afterwards he had to marry the girl', and for the 'lethargic' who were unable to initiate or complete sexual relations there were also particular remedies.[2] Sex was a vital and pleasurable act in both an affirmation and a continuation of life. Celibacy or abstinence were not celebrated in this tradition.

4   How did the 'gentleman's miss' fare in these statements about purity? In nineteenth-century Ireland, the 'gentleman's miss' was public knowledge. She was a women of lower socio-economic rank who was prepared to sell her sexual favours to a gentleman on her own terms.

5   In the minute books of the various poor-law unions there are letters from emigrant women, previously assisted to emigrate to North America and Australia, who sought children left behind in the workhouse. These women were sent out to the colonies as single unmarried individuals, but, on becoming settled and earning a livelihood, sent for their children. [. . .] These

petitions, and there were many of them, reveal the extent which women could conceal unapproved aspects of their lives (illegitimate offspring) from officialdom. [. . .] Indeed these schemes might be an early example of the Irish exporting their problems so that the stereotype of a virtuous and unblemished womanhood remained intact.

6   The presence of the Dublin foundling hospital in the eighteenth century, the use of the workhouse as a dumping ground for unwanted children in the nineteenth century, as well as the many private institutions and orphanages for unwanted and deserted children, would suggest sexual activity outside approved social norms, or practices unable to be sustained in the emerging economic order.

7   Details of illegitimacy and illicit sexual contact are not to be found in the official records of the age. The fact remains that illegitimacy, infanticide and the concealment of births did not come under sustained official scrutiny and are thus presumed not to have existed. [. . .]

To accept the notion that the Irish remained immune from strong and definite demographic trends in Europe is to glide over a vital area of Irish life and to obscure vital elements in the history of women. This includes the realms of work, marriage, sexuality, childbirth and child-rearing, and indeed for many, their very survival.

[. . .] There was not a single norm of sexual alliance in Ireland in this period, but rather a whole series of relationships both casual and permanent (see Table 11.1). In the 'gentleman's miss' situation, the 'miss' had the power to define the terms of her sexual involvement, including provision for the children of the union. By far the commonest sexual alliance was between men and women of the very poorest ranks of society. These were termed 'irregular unions' since they were not recognised by either church or state. However, these destitute paupers believed themselves to be married, since they had paid a small sum of money to a 'couple beggar' and in return he performed a rudimentary ritual over them. It was the

Table 11.1   Sexual transactions in nineteenth-century Ireland

Sex	Power	Gentleman's miss
	Survival	Irregular unions
	Formal exchange	Marriage
	Informal/transient contact	Prostitution
	Forfeit	Nuns
	Pending (hopefully)	Heterosexual contact
	Satisfied	Homosexual relationships
	'Ill', 'deviant' but acknowledged	'Self-polluters', 'hysterics', 'Mad', those who abandoned children
	Unacknowledged	Women guilty of infanticide

joint effort of both man and woman in their unions which made for their own survival and that of any children they might have had. These unions varied in duration. If one partner was deemed to be unsatisfactory the alliance was terminated.

The formal exchange of a chaste dowered woman by her father to a man with land or property was slowly becoming the only acceptable mode of sexual alliance from 1880 onwards. The chastity of the woman sealed the contract and ensured only a legitimate male heir had a claim to the land. These were respectably married women, to be envied in their esteemed position as wives and more importantly in the Irish context, as mothers. There was the same degree of contempt for women who sold sex in transient contact as there was for spinsters who remained on as an unwelcome burden with their married siblings. Women who did Trojan work in schooling, in the administration of hospitals and asylums as religious sisters were hardly recognised at all, as was the case with the other women who were failing to conform to the dominant stereotype of an appropriate feminine destiny.

Three types of sexual alliance will be briefly outlined – the 'gentleman's miss', very poor women with illegitimate children, and finally, aspiring middle-class women.

[. . .] The interest of a gentleman in a woman was her passport to a comfortable life. His sexual pleasure with her, even if short-lived, meant that she had his lifelong interest and protection. She and their children were usually given a small cottage and land while the gentleman lived and, on his death, she obtained legal title to these and sometimes even extras such as orchards or rights of way.[3] Sometimes this union was lifelong, giving rise to subsequent disputes over the legitimacy of the heirs; often it was only for a few years. In the latter cases the gentleman often provided a marriage partner for his former mistress. It was usually someone of his acquaintance of an artisan or labouring background, men for whom the promise of money and land was irresistible. There was never difficulty in procuring husbands for these women, despite their very public loss of virtue, and their very comfortable economic position no doubt overcame prejudices. In general:

> a girl that has been seduced by a gentleman, is not looked upon as being altogether so impure as one who has been led into error by one in her own station . . . the leniency of opinion arose from the possibility that she had weighty reasons for her yielding.[4]

Overall there was a kind of grudging admiration of this woman's economic astuteness, and her ability to take care of her self and her own interests. She never became an outcast as did the middle-class women who broke with the conventions of acceptable behaviour of both their sex and their class.

[. . .] Few were concerned with the fate of pauper women as they carried on with their lives, making deliberate efforts to make themselves invisible to official eyes. Their sexual behaviour was deemed to be outside the bounds of decency and respectability and thus not worthy of public interest or scrutiny. In 1836, in Skull in County Cork it was noted that [the]:

circumstance of having an illegitimate child is thought less of in this parish than elsewhere. They are all too much reduced and in too great poverty to feel the distinction. There is very little feeling of respectability among them.[5]

In the industrial north-east of Antrim, it was noted in the same report that 'the crime of being the mother of a bastard and the misfortune of being a bastard are little thought of here'.[6] Industrial context was very different from the rural one. Land, lineage and virtue were not the prerequisites to wealth and respectability. In an industrial context, fortunes could be easily amassed and status was achieved rather than ascribed.

[. . .] If a woman was impregnated through pre-marital sexual relation, and the man refused to marry her, she was in a most wretched predicament. Her only chance of redemption was if her father provided an extra large dowry 'in order to cover her disgrace'.[7] The size of the marriage dowry, of anything up to one hundred pounds, was viewed as the financial worth of female purity and virtue. However, in practice, the colossal sum paid to compensate for lost virtue only served to circumscribe the conduct of the middling sorts even more. There could be no frolicking with any man, since an 'accident' of any type could render them in a most vulnerable situation. If the man refused to marry them and if their fathers were unable or unwilling to provide them with a dowry then they remained unmarriageable and a humiliation upon the family as well as an economic burden. These women could either conceal their illegitimate offspring, or else remain absolutely celibate until their nuptials. Increasingly after 1850, the middling sorts of folk, farmers in particular, stressed the absolute importance of female virtue. An unvirtuous daughter could be the ruination of an otherwise thrifty and farseeing man.

The daughters of the thrifty and wealthy were continuously watched and gossiped about. This gossip served as a social control on their actions. It also served as a means of letting mercenary-minded men know when somebody's daughter had been impregnated and abandoned and the financial booty that might be in the offing for any man willing to repair the damage by a 'subsequent marriage'.[8] In this sense, sexual prudery in nineteenth-century Ireland had little to do with the Church and all to do with the economics of the emerging middle class. Delayed sexual intimacy for women until marriage was thus to emerge as a most important social [norm] that was vigorously enforced in almost every aspect of life.

Few men were willing to place their wealth and status at risk by attempting to conceal their daughter's shame. Economics, and not sentiment, were the main issues here. There was public contempt also for the man who took a pregnant bride (even if he was the father of the child). He was known as a 'purchased husband', a 'mean fellow', or it was simply stated that he was paid to marry the woman. Generally these men were believed to demean themselves by voluntarily participating in the woman's disgrace and therefore judged as just as morally corrupt. For women who did manage to find a marriage partner all they gained was the slightest shred of respectability. Under this cloak of marriage they could be endlessly exploited and abused without sympathy or comment. Having lost caste there was little social concern with her subsequent fate. [. . .]

The unmarried pregnant woman was in a most wretched condition, depending on the charity of her family for her support. Families less tolerant of her disgrace cast her away from them to become a vagrant. Having no skills and having been shunned by decent society many had to resort to the workhouse or prostitution. Whatever path they chose, theirs was a most difficult lot. An awareness of the vulnerability of pregnancy outside marriage was acute for many young women and the fear of their families' wrath coupled with the astute realisation of their lack of employment prospects in Ireland made many of them extremely conservative in their courtships. [. . .]

The purpose of this short piece is to question the myth of nineteenth-century Ireland as some idealised asexual age, where there were no sexual relations outside marriage, no prostitution, infanticide, or child abandonment nor indeed any forms of sexual deviance. This was not the case. These are issues which long predate the nineteenth century. In the Irish situation we have ignored them totally, filtered them (along with social history generally) out of a very politicised history and thus incorrectly assumed they are of recent origin.

In the nineteenth century there was great variety and complexity in women's lives. The single life pattern for women, of marriage, husband and children was only becoming widespread in the 1880s and was ultimately to reach its fullest expression in the newly independent Ireland and most especially in the 1937 Constitution. Here many roles had been pared away totally, and women received only partial recognition, not as citizens but as mothers. [. . .]

Notes

1   In the Irish context this sense of the superior morality of women had little impact in the social sphere. [. . .]

2   See the records of the Irish Folklore Commission in University College Dublin.

3   For an example, see the indenture made between William Barrett of Culleenamore in Sligo and Letitia Begley of Culleenamore, Spinster. Letitia received a lease for three lives and a considerable amount of property in a will dated 2 March 1822. The indenture concludes 'and it is further agreed that the said Letitia Begley can only have the power of bequeathing the said demesne premises to the children of the said William Barrett begotten on the body of the said Letitia Begley and to no other person whatsoever'. Letitia placed her mark in agreement with the terms in the indenture.

4   First Report of His Majesty's Commissioners for inquiring into the condition of the poorer classes in Ireland, appendix A. HC 1835 xxxii, County Clare Parish Kilfarboy, including town of Miltown Malbay, p. 78.

5   Ibid., County Cork, Parish Skull, p. 27.

6   Ibid., County Antrim, Parish Resharkin, p. 38.

7   Ibid., County Carlow, the Parish of Aghade and Ballin, p. 57. Also see Barony of Kilkenny West, p. 68.

8   A subsequent marriage was marriage after conception of a child, in other words, to a pregnant bride.

Chapter 12

Maria Luddy

■   from 'ABANDONED WOMEN AND BAD CHARACTERS': PROSTITUTION IN NINETEENTH-CENTURY IRELAND, *Women's History Review*, 6/4, 1997, pp. 485–503

[. . .]

PROSTITUTION EXISTED PUBLICLY in the streets, and less openly in the brothels and public houses of the towns and cities of Ireland. For many women prostitution was a way of life, for others it was a casual occupation. It is difficult to provide accurate figures of the numbers of women who worked as prostitutes in any given period. Estimates of the numbers of women engaged in this business varied according to who was telling the story and what particular point they were trying to make. William Logan, a mission worker from Leeds who visited Ireland in 1845, noted that Cork allegedly contained eighty-five regular brothels and 356 public prostitutes. He also remarked that in Cork 'a large number of procuresses abound [. . .] Individuals [. . .] have been known to tender their daughters and other relatives to brothel keepers for money'.[1] Noting that even prostitution paid homage to class distinctions, Logan also mentioned that there were thought to be one hundred 'privateers' who operated from houses not designated as brothels. Indeed the social hierarchy of prostitutes mirrored the class structure of society itself. [. . .] Information provided to Logan in Dublin allowed for 1,700 prostitutes operating in the city, while Belfast was deemed to have 236 prostitutes residing in brothels there.[2] Arrests for prostitution in Ireland between 1870 and 1900 went from 3,673 in 1870, to 2,186 in 1885, to a low of 656 by 1900.[3] [. . .]

That prostitution was a considerable problem in Dublin and elsewhere in Ireland can be gauged by the fact that by 1835 there were at least eleven rescue homes, or Magdalen asylums, attempting to reform prostitutes in Dublin.[4] These existed along with other refuges which took in destitute women. Other Magdalen asylums operated around the country, one even being opened in the small market town of Tralee in 1854 and operated by the Sisters of Mercy. Prostitutes were also to be found in large numbers in all the workhouses of the country. Indeed many guardians feared that some women gained access to the workhouse for the sole purpose of procuring.[5] Towns which housed garrisons also accommodated women who worked as prostitutes. [. . .]

The Irish authorities appear generally to have taken a complacent attitude to prostitution. However, there were, at times, efforts made to clear the streets of prostitutes. For example, the *Freeman's Journal* reported in 1855 that a magistrate complained that Dublin Metropolitan Police (DMP) efforts to clear prostitutes from French Street were of dubious value since they merely had the effect of dispersing the prostitutes into 'respectable locales'.[6] [. . .] In the 1870s a more concerted effort was made by the DMP to close down some brothels. These attempts may have been occasioned by the Contagious Diseases Acts legislation and were often instigated and supported by the public and by the clergy. [. . .] Police activity was often a pretence of vigilance. It was when prostitution involved violence, disturbed the public peace or became too noticeable that it became an issue of public, and hence of police, concern.

The police had many legal codes to help them deal with prostitutes, though there was no legal definition of what constituted a prostitute and prostitution itself was not outlawed. For example, under the Police Clauses Acts of 1847 a woman deemed to be 'a common prostitute or night walker loitering or importuning passengers for the purpose of prostitution', could be arrested.[7] That section was extended under the Towns' Improvements Acts of 1854 to include women being 'otherwise offensive'.[8] Women found themselves, under the Towns' Improvement Act, in the company of all kinds of individuals trying to earn a living, such as fortune-tellers, performers, and beggars. These were individuals who were deemed [. . .] capable of causing public disorder. This section provided the police with broad discretionary powers of arrest. Women could also be taken up under the vagrancy laws. There were also laws against keeping bawdy houses or brothels. The role of the state in monitoring sexual behaviour was practically confined to arrests for public prostitution and solicitation, and hence singled out the lowliest class of prostitutes, those who peddled their wares in the streets, for arrest.

It was, however, under the Contagious Diseases Acts that the broadest powers were given to the police. As is well known, Parliament passed the first of three statutes which permitted the compulsory inspection of prostitutes for venereal disease in certain military camps in both England and Ireland in 1864. In Ireland the areas designated 'subjected districts' were Cork, Cobh and the Curragh camp. In effect the acts subjected women who were on the street to arbitrary and compulsory medical examination. If the woman inspected was infected she was forcibly detained in a Lock hospital for a period of up to nine months and registered as a prostitute. As a result of the introduction of the acts, Lock hospitals were established in both Cork and the Curragh in 1869.

The acts, which applied only to women, were intended to stop the spread of venereal diseases. They remained in force until 1883 when they were suspended, and were finally repealed in 1886. [. . .] Women who were arrested and summonsed were ordered to be examined at a certified hospital. If they refused to be examined they could be imprisoned for a month. [. . .] It could be argued that the women who worked as prostitutes in the subjected districts were permitted to continue their business provided they allowed themselves to be examined, and if necessary treated, for venereal diseases. Those women who worked as prostitutes outside the subjected districts continued to be taken up under legislation dealing with vagrancy and disorderly conduct. [. . .]

Organised opposition to the acts did not emerge until 1869, when the government proposed to extend them. In that year the National Anti-Contagious Diseases Acts Extensions Association, better known as the National Association, was formed. Women established their own organisation, the Ladies National Association (LNA), led by Josephine Butler. In England repeal groups proliferated between 1870 and 1884, and in Ireland too, branches of the National Association and the LNA were formed.[9] While many of the societies in England worked in their specific localities the organisations in Ireland worked on a national basis.

In Ireland membership of the repeal association was generally confined to Anglicans, Quakers, Presbyterians, Wesleyan Methodists and Congregationalists. Many of the members of the LNA, Anna Haslam and Isabella Tod for example, were leading activists in political campaigns to improve the position of women in society.[10] Opposition to the acts from religious bodies came mostly from within the Nonconformist churches whose members saw them as symbolising an acceptance of the double standard of sexual morality. [. . .] Public awareness of the acts in Ireland appears to have been limited as so few areas were affected by the legislation. [. . .]

That there was some public concern about prostitution is without doubt. But in many instances the public had an ambivalent attitude to prostitution. [. . .] That no absolute sexual moral standard was enforced regarding prostitution is evident from the fact that the most common concern about prostitution was its visibility. A correspondent to the *Freeman's Journal* in 1866, as part of a series of correspondence to that paper regarding the 'irrepressible evil', noted that 'for the purpose of decency they [prostitutes] should be kept out of the vicinity of the public ways'.[11] [. . .]

Just as prostitution was an evil which had to be contained, prostitutes were themselves regarded as sites of moral infection. A witness to a hospital commission noted that 'If we allowed these swell ladies from Mecklenburgh Street to flit about in pink wrappers and so on, it would be a distinct inducement to others less hardened to persevere in that life in the hope that probably they would arrive at similar distinction'.[12] Not only might prostitutes be carriers of disease but prostitution itself might be contagious. Within Irish workhouses a 'classification' system was in operation, from the 1850s, which attempted to keep 'respectable' women and girls away from the 'unrespectable'. A report of the Carlow Union from 1854, for example, noted that, 'although there is no separate ward in the workhouse for prostitutes, the master and matron, who are aware of the importance of the matter, do all in their power to prevent prostitutes associating with other females'.[13]

Commentators on prostitution portrayed prostitutes as women whose lives were destroyed by sexual experience. Rescuers never accepted that, in a country which provided few employment opportunities for women, women could choose prostitution as a viable means of earning or supplementing an income. [. . .] Logan stated that prostitutes came usually from the lower classes: 'low dressmakers, and servants; manure collectors, who are sent very young to the streets for that purpose, have also furnished their quota'.[14] [. . . They] were not accepted into brothels unless they were well recommended, usually by another prostitute, and paid eight shillings per week to their mistresses for board; any other money they made was for their own use. He also claimed that sisters often lived together and 'support[ed] their parents and relatives by the wages of prostitution'.[15]

[. . .] Organised prostitutes, those who worked in brothels, were probably a little better off than their street-walking counterparts. For a number of women, managing their own brothel was a lucrative business. [. . .] In Limerick, for example, in July 1836 we find eight women charged with keeping 'houses of ill fame'.[16] For poorer prostitutes, however, conditions could be miserable. The 'Bush' was a wooded place near Cobh where '20 to 25 to 30 women [. . .] lived [. . .] all the year round under the furze [. . .] like animals'.[17] Many prostitutes followed soldiers around from one depot to another. The 'wrens of the Curragh' were a notorious band of prostitutes who lived primitively in makeshift huts on the perimeters of the Curragh camp. The numbers of women living in these conditions varied but up to sixty women were stated to live at the Curragh. Even living in such conditions there was a certain bond of solidarity amongst the women who occupied the 'nests' and they pooled their meagre financial resources.[18] Evidence relating to the 'wrens' also suggests that prostitution was a seasonal occupation. Harvesters sometimes joined the band of women during the winter, while the numbers of women at the Curragh declined during the winter when many of them returned to the city. [. . .]

The first attempts to target sexual vice in itself came from individuals who were concerned with moral reform. Rescue work became an important arena of public philanthropy amongst women in the nineteenth century. The first involvement of women in collective efforts to reform prostitutes and discourage young women from being drawn into a life of prostitution appears to have been the Magdalen asylum established by Arbella Denny in 1765. [. . .] Between 1765 and 1914 at least thirty-three refuges or asylums were formed in Ireland for the rescue of 'fallen women'.[19]

In contrast to religious-run Magdalen asylums, lay asylums seem to have excluded the admission of hardened prostitutes. Lay rescue workers targeted those who were redeemable, young girls who had not yet been hardened into vice. However, rescue workers soon discovered that many of their charges resisted reformation. [. . .] Female moral reformers enclosed their politics within the boundaries of an institution that resembled a family dwelling. When their efforts at redemption failed, or as often occurred, were rejected by the prostitutes, they took in only women whom they deemed salvageable. The case histories provided in some of the annual reports indicate that many of the women appear not to have been prostitutes at all. Many were 'seduced' women, who, on abandonment by their seducers and families, turned to the asylums for protection. It was probably easier to reclaim young and 'seduced' women than hardened prostitutes, and the greater the success rate claimed by the asylums in the reform of penitents the more justification they had for their existence and the greater their claim on the public support on which the lay asylums depended.

That there was an abundance of refuges there is no doubt, and the majority were run by Catholic nuns. The refuges attempted three things: to keep 'fallen women' from public view, to reform the women and to prevent girls and young women from falling into vice.

Magdalen asylums were places of confinement and the women who entered these dwellings were expected to spend at least enough time there to bring about their reformation. Life within these institutions was severely restricted and restrictive. Women were often separated into different classes. In the Dublin Female Penitentiary the classification was carried out with reference 'to their [the inmates'] former education and habits of life',[20] suggesting a social rather than moral classification. In some religious-run asylums classifications were made according to the amount of time spent in the institution and the degree of penitence displayed by the inmate. Not only were 'fallen women' to be separated from the world but they were also to be separated from each other.

Once women entered these refuges, responsibility for their actions was laid firmly on the shoulders of the penitents themselves. A strict regime was followed in the asylums, which stripped the women of their former identity and attempted to mould a new one for them. Penitents were forbidden to use their own names or to speak of their past. [. . .] The women's past had to be abandoned but even in rejecting their past the penitents were never allowed to forget that they had sinned. Their daily life was made up of prayer, labour, recreation and silence. This programme of reform and discipline made no allowance either for maternal feeling. The children of penitents were usually sent for adoption. [. . .] All contacts with the outside world were limited and there were severe restrictions placed on the women's freedom within the institutions. [. . .]

There was, of course, no room for vanity and the most public aspect of vanity, the women's hair, was to be cut on entrance to the asylum. This, it was believed, was 'a means of bringing grace, which the willing sacrifice of their hair – on which they usually set such value – generally brings them'[21] [. . .] Cutting their hair was also a test for their motivation on entering, as the nuns believed that some women entered for the purpose of procuring.

[. . .] The most extensive network of Magdalen asylums, or refuges, was provided by Catholic nuns. The Good Shepherd nuns ran homes in Belfast, Cork, Limerick, New Ross and Waterford. The Sisters of Mercy ran a refuge in Galway and Tralee and an institution in Dun Laoghaire. The Sisters of Our Lady of Charity of Refuge operated an asylum in Drumcondra and a branch of that congregation ran a home from Gloucester Street in Dublin. The Sisters of Charity also operated a home in Cork and one in Dublin. After 1830 no lay Catholic asylum was established to look after prostitutes and those begun earlier in the century were all taken over by religious congregations. The Good Shepherd asylum in Cork appears to have been the only religious-run asylum established to meet the demand for a refuge resulting from the implementation of the Contagious Diseases Acts in the 1860s. It is clear that the Catholic hierarchy, and the Catholic public, felt that the only worthwhile impact to be made on fallen women could come from nuns.[22]

However, these religious-run asylums failed in their attempts to reform 'fallen women'. If we examine the numbers of women who entered and left these institutions the inability of Magdalen asylums to effect their objectives is obvious. In a breakdown of the inmates of seven asylums run by religious congregations during the nineteenth century it can be seen that overall these asylums catered for a total of 10,674 women over the period 1800–99. Of this number approximately 2,219 entered an asylum more than once. This is an underestimate, as not all the registers account for repeats. The majority of women who entered these refuges did so voluntarily, approximately 7,110, or just over 66 per cent, and a number of women re-entered, some as often as ten times.[23] From the available evidence it seems that entering a refuge was, for the majority of women, a matter of choice. While it is true that many destitute women had only the workhouse or the Magdalen asylum to turn to in times of utter distress, it would appear that the second was the favoured option of many. The length of stay in the asylums varied from one day for some women to an entire lifetime, of thirty or forty years, for others. It was generally women who entered in their teens or who were in their thirties or older, who remained in the homes. The decision to stay was made by the women themselves and although the nuns certainly did not encourage women to leave, they had little choice in the matter if the woman was determined to go. It would seem, from the number of re-entries, that some women may have used the asylums as a temporary shelter and once they were able to return to the outside world they did so. For others, the stability of life within a refuge, the order and discipline imposed, may have bought a sense of security, and made it an attractive option to remain.

Referrals to Magdalen asylums often came from religious, either priests and in some cases bishops, or nuns in other convents, as well as from hospital matrons and employers. Referrals were also made by family members, particularly parents who sent their daughters to a refuge, a practice which became more common as the century progressed. About 14 per cent or 1,309 women were expelled from the refuges.[24] Insubordination, violence, madness or a refusal to attend to religious duties or ceremonies were the reasons usually given for dismissal. A small number of penitents were dismissed for engaging in lesbian relationships, or 'particular friendships' as they were termed, within the home. Whether this involved actual sexual activity or not remains unrecorded. It was undoubtedly difficult for the nuns to control many of the penitents and they were probably glad to see the back of many of them. Expulsion did not mean that a penitent would not be taken back into the refuge again at a later stage. Indeed the nuns did not operate on any discriminatory basis and seem to have taken in any woman who came to their doors.

[. . .] The decline in prostitution noticeable in the police statistics may reflect some influence of the purity movement which was active from the 1880s. But it is more likely that rising educational standards, increased work opportunities and declining population, witnessed particularly in high levels of female emigration, were more influential. There was also a myriad of other societies which may have helped reduce the number of prostitutes operating in the country. A number of institutions were established which took in poor girls and trained them for employment in an effort to prevent them from falling into vice.

Perhaps the most effective force in reducing the level of prostitution was the new morality that was developing strongly amongst the Catholic population. The values of the propertied came to dominate in Irish society. Those who survived the Great Famine of 1845–51 were disproportionately farmers and other property owners, amongst whom cautious attitudes were becoming ingrained. This more calculating outlook found expression in such practices as dowry payments, impartible inheritance and a comparatively late age at marriage, and reticence in areas of sexual activity.[25] An ideology of sexual abstinence for the sake of the land eventually became the accepted basis for sexual morality of the entire society. This was a morality imposed by the family and the community, and reinforced by the teachings of the Catholic Church.

[. . .] The function of the Magdalen asylums was to change in the twentieth century, where they became increasingly homes for unmarried mothers, rather than for prostitutes.[26] The lay population saw these refuges run by nuns as institutions of repentance, of possible 'cure', and in the twentieth century as hiding places for 'shame filled' daughters. As the nuns had acquired authority over Catholic children through education, the Catholic community gave them the authority to mould and influence their wayward daughters and to keep them, and particularly their families, in an age which was becoming increasingly concerned with the concept of 'respectability', from public shame. [. . .]

Prostitutes, however, were not without some forms of resistance. They exercised their own forms of rebellion, resistance or nonconformity. They changed their names to confuse the authorities. They moved around from town to town. There was solidarity, seen particularly in the case of the 'wrens' of the Curragh. [. . .]

Prostitutes were, and are, referred to in many ways by commentators, rescue workers, etc. Amongst the descriptive names used were 'women of bad character', 'prostitutes', 'women of abandoned character', 'unfortunate women', 'dirty persons', 'destitute women' and the 'fallen'. Within the rescue homes they were termed penitents, Magdalens, and children. The range of names applied to women who worked as prostitutes relates the ambiguity, ambivalence, hypocrisy and disgust the public often felt towards these women. Ideally the public preferred not to think about, and certainly not to see, them at all. Confinement and reform were the ideal means of dealing with these women. Few individuals in nineteenth-century Ireland made any serious attempt to deal with the true causes of prostitution.

Notes

1   William Logan, *The Great Social Evil: Its Causes, Extent, Results and Remedies*, London, 1871, pp. 48–52.
2   Ibid., p. 95.
3   *Judicial and Criminal Statistics for Ireland*, 1871, 1886, 1901.
4   See Maria Luddy, 'Prostitution and rescue work in nineteenth-century Ireland', in Maria Luddy and Cliona Murphy (eds), *Women Surviving: Studies in Irish Women's History in the 19th and 20th Centuries*, Dublin, 1990, pp. 51–84.
5   *Annual Report of the Commissioners for Administering the Laws for the Relief of the Poor in Ireland*, H.C. 1854–1855 (1945), xxiv.
6   *Freeman's Journal*, 30 July 1855; 5 June 1857; 5 May 1880. [. . .]
7   10 & 11 Vic. c.89, s.28.
8   17 & 18 Vic. c.103, s.72.
9   See Maria Luddy, 'Women and the Contagious Diseases Acts in Ireland', *History Ireland*, 1, 1, 1992, pp. 32–4.

10   For the lives of Tod and Haslam see Mary Cullen and Maria Luddy (eds), *Women, Power and Consciousness in Nineteenth-Century Ireland: Eight Biographical Studies*, Dublin, 1995, pp. 161–230.

11   *Freeman's Journal*, 14 September 1866. See other letters in the same paper, 7, 15, 18, 19, 20, 24, 25, 28, 29 September and 1, 3, 5 October 1866, all on the same subject.

12   *Dublin Hospitals Commission: Report of the Committee of Inquiry*, H.C. 1887, xxxv, [c.5042], p. 94.

13   *Annual Report of the Commissioners for Administering the Laws for the Relief of the Poor in Ireland*, H.C. 1854–1855 (1945), xxiv.

14   Logan, *Great Social Evil*, pp. 49–50.

15   Ibid., p. 49.

16   *Limerick Chronicle*, 9 July 1836.

17   Evidence of Mr Curtis, *House of Commons Select Committee on CDAS*, 1882, (340) ix, Q. 11,256.

18   See Maria Luddy, 'An outcast community: the "wrens" of the Curragh', *Women's History Review*, 1/3, 1992, pp. 341–55.

19   See Maria Luddy, *Women and Philanthropy in Nineteenth-Century Ireland*, Cambridge, 1995, ch. 4.

20   Annual Report, Dublin Female Penitentiary, 1814, p. 6.

21   *Guide for the Religious Called Sisters of Mercy*, London, 1866, p. 58.

22   Luddy, *Women and Philanthropy*, p. 127.

23   Luddy, 'Prostitution', pp. 71–5.

24   Ibid., p. 75.

25   B. J. Graham and L. Proudfoot (eds), *An Historical Geography of Ireland*, London, 1993, pp. 158–84.

26   Tom Inglis, *Moral Monopoly: The Catholic Church in Modern Irish Society*, Dublin, 1987.

Chapter 13

David Fitzpatrick

■ from **WOMEN AND THE GREAT FAMINE**,
in Margaret Kelleher and James H. Murphy (eds),
Gender Perspectives in Nineteenth-Century Ireland:
Public and Private Spheres, Dublin, 1997, pp. 50–69

[. . .]

MORTALITY IS THE LEAST AMBIGUOUS index of the human cost of famine. It is scarcely surprising that no comprehensive record exists of the number of male and female deaths attributable to the Irish famine. Even if every death had been accurately recorded, the proportion caused by famine-induced deprivation or infection would remain conjectural. Nevertheless, the Irish case is documented by remarkably detailed 'tables of deaths' for each year between 1841 and 1851, recording the age and sex of those dying in each county (subdivided by deaths in rural districts, in towns and in public institutions). [. . .]

Since the impact of famine varied sharply between regions, it is essential to document the female experience in local context. The contrasts evident for Ireland as a whole are confirmed by mortality in Fermanagh, as summarised in Table 13.1. With the exception of the age group most affected by childbearing, women were substantially underrepresented in all categories by comparison with the county's population in 1841. Despite the surplus of women among surviving adults, the female advantage in rural mortality was particularly pronounced for those aged over thirty-five years. As in Ireland overall, the female component of mortality diminished slightly after 1845, except in the case of children. These relative gains were most notable in the case of middle-aged and younger women in rural districts. In the town of Enniskillen and in public institutions, however, there was a slight increase in the female contribution.[1] Further evidence of famine mortality is provided by the manuscript register of deaths in the workhouse and its auxiliaries in Enniskillen Union.[2] This district provides an instructive example of the ubiquity of suffering, which affected Catholics and Protestants in almost equal measure and culminated in the loss of about a quarter of the population between 1841 and 1851.

By comparison with the proportions of women admitted to the workhouse up to July 1847, female mortality was relatively light among younger adults (Table

Table 13.1   Female percentage of deaths and population in Fermanagh, 1841–51

Category	Period	Age					
		0	1–14	15–34	35–49	50+	Total
DEATHS	1841–5	44.1	46.0	54.7	48.6	46.9	47.6
	1846–5I	44.9	47.5	48.9	46.5	44.5	46.5
Institutions	1841–5	*44.4	*44.4	*45.0	*40.0	*35.3	39.1
	1846–51	50.0	46.0	55.6	52.7	44.8	47.9
Civic	1841–5	42.6	44.1	*54.2	*19.0	*48.3	42.9
	1846–51	36.3	48.2	48.7	37.1	44.4	44.5
Rural	1841–5	44.2	46.2	55.0	50.4	47.1	48.2
	1846–51	44.5	48.6	47.0	44.9	44.5	46.0
POPULATION	1841	48.2	48.9	52.5	52.0	51.4	50.8
	1851	50.1	49.2	51.4	53.2	52.5	51.0
Civic	1841	49.7	51.1	55.2	55.9	54.9	53.9
	1851	54.5	50.1	56.3	55.5	55.9	54.3
Rural	1841	48.1	48.8	52.4	51.8	51.2	50.7
	1851	49.8	49.1	51.1	53.1	52.4	50.9

Note: [Statistics for total deaths and population were derived from the reports of the Census of Ireland for 1841 and 1851 (HCP).] The only 'civic' district in Fermanagh was the town of Enniskillen. Asterisked figures represent populations of less than fifty.

13.2). This also applied to older inmates at the height of the crisis; only in the aftermath of the famine did women account for a majority of pauper deaths.[3] In Fermanagh, as in Ireland generally, women seem to have been more likely than men to survive the ravages of famine.

A contrasting urban pattern emerges from Table 13.3 for the city of Dublin, one of the few populations that actually increased between 1841 and 1851. This growth of population was a by-product of in-migration, masking considerable excess mortality in 1847, and especially during the cholera epidemic of 1849. The city had a substantial female majority of 55.0 per cent in 1841. Against the national pattern for civic districts, that majority declined to 53.9 per cent in 1851. In both census years, nearly three-fifths of those who had reached fifty were women. In Dublin, as in Irish towns overall, the female minority of deaths increased slightly in each age group after 1845. The returns of burials in Glasnevin cemetery, a major repository for northside Catholics from 1832 onwards, indicate that women were more likely than men to die poor.

Table 13.2   Female percentage of deaths and recipients of poor relief in Enniskillen Union, 1845–54

Category	Period	Age					
		0	1–14	15–34	35–49	50+	Total
ENNISKILLEN WORKHOUSE							
Deaths	1846–7	66.1	44.5	61.2	59.6	37.3	47.9
Deaths	1848–50	34.0	45.6	59.0	59.0	52.3	49.4
Deaths	1851–4	*61.1	46.9	48.3	*58.6	58.2	53.0
Admissions	1845–7	54.5	46.0	69.0	67.7	47.8	54.5
Outdoor relief	1848	None	54.4	75.1	81.4	75.8	76.3

Note: [. . .] The Record of Deaths, Indoor Relief Register and Outdoor Relief Register for Enniskillen Union are in the Public Record Office of Northern Ireland, Belfast, BG 14/KA/I, BG 14/G/I and BG 14/EA/I. The [abstracted] records of admissions to the workhouse terminate in early July 1847, and those for outdoor relief cover January to March 1848. Asterisked figures represent populations of less than fifty.

Table 13.3   Female percentage of deaths and population in Dublin city, 1841–51

Category	Period	Age					
		0	1–14	15–34	35–49	50+	Total
Deaths	1841–5	43.8	48.2	47.7	43.7	47.6	46.8
	1846–51	45.6	49.4	48.7	45.7	48.4	48.2
Population	1841	48.7	50.1	57.5	55.5	58.5	55.0
	1851	49.5	49.6	55.7	54.1	58.0	53.9

Note: [Statistics for total deaths and population were derived from the reports of the Census of Ireland for 1841 and 1851 (HCP).]

Table 13.4 indicates that the female component was almost invariably lower in the general plot than in the poor plot, where space could be secured for only 1s. 6d. Widows, always vulnerable to isolation and poverty, probably account for the overrepresentation of older women in the poor plot, both before and during the famine. For the destitute, however, burial was more likely to occur in an unbought and unmarked grave adjacent to the workhouse. The registers for North Dublin Union show that women accounted for just under half of the deaths recorded during the famine, whereas rather more women than men gained admission to the workhouse. Among children and older inmates, women had a slightly higher risk of death than their male counterparts.[4] These findings suggest that the general female advantage in adult mortality did not apply to Dublin's elderly poor, and

Table 13.4 Female percentage of deaths and recipients of poor relief in North Dublin, 1841–51

Category	Period	Age					Total
		0	1–14	15–34	35–49	50+	
BURIALS IN GLASNEVIN (ROMAN CATHOLIC) CEMETERY							
Poor plot	1844	48.2	52.4	56.8	51.2	61.1	53.6
Poor plot	1847	45.7	50.7	56.4	50.9	59.2	53.4
Poor plot	1849	45.3	47.3	46.7	59.8	67.7	53.8
General plot	1844	41.2	49.2	54.7	50.4	57.2	50.5
General plot	1847	45.0	50.5	49.7	50.0	50.8	49.7
General plot	1849	35.1	46.7	46.9	57.5	53.1	48.9
NORTH DUBLIN WORKHOUSE							
Deaths	1845–8	46.4	49.3	57.7	48.8	48.6	49.6
Admissions	1844–50	46.3	44.4	57.1	53.7	45.1	50.7

Note: [. . .] The Indoor Relief Register for North Dublin Union is at the National Archives, Dublin; the burial registers were kindly made available by the keepers of the Glasnevin cemetery. The age bands for Glasnevin burials in 1847 are 0, 1–19, 20–39, 40–9, and 50+. The statistics for admissions to the workhouse, and for Glasnevin burials in 1849, are derived from a sample of one in ten.

that Dublin women fared relatively badly during the famine and the cholera epidemic. In regions more drastically affected, however, women proved more resilient than men.

[. . .] The allocation of resources between men and women was governed by many agencies, including the family, employers, landlords, ratepayers and the state. The role of the state was critical in determining which subgroups of the poor should be given preferential access to relief, whether in the form of wages, food, or board and lodging. The schemes for public employment in 1846–7, administered by the Board of Works, were largely directed towards able-bodied men, who accounted for 83 per cent of recorded recipients in late January 1847. The 27,507 female wage-earners represented only 5 per cent of the workforce, a proportion subsequently reduced as a result of more rigorous exclusion of family dependants from employment.[5] In the absence of adequate alternative relief for those most vulnerable to destitution, committees in some localities had signed on far higher proportions of women, boys and elderly men: in Castlebellingham, Co. Louth, the female proportion apparently reached 35 per cent. Even there, however, wages were much higher for adult men than for women, though boys were yet worse off.[6] The manifest futility of paying cash to able-bodied men with superior 'endowment', while virtually ignoring those most in need, was a major factor in inducing the government to curtail public employment and vastly extend relief in kind through the 'soup kitchens'.[7] No record was kept of the sex of those receiving 'rations'; but the administrators directed relief towards families rather than individuals, and attempted to prevent male recipients from excluding their dependants from benefit. The relief commissioners justified their unpopular decision to provide cooked rather than raw meals by claiming that men had sold uncooked rations and become 'drunk upon the proceedings, leaving their children to starve'. The State, confronted by enraged mobs intent on wrecking soup kitchens, thus presented itself as the defender of those with inferior entitlements, against the arrogation of further benefits by persons already better endowed. The administration did not fully merit its self-image as fairy godmother to Ireland's oppressed dependants: the Temporary Relief Act of 1847 specified that male heads of family would normally collect the rations on behalf of their wives and children.[8] Had women been supplied directly with uncooked food, female and family claims might have been more effectively asserted through government of the hearth. Nevertheless, the tendency of state intervention was to undermine local hierarchies by redirecting much of the available free food to those lacking recognised entitlements.

It was through the much vilified poor law that the government most strenuously and effectively enhanced the entitlements of the weak, and to some extent of women. The rules for admission to the workhouse, and especially for provision of 'outdoor relief' once the soup kitchens had been closed down, were designed to penalise able-bodied adult men. So long as public employment or rations were available, the poor law provided only secondary relief for those otherwise disqualified. But from October 1847 onwards, almost all public assistance was managed by the Boards of Guardians or Vice-Guardians nominated by the poor law commissioners. Under the Poor Law Amendment Act of June 1847, able-bodied men could secure relief only if destitute, unemployed and virtually landless, and solely as inmates of the workhouse. Admittedly, the exclusion of able-bodied men from outdoor relief in kind was relaxed in the majority of unions because of insufficient space in the workhouses; whereas no outdoor relief for either sex was normally permitted in twenty-five unions.[9] Nevertheless, the allocation of poor relief was biased in favour of vulnerable classes such as widows, unhusbanded mothers and their children.

[. . .] Returns from immediately before and after the famine indicate that the female component of Ireland's workhouse population was 53.4 per cent in 1844 and 59.5 per cent in 1851. The age-breakdown available for 1844 confirms the prominence of women among inmates between fifteen and fifty, and their relative scantiness among the young and the old.[10] Thus poor relief appears to have favoured women over men among able-bodied adults, but no female advantage is demonstrable for the more vulnerable age groups. While offering a lifeline and often a deathline for both children and veterans, the workhouses of Ireland seem to have favoured male applicants when catering for those dependent classes.

[. . .] Temporarily but undeniably, the devastation of famine diminished the recognised value of children as future benefactors. The female endowment of potential motherhood was therefore devalued, a process reinforced by the reduction in fecundity resulting from malnutrition and consequent amenorrhoea during famines.[11] The decline in fertility [. . .] was compounded by a sharp drop in the number of marriages reported in 1847.[12] The reductions in nuptiality and fertility, though relatively unimportant in improving the survival chances of adult women, signified rapid deterioration in the most important of female exchange entitlements. The diminished appeal of childbearing and marriage was parodied in the reports of 'outrages' for 1847, which revealed an increase in infanticide but reductions in rape, attempted rape and abduction.[13] The devaluation of female services within families was compounded by the razing of cottages, the dissolution of households, and therefore the redundancy of managerial skills. On the roadside or in the workhouse, the power of the domestic administrator was negated.

[. . .] The intention of this essay is to provoke discussion of the evidence for discrimination against women in Irish history, by comparing male and female suffering and survival during an unexampled economic, social and familial crisis. To the extent that the incidence of mortality indicates relative victimhood, women had a marked initial advantage which was extended during the famine. The allocation of official relief, at least through the workhouse, favoured women among younger adults but males among children and the elderly. The state thus protected and enhanced the entitlements of dependants in general, and of non-dependent women. These relief measures affected a society in which the superiority of male endowments was less obvious than is usually assumed. If household and family services are analysed along with assets and skills with a monetary exchange value, the apparent differential in pre-famine entitlements is greatly diminished. The effect of famine was to reduce the value of most of these endowments, while increasing the demand for the provision of affection and solace, perhaps a female speciality. The roughly equal access of the sexes to emigration suggests that women were not effectively excluded from the most efficient path to survival and revival. If women were indeed the victims of systematic discrimination during the Irish famine, the evidence in support of that hypothesis has yet to be assembled.

Notes

1   These comparisons with pre-famine mortality are somewhat spurious, since the number of deaths recorded between 1841 and 1845 was only 138 in institutions and 226 in the town of Enniskillen.

2   The registers for Enniskillen were analysed by Desmond McCabe for the National Famine Research Project. The provisional statistics given in this paper are cited with the permission of my colleagues in the Project, which was supported by the Irish government's National Famine Commemoration Committee.

3   By 1851, according to the census, the female proportion of Enniskillen's workhouse population had risen to 60 per cent. The relative increase in female deaths therefore reflected an increasingly female intake.

4   These comparisons are approximate, since the available analysis (by Catherine Cox, for the National Famine Research Project) refers to a sample of admissions between 1844 and 1850 which does not represent the precise population from which those dying between 1845 and 1848 were drawn.

5   Correspondence [. . .] relating to the Measures adopted for the Relief of Distress in Ireland: Board of Works Series, Second Part, pp. 48–9, in HCP, 1847 [797], lii; Thomas P. O'Neill, 'The organisation and administration of relief, 1845–52', in R. Dudley Edwards and T. Desmond Williams (eds), The Great Famine, Dublin, 1956, p. 232.

6   Christine Kinealy, *This Great Calamity*, Dublin, 1994, p. 96. The return for Castlebellingham, in the barony of Ardee, enumerated 7,042 women and girls, 9,608 men and 3,606 boys on public works in the week ending 30 January 1847. The incomplete general return for the same week, cited in the previous note, showed only 155 women, 1,138 men and 324 boys for the entire barony, whose population in 1841 was 28,704.

7   See David Fitzpatrick, 'Famine, entitlements and seduction: Captain Edmond Wynne in Ireland, 1846–1851', *English Historical Review*, CX 437, 1995, p. 601.

8   See Kinealy, *This Great Calamity*, pp. 146, 149–50.

9   James S. Donnelly, 'The administration of relief, 1847–51', in W. E. Vaughan (ed.), *A New History of Ireland*, vol. V, *Ireland under the Union, I, 1801–70*, Oxford, 1989, pp. 317–20.

10 For various age groups, the female proportions of inmates relieved between 10 January and 9 April 1844 were 46.4 per cent (under 15); 69.2 per cent (15–34); 67.7 per cent (35–49); 46.8 per cent (over 50): *10th Annual Report of the Poor Law Commissioners*, pp. 352–4, in HCP, 1844 [560], xix. The returns for 30 March 1851 were published in the *General Report* of the 1851 census, p. xxi.

11 Michael W. Flinn, *The European Demographic System, 1500–1820*, Brighton, 1981, p. 31.

12 The *General Report* of the 1851 census, pp. 658–61, reveals that the number of marriages reported by surviving family heads declined from 34,433 in 1846 to 25,906 in 1847, thereafter somewhat recovering. The number in 1847 fell 25 per cent short of the mean annual figure for 1841–6. Corresponding provincial reductions were 36 per cent in Munster, 31 per cent in Connaught, 18 per cent in Ulster, and 17 per cent in Leinster. A similar change is evident in the Registrar-General's returns, restricted to non-Catholic marriages, showing a decline of 26 per cent between 1846 (9,344 marriages) and 1847 (6,943), followed by 9,048 in 1848 and 9,493 in 1849 (*Thom's Official Directory*, Dublin, 1850, p. 191).

13 The pattern is somewhat spoiled by the reduced incidence of concealment of birth and desertion of children, crimes which (like infanticide) were more prevalent in 1844 than during the famine. The number of reported infanticides was 135 in 1844, 107 in 1845, 100 in 1846 and 131 in 1847. Corresponding figures for other crimes were as follows: rape, 114, 102, 105 and 35; attempted rape, 43, 50, 49 and 23; abduction, 28, 17, 18 and 10; concealment of birth, 64, 63, 66 and 55; desertion of children, 191, 125, 147 and 116. See National Archives, Irish Crime Records, i, *Returns of Outrages reported to the Constabulary Office*.

Chapter 14

Áine McCarthy

■   from HEARTHS, BODIES AND MINDS:
GENDER IDEOLOGY AND WOMEN'S COMMITTAL
TO ENNISCORTHY LUNATIC ASYLUM, 1916–25,
in Alan Hayes and Diane Urquhart (eds) *Female Experiences:
Essays in Irish Women's History*, Dublin, 2000

[. . .]

TOWARDS THE END OF THE eighteenth century a fundamental change occurred in the way madness was perceived in Great Britain.[1] Until this time 'lunatics' were considered to be unfeeling, ferocious animals who needed chains, straitcoats, bars on locked cells and physical brutality to keep them in check. However, under new ideas of 'moral management' implemented thoughout the British Isles in the nineteenth century, the mad came to be regarded as sick human beings, objects of pity not fear, and capable of defeating their madness if subjected to kindly surveillance and care in comforting surroundings. Reformers posited 'asylums' as a suitable environment for this care, not the jails, workhouses or private madhouses in which the mad had previously been housed.

Enniscorthy District Lunatic Asylum, opened in 1869, was one of twenty-one Irish poor-law institutions built as part of the great wave of asylum construction in nineteenth-century Britain. Throughout that century, accommodation in Irish lunatic asylums continuously expanded, so that by 1901 there were almost 17,000 inmates in asylums originally planned for less than 5,000. Enniscorthy Asylum also grew rapidly: first admission rates per 10,000 population increased from 3.69 in 1871 to 6.14 in 1911, a percentage increase of 166 per cent. By 1916, there were 556 people in the asylum, 286 women and 270 men and the institution remained full for the period 1916–25.[2]

[. . .] Alongside the ideological changes of moral managment came a fundamental shift in the symbolic gendering of insanity, from male to female. The repulsive madman who had been the prototype and cultural representation of the lunatic was replaced by the youthful, victimised and sexualised madwoman.[3] As the nineteenth century progressed asylum doctors, eager for scientific legitimisation in an increasingly positivistic age, linked their classifications of insanity to discoveries about women's reproductive systems, so that several distinctive forms of female insanity were 'diagnosed at this time: puerperal mania, ovarian madness, insanity of lactation, climacteric melancholia.[4]

Ireland, under British rule during the nineteenth century, experienced these developments and the fact that fewer women than men entered Irish asylums did nothing to dissuade Irish doctors that women were more vulnerable to madness. The first Irish doctor to write a major treatise on insanity and the most prominent of the early Irish disciples of moral treatment was Dr William Hallaran of Cork. Hallaran was thoroughly convinced of female susceptibility to madness, writing in 1818 that: 'This cannot be wondered at when we take into account the many exciting causes to which females are more particularly exposed . . .'. Men, however, even when predisposed to insanity through heredity or other factors, would find that 'their superior powers of resistance' would overcome any latent tendencies they might have.[5] As the century wore on such concepts began to be taken for granted, so that by 1874 a standard textbook on psychological medicine could affirm the connection thus:

> Women in whom the generative organs are developed or in action are those most liable to hysterical disease. Indeed, the general fact is so universally acknowledged and so constantly corroborated by daily experience, that *anything in the nature of proof is unnecessary*.[6] [my emphasis]

By the early twentieth century, the concept of insanity had become so flexible that it could be stretched to encompass almost any behaviour. In the period 1916 to 1925 the main 'categories of insanity' ascribed to inmates in Enniscorthy Asylum were mania (54 per cent total, 47 per cent of women), melancholia (28 per cent total, 36 per cent women), congenital mental deficiency (8 per cent total, 8 per cent women) and epilepsy (4 per cent total, 4 per cent women). A small number were given another category like senile dementia. These classifications – particularly those of mania and melancholia which between them accounted for the vast majority of admissions – were vague in concept and had little scientific basis. [. . .]

Men were committed to Enniscorthy Asylum in greater numbers than women during the period 1916–25. This was a reversal of the situation in other countries like Britain, parts of Europe and the US. [. . .] But this fact did not lead doctors at this asylum to question the link between femininity and madness. Careful notes were made in the casebooks about the biology of their female patients. One of the first questions put to a woman on committal was the pattern of her menstrual period and details of regularity and quantity of the blood were duly noted: 'menses are on and very profuse'; 'says she has not been regular in this way for some months past'; 'menses regular but light'.[7] Such a focus on female biology placed the problem of madness within the woman's person, rather than the social reality of her life. Sis Berry's admission form, for example, cites 'menopause' as her cause of insanity. However a doctor's conversation with her sister suggests that life stresses, not biology, may have been the root of her trouble, as, according to her sister, Sis's husband 'never agreed with her and always gave her a hard time'.[8]

Many of those who were admitted with puerperal mania were suffering from physical gynaecological problems rather than mental symptoms. [. . .] Anastasia

Jones, a single woman of thirty said to be congenitally mentally deficient, related on admission how nine months previously she had been constantly 'annoyed' by a national soldier and that eight days before her committal she had given birth to an illegitimate child. She had experienced a very difficult labour with a forceps delivery leading to severe puerperal rupture which extended to her rectum. The rupture had turned septic. Her physical condition was treated and she made a good recovery, leaving the asylum two years later.[9] [. . .]

The family was the primary economic and social unit in early twentieth-century Ireland [. . .] and [contemporary] gender ideology located women firmly in the domestic realm. [. . .] This ideology held almost universal sway across different social classes and groupings. Analysis of the records makes it clear that many casualties of this strict gender ideology ended up in the asylum; both those who rejected and those who too wholeheartedly embraced their gendered role within society were vulnerable to committal. [. . .]

The declining economic and social position of Irishwomen as land became the distinguishing criterion of status has been well documented. [. . .] Unmarried women were of little benefit to a household, indeed they were often a financial burden if money was short. Socially they were objects of pity, ridicule or even revulsion. Unsurprisingly, the casebooks show that many single women, adrift and purposeless, ended up in Enniscorthy Asylum. Fifty-six per cent of female admissions during this period were single. In some such instances, evidence of madness was scant. Annie Stafford and Mary Cullen, for example, both single women who complained about 'persecution' by family members who wanted them out of the house, were committed for expressing their anger and despair – Annie for threatening to kill her sister, Mary for threatening to end her own life, because 'her father treated her so badly'. Both were noted in the casebooks to be 'quite rational in manner', but both lived the remainder of their long lives, and eventually died, in the asylum.[10]

[. . .] Underpinning female gender ideology was the fear of 'illegitimate' pregnancy and those who found themselves in this plight were thrown back on the mercy of their families for economic survival. Many parents, particularly those of the middle classes – fearful of public contempt or reluctant to support the economic burden of an unmarriageable daughter – cast their daughters from their homes. Many of these castaways ended up in the workhouse or worked in prostitution. Another option was the asylum.[11] Almost half the women in Enniscorthy whose admission forms or case records make reference to childbirth or miscarriage were single. Some of them never left the asylum afterwards and no mention is made of what happened to their children.

Many of these women were troubled by thoughts of their sexual 'misconduct' and real or imagined slights about alleged illegitimacy. Ellen Morris was so disturbed about what her neighbours said about her that she kept a knife under her pillow. She told a doctor 'she never had a bastard and always was decent and respectable'.[12] [. . .] Margaret Cummins told the doctor on admission that it was 'love for the boys' which had brought her to the asylum.[13] Whatever the truth about their mental condition, one consequence of labelling these sexually nonconformist women as mad and locking them away in the asylum was that their threat to the ideology of femininity was neutralised.

[. . .] Though women who married and had children were conforming to their gender role, this did not leave them immune from unhappiness, the taint of madness or the fate of the asylum. It appears that marriage was less advantageous to women's mental condition than men's: 34 per cent of women admitted to the asylum were married, compared to 25 per cent of men.[14] [. . .] Women such as Joan McCarthy, described as 'flighty, cheeky and resistive' on admission, who had 'threatened violence to her husband' and 'will not mind her children' was committed for 'trying to get away from home'.[15]

The trouble could begin as early as the 'match'. [. . .] Margaret Doyle, on admission, told the attendants that she hardly knew her husband before marriage and that she had been forced by her people to marry him. When her father and brother called to see her, she became 'very excited and screamed at the top of her voice', telling her father that 'he forced her to marry against her will and that the result now was that she was in the asylum with her mind lost'.[16] The night following this visit she attempted suicide by tying a sheet around her neck.

[. . .] Some of the women admitted were said to be hungry, though their husbands worked. Drink was often a culprit. Mary Ellen Doyle, for example, was in poor physical health when admitted and her house was said by the RIC to be very damp. When her sister visited the asylum she reported that Mary Ellen's husband drank and that she was left very little to live on and was often 'almost in want'.[17] [. . .]

Conflict between spouses could also lead to committal. Anastasia Hogan was admitted with 'delusions with reference to her husband being unfaithful to her. She frequently gets fits of violence, striking her husband and accusing him of unfaithfulness'.[18] The police who brought her in stated that her husband claimed she had attempted serious assault on him, struck her child and accused him of unfaithfulness 'without any cause'. Anastasia alleged that her husband beat her, called her names and was unfaithful. It was a case of his word against hers, but it was she who was committed.

In both farming and working-class communities, the woman usually 'married in' to her husband's family and she had to adapt to their ways. This made conflict with in-laws extremely common. The story of Sarah Ryan is an illustration of this, as well as the way in which the asylum could be used as a dumping ground for the unwanted. Admitted to Enniscorthy because her husband considered she 'romanced a lot, does not speak a sensible word and believes if at home she w[oul]d be a danger to herself and children', Sarah was found to be quite rational and was let out on probation a couple of months later. Her husband, however, re-admitted her within two weeks, with her weeping that she would 'never forgive' him. The casebook recorded her as saying her in-laws are:

> very interfering, [she] thinks they look on her as inferior and are always finding fault with her. Thinks her husband is fond of her and they could live happily if it wasn't for his relatives. [. . .]

The prevailing gender ideology was given religious endorsement by the Roman Catholic Church, which emphasised the 'natural' female virtues of obedience, servility and self-sacrifice for women and repressed the reality of female sexuality. At the same time, there was an undercurrent of obsession with women's bodies as a source of sin, by which was meant sexual misconduct. The admission forms of many women admitted to Enniscorthy Asylum in the period 1916–25 quoted 'symptoms' which exaggerated the religious devotion expected of them to an unacceptable extent. Bridie Hayes, for example, was admitted for not staying in her bed because God had directed her to go out; Nellie O'Keefe because she had a vision of the Sacred Heart; Margaret Butler for singing hymns and believing that the Devil told her she was going to be damned and Teresa Nolan for feeling 'hopeless' over concealing a 'sin' in confession, that she had pre-marital sex the previous summer. She had been too ashamed to tell the priest and now lived in fear of being 'damned forever'.[19] [. . .]

Some of the women with religious symptoms had rejected religion outright and it seems that this alone could be reason enough for their committal, especially if it was a deviation from previous behaviour. Mary O'Neill, a 56-year-old farmer's wife, had been 'formerly of a very devout disposition, now she won't pray at all'.[20] Bridget Welsh was admitted weeping incoherently and saying 'I'm a virgin like the mother of God and my husband is like St Joseph'. She had been a devout Catholic all her life and her madness manifested when she engaged in 'unseemly conduct' during divine service and began cursing, blaspheming and refusing to go to mass on Sunday.[21]

Many of the women who suffered religious 'symptoms' also refused food. Katie Quigley, for example, believed that every time she ate she was committing a sin.[22] This linking of eating and sin was not uncommon. Hannah Riley was admitted because 'it was nearly impossible to keep her away from the chapel' and she stated that the 'only food she lived on was the Blessed Sacrament'.[23] [. . .]

By the early twentieth century, the financial burden of asylums was weighing heavily on local management boards. Within Enniscorthy, like the other district asylums, this translated into a bare, unadorned environment, with few comforts. Basic neglect was sometimes in evidence: unpainted walls, worn floors or bedsteads which needed cleaning and enamelling.[24] Diet was basic, mostly bread and potatoes, and followed the usual practice in rural Ireland of giving more food to men.

[. . .] Communal asylum life was supposed to promote reintegration into society. This was dependent on the patient's ability to relate well to other inmates and staff. An asylum inspector summed up the expectations of the system: 'The conduct of the patients was admirable. There was no noise or excitement.'[25] Any noise, heightened emotion or violence was seen as a failure and the casenotes show that doctors found such behaviour particularly unacceptable in women. [. . .] As well as being submissive, inmates, especially the women, were expected to be neat and tidy in dress and personal habits. Margaret Hicky's 'untidiness and dishevelled hair' for example, were enough to secure her committal, even though the doctor admitted that she 'did not show much signs of insanity further than [that]'.[26]

There is no reference to theories of madness in the casenotes, no consistent framework within which the 'progress' of an inmate was evaluated, only the doctor's own values and prejudices. [. . .] Only those who conformed were considered to be improving and would therefore stand any chance of release; those who protested their lot of being deprived of liberty and subjected to a barrage of rules were considered to be still suffering from their madness. Six months after her admission, for instance, Elizabeth Kearns was said to be 'somewhat better in mind'. The reason? 'She is not so full of complaints and is doing a little work'.[27]

Work was presented as therapy and the inmates in the asylum received no payment for their labour. [. . .] Work was allocated on strictly gender-divided lines, with men working on the farm, in the Kilcarbery vegetable garden or in the workshops and women dressmaking, repairing stockings and underclothing, working in the laundry, the kitchen and dining hall.[28] [. . .]

Drugs were rarely used but were prescribed more frequently to women than men. A 1905 review of sedatives and narcotics used in the treatment of the mad agreed with the contemporary opposition to 'drugging'. However, it made one exception: the use of a depressant in cases of 'moral insanity', which in the writer's experience were 'always female'. [. . .]

Celibacy was strictly enforced in the asylum and there was strict segregation of the sexes into separate wards, dining halls and dayrooms, to the extent that a female attendant could not enter one of the male wards without special permission. [. . .] The inmates came into intensive daily contact with the attendants, whose job it was to focus on correction of behaviour: uncleanliness, slovenliness, disorderliness, bad sexual habits and destructiveness were all to be eradicated. [. . .]

Once committed to the asylum, an inmate could only leave with the permission of the authorities and often the agreement of family too. Many railed against their incarceration, as this [undated] letter from Elizabeth Nolan, known as Elsie, who was committed to the asylum in 1923, shows:

> My dear brother,
>
> Just got your letter and am glad you are well its high time I left here as the time is up so you had better write to the doctor to make some arrangment [sic] about bring me back every day I expect to get back and it ends just the same till, I know nothing about the place except that you at least should bring me back or tell me why you put me here [. . .] It's the same thing day after day. I can hardly write with everyone speaking and I think it very unfair of you to leave me here so long [. . .] Anyhow the sooner you get me home the better it will be for me unless of course you want to get rid of me altogether[.]
>
> Yours Elsie[29]

On the other hand, a number of women were discharged even though the authorities still considered their mental condition to be troubled. This was almost always because they were required for domestic duties at home. Katie Grant had been in the asylum for seven years when her brother took her out. His wife had died and he needed 'someone to keep house for him'.[30] The authorities let her go, but her housekeeping skills must have left something to be desired, because she was back within a week. [. . .] This category made up only a small minority: just 6 per cent of the women discharged. While we know that 44 per cent of the total sample died in the asylum, 40 per cent were discharged and of these, the vast majority were said to have 'recovered' (70 per cent) or to have been 'relieved' of their symptoms (24 per cent). Some of these, fewer than 10 per cent, returned to the asylum later in life but the vast majority did not. [. . .]

A number of interlinking discourses framed knowledge about, and regulated the experience of, the women who were committed to Enniscorthy Asylum in the period 1916 to 1925: discourses of medicine, sexuality, femininity and domesticity as well as madness. [. . .] To say that gender ideology was a central factor in the dynamics of committal and incarceration is not to claim that it provides a full explanation of these processes. But what emerges clearly from this study is the struggle endured by so many of these women who were labelled mad, as they tried to cope with familial misfortune, with economic insecurity and powerlessness in a society that allowed them little scope for independence or autonomy, with a gendered code of behaviour which was, for many, impossible to sustain. [. . .]

Notes

1   Throughout this article I use the word 'madness' rather than the favoured language of the time (lunacy, insanity) or of today (mental illness). [. . .]
2   *Annual Reports of Enniscorthy Lunatic Asylum, 1916–1925*. Annual reports and casebooks are held in St Senan's Mental Hospital (formerly Enniscorthy Lunatic Asylum).
3   Elaine Showalter, *The Female Malady*, London, 1987, p. 8.
4   Puerperal mania was believed to be caused by septic poisoning during childbirth; ovarian madness by 'inflammation' of the ovaries; insanity of lactation was brought on by prolonged breastfeeding and climacteric melancholia by menopause. [. . .]
5   W. H. Hallaran, *Practical Observations on the Causes and Cure of Insanity*, Cork, 1818, p. 50.
6   J. C. Bucknill and D. H. Tuke, *A Manual of Psychological Medicine*, New York, 1874, p. 347.
7   Casebook, PN (Patient Number) 4019, 3721, 3310. In order to protect anonymity the names of all inmates have been changed.
8   Casebook, PN 3972.
9   Casebook, PN 4290.
10   Casebook, PN 3872.
11   Dympna McLoughlin, 'Women and sexuality in nineteenth-century Ireland', *Irish Journal of Psychology*, 15/2–3, 1994, p. 273.
12   Casebook, PN 3431.
13   Casebook, PN 3774.
14   Compiled from Annual Reports of Enniscorthy Lunatic Asylum, 1916–1925.
15   Casebook, PN 3990.
16   Casebook, PN 3576.
17   Casebook, PN 3924.
18   Casebook, PN 3721.
19   Casebook, PN 4142, 3650, 3462, 3978.
20   Casebook, PN 4019.
21   Casebook, PN 3810.
22   Casebook, PN 4305.
23   Casebook, PN 3818.

24   Annual Memoranda of Inspection of Enniscorthy Asylum, 1919, 1924 and 1925.
25   Ibid., 1924.
26   Casebook, PN 3622.
27   Casebook, PN 3763.
28   Annual Memoranda of Inspection of Enniscorthy Asylum, 1925.
29   Letter found in casebook PN 4218.
30   Casebook, PN 4305.

Chapter 15

Greta Jones

■   from MARIE STOPES IN IRELAND: THE
MOTHER'S CLINIC IN BELFAST, 1936–47, *Social
History of Medicine*, 5/2, April 1992, pp. 255–77

[. . .]

HISTORIANS OF EUROPE'S POPULATION have pointed out a
demographic transition occurring in the late nineteenth and early twentieth
centuries.[1] After a period of rapid rise, the birth rate in many European countries
started to fall. At first this occurred chiefly among the better off social groups but,
by the end of the First World War, it had reached the working classes. It is
believed that at least some of the decline can be attributed to the use of artificial
birth control. Older traditional means of controlling birth were gradually replaced
by artificial birth-control devices manufactured large scale for a market.[2]

Ireland was unique in two ways. Its demographic history was different from
the rest of Europe. Second, the position in Ireland was further complicated by
partition in 1922. In the Irish Free State (Saorstat Éireann), comprising twenty-
six counties which became independent, propaganda and advertisement for birth
control was made illegal in 1929 under the Censorship Act and the importation
of contraceptives banned in 1935 under the Criminal Law Amendment Act.[3]
Northern Ireland, comprising six counties in the north-east, had a domestic
parliament at Stormont but remained within the United Kingdom. There, whilst
there was considerable disapproval and opposition to birth control, no attempts
were made to ban it. Northern Ireland became, therefore, the site of the first
birth-control clinic in Ireland: the Mother's Clinic funded by the Marie Stopes
Society for Constructive Birth Control. This clinic opened its doors in Belfast in
1936.

[. . .] As regards the means of fertility control [in Ireland] we are dependent
in the early stages upon largely impressionistic evidence. Nonetheless there is some.
As in other parts of the British Isles, in the late nineteenth and twentieth centuries
birth-control devices or abortifacents were distributed via advertisement columns
in the press. Before the Censorship Act of 1929 these could be found in the Irish
papers. For example, in the *Cork Free Press* an advertisement appeared in May 1912,

for 'Widow Welch's Female Pills' described as 'prompt and reliable for ladies. Able to cure all female complaints', along the lines of similar advertisements for abortifacents in Britain. In October 1920, an advertisement in the *Dublin Evening Mail* offered 'rubber goods, sprays, douches and enemas' together with a pamphlet detailing their use, 'The Manual of Wisdom'. Even after the disappearance of this sort of advertisement from the Irish papers published in the Free State, they were available to Irish men and women in British newspapers distributed in Ireland.

Moreover, prosecutions under the Criminal Law Amendment Act reveal a trade in contraceptives. The *Birth Control News* reported on these prosecutions in 1936:

> In several cases the maximum penalties have been imposed. In one case fines amounting to £250 were imposed together with six months hard labour and other terms of imprisonment in default of payment; in another fines amounting to £200 with six months hard labour; and in a third a fine of £100.[4]

[The paper] also reported seizures at the ports. In April 1936 a quantity of quinine pessaries were seized by the Customs and Excise from Henry Bell Ltd. Although some confusion and dispute existed as to their purpose (they were in fact contraceptives) they were eventually destroyed. Interestingly enough, as a comment on medical practice in the Free State, four prescriptions from medical [doctors] were produced by the chemists, in their defence.[5]

There is also some, admittedly impressionistic, information of the knowledge of contraception after its prohibition. Professor John Busteed speaking to the Statistical and Social Inquiry Society of Ireland in 1937 believed, 'it is a fact that during the past two years a remarkable distribution of the literature and knowledge of the subject [birth control] has been quietly proceeding among the Irish middle classes'.[6] Although Busteed argued, at least publicly, that this birth control was exclusively by methods approved by the Catholic Church, the trickle of visitors to the Belfast Clinic from over the border and the correspondence between individuals and the Family Planning Association (FPA) in the 1950s, indicate otherwise. [. . .]

Writing to Stopes in 1940, Catherine Armstrong, the resident nurse, described 'a farmer's wife who has had seven children. Years ago she had been advised by a friend who had come from South Africa to use a sponge. She had done so but it had not prevented pregnancy.'[7] This was because the women cut and inserted it without basic anatomical knowledge, a situation rectified by the nurse. [. . .] In addition to these home-made remedies, condoms, coitus interruptus and abortion were mentioned by the clinic patients in the 1930s.

[. . . I]n an examination of letters written to Marie Stopes in the inter-war period [, . . .] compared with surveys of this period, correspondents to Stopes were more willing to admit recourse to abortion.[8] [. . .] Three of the nine surviving case sheets mention abortion [as did] four of the fifty-nine cases mentioned in letters from the clinic nurse to Stopes. In many of these cases a woman might have had several abortions. In fact, the Belfast clinic had some difficulty in persuading some who called at the door that it was not providing an abortion service. Armstrong wrote to Stopes, 'you will see we had three pregnant mothers on Wednesday. They had all noticed our advertisement and came hoping to terminate an unwanted pregnancy, not understanding our work'.[9] [. . .]

It was the Criminal Law Amendment Act which acted as a catalyst for Marie Stopes to open a birth clinic in Northern Ireland. In response to events in the Dáil and Senate, she wrote to the *Irish Times*. They refused to publish her letter which, in effect, contravened the 1929 Censorship Act. She wrote:

> [. . .] the interference between the medical practitioner and his patients on the part of the pharmaceutical chemists who refuse to sell medically necessary and proper goods fosters the existence of a 'vile underground trade' [. . . and m]ake the trade totally unprofitable by giving knowledge to women that the best contraceptive in the world costs almost nothing and can be purchased from every grocers shop. It is pure olive oil[10] [. . .]

Marie Stopes's venture in Ireland was undoubtedly influenced by her previous conflicts with Catholicism. Her experiences in this respect had been entirely negative. Not only was there an active lobby in Parliament of Roman Catholic MPs who attempted to stop or delay any legislation intended to make birth control more easy to obtain, but the use of local-authority maternity and child-welfare clinics as conduits for birth-control information was often impeded by Roman Catholic influence inside or outside the Council [Council of the Pharmaceutical Society of Ireland].[11]

Stopes's Belfast clinic was, however, only possible because of the existence of an indigenous birth-control movement in the shape of a branch of the Northern Ireland Society for Constructive Birth Control. There were various reasons for the growth of the birth-control movement in Ireland. Among Church of Ireland Protestants at least, the misgivings about birth control were removed or at least mitigated by the Anglican Lambeth Conference of 1930, which gave recognition to birth control under certain strict conditions. This may have been insignificant for the non-church-attending working class Protestants of Belfast, but it helped develop a climate of opinion more favourable to the practice of contraception among the middle classes. [. . .] Moreover, patrons of the Belfast Mother's Clinic included a number of clergymen, among them W. S. Kerr, the Dean of Belfast.

Second, in spite of the political difficulties which subsequently affected the clinic, it had support among liberal unionists. Its political patrons included Harry Midgeley, a prominent member of the Northern Ireland Labour Party and a member of Belfast City Council's Maternity and Child Welfare Committee. [. . .]

A third influence was the Belfast tradition of philanthropic social work. A motivation behind this charitable impulse was the belief that birth control could be used to alleviate the poverty of the working class. A clergyman from Belfast's Sandy Row wrote to Stopes that he was 'very much interested in the subject and feel some such movement as you have started is very much needed in working-class centres of population particularly'.[12]

Stopes, in fact, saw her clinics as aimed at poor women. It was assumed that the better off would make private provision.[13] But this view of birth control as another form of charitable provision was double-edged. The proselytising of birth control as the cure for poverty was one reason for the Labour Party's rejection of the demands that it throw its weight behind the movement for free access to birth-control advice for the working class women – a reluctance eventually overcome by the persistence of its women members. Stopes's eugenic connections also aroused suspicion in some quarters.[14] [. . .]

The financial position of the clinic and the future of birth-control advice in Ireland would have been secure if assistance from government and local authority could have been obtained. The position in Britain was that a memorandum from the Ministry of Health in 1930 to Maternity and Child Welfare Clinics, whilst discouraging any general contraceptive advice, stated: 'it may be given out only when further pregnancies would lead to bad health and in a separate session'.[15] This memorandum also allowed for the establishment of birth-control clinics by local authorities or assistance to be given to existing ones.

However, this was not mandatory on local authorities. [. . .] In Northern Ireland all approaches to the government were repulsed on the grounds that the memorandum did not apply because of the existence of a separate domestic parliament. The real reason was the morally contentious nature of the issue, particularly for Catholics.

[. . .] In November 1936, Marie Stopes's Mother's Clinic opened at 103 The Mount, in a working-class district of Belfast near the Harland and Wolff shipyards and not far from the city centre. The clinic offered advice to married women. Consultation was free but the patient had to meet the cost of appliances. These could include the cervical cap,[16] pessaries or sponges. A full-time nurse was in attendance and a medically qualified officer who was part-time. Stopes insisted that the clinic be staffed by married women. They had to be free from all suspicion of involvement in abortion and also had to stay clear of commercial pressure or private experiment. They also helped infertility. A management committee saw to the day-to-day running and raised money by voluntary efforts, such as sales and entertainments. The bulk of running costs had to be raised by annual subscription from its supporters or by other fund-raising activities. [. . .] Stopes ruled these clinics with a rod of iron and closely supervised everything. The nurse sent her almost weekly letters and copies of all case sheets, the majority of which, unfortunately, have not survived. [. . .]

In the absence of political support it was the efforts of three women doctors that were crucial in getting the birth-control movement off the ground in Ireland. The first, Eveline McDaniel, had gone to Marie Stopes's clinic in London in 1934 to acquire training in birth-control techniques. It was she who became the clinic's first doctor, from 1936 to 1940. She was replaced by Charlotte Arnold, who served the clinic until its closure in 1947. Parallel to this Olive Anderson had, from 1940, given advice on birth control at her maternity clinic in the Royal Victoria's Maternity Hospital, Belfast. This work was entirely voluntary on her part, and received no recognition or financial payment from the hospital. In 1951 Anderson and Arnold provided Northern Ireland with another birth-control clinic. [. . .]

In the 1935 report of the Chief Medical Superintendent of Belfast, C. H. Thomson, comment was made on Belfast's high rate of maternal mortality.

Thomson linked this to poor nutrition and to the high birth rate. [. . .] Another factor was the prevalence of the unqualified midwife or 'handy woman'. However:

> A further cause of Maternal Mortality which a National Committee should investigate is that of abortion. Nine maternal deaths occurred from this cause – all were married women in their thirties and six of the nine were poor. Some had families of six, seven, eight or ten children.[17]

The medical consequences of frequent pregnancy also impressed themselves upon Professor Lowry, the Royal Maternity's gynaecologist. It was Lowry together with Mrs Rowland Hill and Mrs Garrod who made the first approaches to Stopes. According to Lowry, 'I see scores of women every year at the Maternity Hospital who should be in attendance at a birth control clinic.'[18] [. . .]

However, birth control was not respectable. As one member of the Clinic Committee reminisced: 'In Belfast forty years ago few medical men (apart from those on the university staff) were prepared to come out publicly in support of birth control although they might privately agree with the need . . .'.[19] A good many of the women who attended the clinic complained that the doctor had advised them to avoid pregnancy but had not told them how, nor would be drawn on the question. [. . .]

Roman Catholic opposition was clear. The opening of the clinic was denounced from the pulpit of the Roman Catholic Churches of Belfast.[20] In spite of this, the Mother's Clinic had a few Roman Catholic patients much to Stopes's delight. [. . .] Moreover, even given the expense of travel, a number of women from the Irish Free State attended the Belfast Clinic. [. . .]

It is clear that many women already knew of, or practised, some form of fertility control prior to attending the Mother's Clinic. As well as abortion, breast-feeding was mentioned as being used to avoid pregnancy – in one case for fourteen months.[21] In other cases abstinence, coitus interruptus, sponges and condoms are recorded in the patient's history.

In these cases what motivated women to attend was the ineffectiveness or dangers of these methods. Often added to this was a breakdown in consensus between husband and wife about contraception. Abstinence, for example, caused strains. Armstrong described to Stopes 'a poor woman [who] is a nervous wreck due to the fear of further pregnancy. She also says it is raising trouble between her and her husband as she is terrified if he comes near to her at all.'[22] In another case a period of abstinence of four months had led to rows between husband and wife. Where condoms had been used it was often the husband's abandonment of them – usually against the wife's wishes – which led to a clinic visit.

Coitus interruptus, also, for some women, was a routine means of controlling fertility. One woman aged forty-nine attended the clinic for the first time because both her mother and sister had become pregnant at that age. Coitus interruptus had been used throughout her reproductive life but not always successfully and she was not prepared to chance a late pregnancy.[23]

Attendance at the clinic was therefore to find an effective means of contraception and, sometimes, when agreement between husband and wife had broken down. It was not always the case that it was a female decision. In one case a woman was referred by her husband because his doctor attributed the man's mental breakdown to coitus interruptus. [. . .]

However in a good number of cases the initiative was the woman's and the aim to redress an unsatisfactory domestic situation which had been made worse by high fertility. [. . .] One woman was brought by her mother, 'who says it is breaking her heart to see her daughter having so many children to a lazy, good for nothing man'.[24] [. . .]

In 1947 the Belfast Mother's Clinic closed. Stopes's expenses had increased as a result of the war and the Irish clinic had always depended upon a subvention from headquarters, which Stopes was reluctant to continue after 1945.[25] Thereafter women who sought contraceptive advice had to rely upon a sympathetic general practitioner or upon Olive Anderson's clinic at the Royal Maternity Hospital, which, as she wrote, 'was not openly recognized as a contraceptive clinic'.[26]

Notes

1   Ansley J. Coale and Susan Cotts Watkins (eds), *The Decline of Fertility in Europe*, Princeton, 1986. [. . .]

2   [. . .] Diana Gittins, *Fair Sex: Family Size and Structure 1900–39*, London, 1982.

3   In 1948 the Irish Free State changed its name to the Republic of Ireland.

4   *Birth Control News*, XV/4, September 1936.

5   *Birth Control News*, XIV/8, April 1936.

6   Professor John Busteed, 'The problem of population': Statistical and Social Inquiry Society of Ireland, paper read on 19 March 1937.

7   BL Add. MS 58,619, Armstrong to Stopes, 21 June 1940.

8   Claire Davey, 'Birth control in Britain during the inter-war years: evidence from the Stopes correspondence', *Journal of Family History*, 13, 1988, pp. 329–45.

9   BL Add. MS 58,619, Armstrong to Stopes, 29 March 1940.

10 *Birth Control News*, XIII/9, March 1935.

11 In 1929 there were 25 Roman Catholic MPs who campaigned against birth control (17 Labour, 5 Conservative, 3 Nationalist). Stopes greeted any loss of seats by them with undisguised glee.

12 BL Add. MS 58,620, Letter from John McCaffrey to Stopes, 1 July 1936.

13 It is very difficult to judge whether this is true in the absence of most of the case sheets recording husband's occupation. The nine surviving case sheets indicate working-class families, as do the letters. However, even here the wives of a farmer, shopkeeper, and businessman are recorded as patients.

14 For the connection between social policy and eugenics, see G. Jones, *Social Hygiene in Twentieth Century Britain*, London, 1986.

15 *Birth Control News*, September 1930, p. 72.

16 Stopes preferred the small high-domed cervical cap to the Dutch cap used by the FPA. 'Dutch cap' was, however, generally used as the name for all female occlusives.

17 Report of the Medical Superintendent of Health of the County Borough of Belfast, 1935, p. 9.

18 BL Add. MS 58,620, Lowry to Stopes, 13 February 1936.

19   Wellcome Institute, Woodside File CMAC GC 39/4, Moya Woodside's remi-
      niscences of the Belfast Clinic, 6 August 1981.

20   *Manchester Guardian*, 5 October 1936.

21   BL add. MS 58,619, Armstrong to Stopes, 31 December 1945.

22   Ibid., Armstrong to Stopes, 9 February 1940.

23   Ibid., Armstrong to Stopes, 5 January 1940.

24   Ibid., Armstrong to Stopes, 9 March 1945.

25   It took £241. 02*d.* to run the clinic in 1938. This included a nurse's annual
      salary of £156 and the cost of free treatment, £34. Patients were charged for
      appliances, although in some cases this was waived. In addition, a doctor's part-
      time expenses were met. All of this was raised by voluntary effort. In 1938 new
      subscriptions to the clinic were £27. 19*s.*, and renewed, £135. 9*s.* 2*d.* However,
      there was still a deficit of £68 11*s.* which had to be met from headquarters. The
      clinic never broke even and local authority support would have been of great
      importance. BL Add. MS 58,620. Clinic accounts year ending 31 August 1938.

26   Wellcome Institute, Family Planning Association Papers A 13/2. Letter from
      Anderson to the FPA, 10 August 1950.

PART FOUR

Religion

THE ROMAN CATHOLIC CHURCH became increasingly structured in the post-famine period, with a growing number of priests and female religious joining the institutional church body. The rise in literacy and popular literature also helped to spread Catholic doctrine. This was not without implications for Irish women. From an early age Irish girls were taught to be chaste, obedient, respectable and docile. Nowhere were these virtues more apparent than in the female religious. Convents offered single women one of the few avenues for gaining respectability and power. Twinned with this was the idea that entering a convent granted high social status on the noviciate and her family. The nineteenth century certainly witnessed an unprecedented increase in the numbers entering convents. But were all women religious equal? It seems not, as there were clear distinctions amongst women serving in a religious community, between the choir and lay sisters. This provides an interesting illustration of how the idea of separate spheres cannot be solely restricted to men and women.

Throughout the twentieth century, although the general perception of female religious may have been of a conservative figure, undoubtedly a number possessed significant influence and power and this was enhanced as their contact with the outside world increased. Although there was a slowing down in the number of women choosing a religious life in the early years of the century, this was still a comparatively popular vocation. Within the Catholic Church, therefore, religion clearly offered opportunities for advancement and public service.

Within the Protestant churches similar opportunites also existed. Women, for instance, played a crucial role at a congregational level. Upper-class women undertook an important role in financing church building, exercising social and religious influence in their own localities and developing avenues for religious-based philanthropic activity. Women from the lower social orders also played a role in housing visiting itinerant preachers, organising female prayer meetings and working as class teachers. Thus, to presume that women have played no part in church work, bar attending church services, is to overlook both their philanthropic and proselytising work. Church-based philanthropy is, for example, apparent in the development of the Salvation Army in Ireland. In the name of religion, women played a key role in Salvationist rescue work, establishing a comprehensive network of refuges for single mothers, the homeless, the ill and the destitute.

The influence of religion was, undoubtedly, far-reaching. Women were not only involved in proselytising, philanthropy, and social work, but were affected by contemporary church doctrines. For instance, the establishment and subsequent development of the Irish Free State in the 1920s and 1930s witnessed the passage of many legislative measures which reflected Catholic social teaching. One consequence of this was the valuation of the role of wife and mother above all other. Thus when considering women's position in the nineteenth and twentieth centuries the heady impact of religion is clearly apparent, influencing both individuals and the state.

Suggestions for further reading

Caitríona Clear, *Nuns in Nineteenth-Century Ireland*, Dublin, 1987.

Tony Fahey, 'Nuns in the Catholic Church in Ireland in the nineteenth century', in Mary Cullen (ed.), *Girls Don't do Honours: Irish Women in Education in the Nineteenth and Twentieth Centuries*, Dublin, 1987.

Suellen Hoy, 'The journey out: the recruitment and emigration of Irish religious women to the United States, 1812–1914', *Journal of Women's History*, 6/7, 4/1, winter/spring 1995.

Maria Luddy, 'Presentation convents in County Tipperary, 1803–1900', *Tipperary Historical Journal*, 1992.

Mary Peckham Magray, *The Transforming Power of the Nuns: Women, Religion and Cultural Change, 1750–1990*, Oxford, 1998.

Marie O'Connell, 'The genesis of convent foundations and their institutions in Ulster, 1840–1920', in Janice Holmes and Diane Urquhart (eds), *Coming into the Light: The Work, Politics and Religion of Women in Ulster, 1840–1940*, Belfast, 1994.

Liam O'Dowd, 'Church, state and women: the aftermath of partition', in Chris Curtin, Pauline Jackson and Barbara O'Connor (eds), *Gender and Irish Society*, Galway, 1987.

Joan Thompson, 'The Women's Auxiliary of the Irish Baptist Foreign Mission, 1929–51', *Baptist Historical Journal*, series 1, 10, 1977–8.

Chapter 16

David Hempton and Myrtle Hill

■   from 'BORN TO SERVE': WOMEN AND
EVANGELICAL RELIGION, Chapter 7 of *Evangelical
Protestantism in Ulster Society, 1740–1890*, London and
New York, 1992, pp. 129–42

[. . .]

R ECENT HISTORICAL STUDIES, concerned to shift the focus from the institutional and political aspects of religion to its broader social and cultural content, have drawn attention to the variety of ways in which women experienced religion and have stressed their important contribution to the religious community. While the growing interest in the role of women in history generally has been impeded by the deficiency and flaws of historical material, the prolific sources of denominations such as Methodism and the Society of Friends, and the wealth of material left by voluntary religious agencies, have proved irresistible to historians. Although in terms of personal and social constraints, evangelicalism's repression of sexuality, emphasis on domestic virtues and opposition to many forms of popular entertainment, had a restricting effect on the contribution of women to the wider secular society, there is much evidence to support the suggestion that evangelical religion was more important than feminism in enlarging women's sphere of action during the nineteenth century.

[. . . Women] achieved a temporary position of influence in the early stages of the evangelical revival which was not sustained into the nineteenth century, when male ministers, trustees and administrators regained full control. By that stage, however, a vast array of voluntary religious associations had opened up new opportunities for female endeavour which did not encroach on the activities of men. [. . .] However, early acceptance, or at least tolerance [to female preaching], soon gave way to caution and then condemnation, as women's position within Methodism reflected its growing respectability and organisational stability. The 1802 Conference decreed it 'contrary both to scripture and to prudence that women should preach or should exhort in public'.[1] It seems that this decision was not entirely effective, but by the mid-nineteenth century female preaching had had its day both in Ireland and in England, where it had been even more common.[2]

In Ireland, it is plain that those preachers who most ardently supported their female counterparts were themselves 'enthusiasts' who frequently found themselves out of favour with an increasingly conservative Dublin leadership.[3] Those women who did continue the practice confined their activities to their own sex. Thus, while Alice Cambridge had addressed mixed congregations in the late eighteenth century, including a regiment of soldiers, together with their wives and children,[4] by the 1830s male followers of Anne Lutton were reduced to dressing in women's clothing in a vain attempt to hear her preach.[5]

Women's preaching should thus be seen as exceptional and transitional rather than officially sanctioned and accepted. Even at the peak of their influence women preachers were seen as itinerant supporters in virgin territory, as with the nineteenth-century overseas missionary movement, and were never accepted as regular preachers to settled congregations. The public activism of strong-willed individuals was possible only in periods of disruption or innovation. [For example], female Ranters, Congregationalists and Baptists similarly took advantage of hierarchical breakdown in the Civil War period, but with the return to social and ecclesiastical stability these 'anomalies' were removed. In the early nineteenth century, the new generation of Methodists, with property considerations and growing, established congregations, was eager to defend itself from accusations of hysteria and sentimentality. As the movement became more institutionalised and respectable, a denomination rather than a voluntary association, men took over the dominant positions and women again assumed supportive and background roles.[6]

Even when female preaching was common women never succeeded in altering, nor indeed attempted to alter, the conventional relationships between men and women within religious communities.[7] For, while their opponents reviled them for casting off the virtues of their sex, their supporters were equally careful always to refer to them in terms of their womanhood. Thus they were portrayed as either exemplifying or denying their 'nature'. Anne Preston, her supporters said, lived a 'life of feeling',[8] Alice Cambridge was neat, plain and greatly opposed to evil-speaking.[9] When speaking of Anne Lutton, the Victorian Methodist historian C. H. Crookshank felt it necessary to explain how such a woman, 'of respectable parents and trained in fear of the Lord', overcame her 'natural' female reticence. [. . .] Anne Lutton's correspondence suggests that she shared these sentiments.[10] The 'essential' nature of woman was thus accepted by both sides as determining the extent and nature of her activities. Modesty and humility precluded any prominent public role and the predominance of emotion over reason was regarded as a further limitation of the value of her contribution. Gideon Ouseley, although a known supporter of female preaching, remarked of a young woman preacher that while she was good at recounting her own experience and blessings, 'her knowledge was not equal to her zeal and some of her remarks were confused and incoherent'.[11] Wesley too felt that the exposition of texts was a male preserve, requiring logic, reasoning and sustained argument. [. . .]

These perceptions of male and female 'natural' attributes perpetuated the division of roles in areas other than the pastoral office. Despite the Quaker theory of equality, for example, men's meetings dealt with matters relating to property, including meeting-houses and burial grounds, and with negotiations with the state and the established church.[12] Generally speaking, matters of policy, the intricacies of doctrine and public debate were regarded as male concerns, while teaching, persuading and background supportive work were considered more appropriate for women. It was only with the rise of voluntary religious agencies at the beginning of the nineteenth century that new opportunities in these areas opened up.[13] Meanwhile, it was as wives and mothers that women's influence was most obviously disseminated through society, and through which undramatic but pervasive contributions were made to the vitality and spread of popular Protestantism. [. . .]

The intensification and diversification of evangelical activity in the nineteenth century greatly increased the opportunities for women's participation. Through the network of voluntary societies and organisations which clustered around the religious denominations, many women were given an opportunity to engage in social and administrative work in their communities. The domestic sphere widened to take in Sunday schools, foreign and domestic evangelistic missions, temperance, educational, Bible and tract societies. The various reports indicate the areas in which it was felt women could be particularly successful: teaching, sponsorship, promotion and persuasion. Sunday-school teaching rapidly became an acceptable occupation for women in many areas. It was a leadership role which offered an important outlet for piety as well as a position within the community, but one which could also be regarded as an extension of the traditional domestic duties of guidance and teaching. [. . .] There was clearly a disproportionate number of females working in this area, and schools for female teachers were operational from the early nineteenth century. The Hibernian Bible Society noted that working-class men were much more open to persuasion from lady visitors when it came to buying Bibles[14] and the impressive distribution statistics recorded during these years owed much to the efforts of these voluntary labourers. The 1830 report of the Religious Tract and Bible Society noted the success of the Ladies' Association in promoting the circulation of tracts and books and in establishing libraries.[15] Similarly, the Ladies Society of the London Hibernian Society was by 1830 running 190 schools with some 8,000 scholars, and the Ladies Auxiliary to the Irish Society employed a small army of scripture readers.[16] Into this mixture of spiritual and practical work women brought their traditional domestic skills and applied them in a wider field. Their efforts did not go unappreciated, especially by those voluntary societies which struggled against the rigidity of ecclesiastical hierarchies. The records of the Church Missionary Society, for example, reveal the way in which women's auxiliaries were used to establish a base in Ireland, getting around the barriers imposed by the Church on male-dominated societies which were regarded, especially in Anglican circles, as a threat to episcopal authority.[17] Ladies' auxiliaries also helped establish the ubiquitous penny-a-week subscription as the main resource of the evangelical religious societies. It was in the area of finance, in fact, that women proved themselves to be indispensable assets. By helping to unleash the 'power of the purse' in a systematic and regular fashion women were at the very heart of a remarkable Victorian industry of religious and moral campaigns in Britain and in Ireland.[18] Apart from direct, individual donations, the collectors of penny-a-week subscriptions were invariably either women or clergymen and they also acted as treasurers to local branches and as organisers of the more traditional fund-raising events such as bazaars and the sale of 'fancy work'.

Specifically female philanthropic societies, both evangelical and non-evangelical, also flourished in the mid-nineteenth century, and this type of involvement, while still largely secondary and supportive in nature, and still within the traditional arena of charity and benevolence, was important in offering an outlet to women's industry and talent outside the home and family circle. [. . .] Ultimately this led to a social extension of their perception of Christian duty. Pious platitudes may often have been served up with the soup or administered with dressings, but there is at least some evidence of individuals going beyond the narrow constraints of proselytism. Societies such as the Belfast Ladies Relief Association may have been mainly concerned to 'imbue the minds of the scholars with the truth and spirit of the gospel', but the industrial schools they set up, supplied by lady teachers and superintendents, offered more concrete benefits to famine-stricken communities.[19] [. . .]

In the field of foreign missions, women were at first confined to supportive committees and auxiliaries and to fund-raising for male missionaries, whose reports were generally designed to appeal to a maternal nature. However, the Zenana Mission, founded by the Presbyterian Church in 1873, promised women a more central and challenging role.[20] Under its full title, 'the Female Association for Promoting Christianity among the Women of the East' it sent out female missionaries. As well as offering traditional medical, educational and child care facilities, this mission had a particular concern for the Zenana, that is, the part of the Indian household set aside for women, and to which men, including evangelical missionaries, had no access. While the setting up of the female mission was therefore essential to fulfil missionary objectives, it also gave local women the opportunity to consider the position of their eastern counterparts and to experience a different culture. Although the actual number of female missionaries leaving Ireland for Calcutta was small, home-based branches were kept well informed. By its second year the mission had 124 congregational auxiliaries in Ireland with over 6,000 members.[21] The idea of women missionaries became more acceptable as the century progressed; in 1887, the queen's golden jubilee year, it was reported that there were about 500 female missionaries in India attached to a variety of denominational societies.[22] The majority of these were native teachers and Bible women taught by Europeans, but a door had been opened through which many women would pass in the following decades. The new venture required courage and assertiveness, and undoubtedly brought fulfilment. It was stressed, however, that their teaching of the gospel was secondary to the primary medical and educational functions of women missionaries, and thus they remained firmly within traditional female boundaries.

The annual reports of the Zenana Mission offer an intriguing glimpse into the respective roles of the sexes in late-Victorian religion. The first report confirmed that the mission had an all-female general committee, female secretaries and treasurer, and a committee of ministers available for consultation.[23] However, at the annual general meeting, all the speeches were made by men, and the images which the women held of themselves were often a pure reflection of those held by their male counterparts. 'We are born to serve the world' was the rallying cry offered by one Zenana missionary. So, although these particular women had to undertake arduous training, in a new language, in kindergarten methods and in medicine, and although their letters are suggestive of the difficult adjustment to the climate, food and culture in which they found themselves, the language in which their experiences are couched reaffirms their perception of women's subordinate role and their willing acceptance of male perceptions of their worth. The importance of language, imagery and symbolism in perpetuating conventional gender roles should not be overlooked. [. . .]

It is this continuing emphasis on traditional feminine virtues by the men who ran the evangelical voluntary organisations, and for whom the 'essential' nature of men and women predetermined religious as well as social roles, which most clearly emerges from a reading of the sources. The controversial nature of many religious meetings, with their emphasis on action and resolution, reinforced these perceptions, particularly in Ireland. In contrast to their own heated political debates, it was suggested that 'the religion of a woman ought to be an impassioned weakness, and that sweet spirit which was typified by the dove should spread its wings upon her'.[24] The *Belfast People's Magazine* also stressed the moral superiority of women, and the duties incumbent upon them.

> Let all females be persuaded, that God did not intend them, by any means, for mere servile purposes, but designed them to be truly helpmates to men; and, therefore, let them with a religious regard to the end of their creation, study by every winning grace, by every angel virtue, to lead those with whom they may be connected to happiness both here and hereafter.[25]

Women's power to influence men – for good or evil – was clearly recognised, but any evaluation of their worth placed them in a complementary and submissive relation, for 'upon the virtues of women much of that of man depended, and the religious habits of the sex could not fail to exercise a salutary influence'.[26] Similarly, while evangelicals encouraged the participation of women in many areas, it was clear that their moral authority was to be used not to erode traditional boundaries, but as an instrument in the regeneration of the wider society. Women provided much of the funding, the administrative expertise and the social skills necessary to maintain the popular status of evangelical societies, but men retained their official status and continued to exercise authority and determine policy. Traditional arrangements and traditional values were not only retained but upheld by evangelical theology, and the extension of women's influence was interpreted in purely spiritual terms. On the whole, women accepted, even welcomed, the cultural role conferred upon them by Ulster evangelicalism. They also picked out aspects of Christ's personality with which to identify and unquestioningly drew upon the prevalent cult of evangelical domesticity, which after all offered tangible benefits when set alongside the domestic circumstances of women exposed to rougher and more irreligious households.

Women's contribution to popular Protestantism in this period is not easily reduced to facile categories. They certainly provided ammunition for critics, particularly in the early stages of evangelical enthusiasm, but as evangelicalism took on an aura of respectability, with congregations becoming more settled and the dignity of the pastoral office replacing the excitement of the circuit horse-rider, women became less controversial but more central to evangelicalism's social creed.

Inevitably, the limits of women's actions were circumscribed by men, and the much-vaunted importance of female example in terms of piety, humility, and service was widely disseminated through family and social structures. But in these traditional areas women were not simply victims but willing participants in a campaign of moral reformation. It is, however, in the relation between popular Protestantism and home life that their presence was most significant. In a faith which relied strongly on idealised notions of domesticity, this should not be under-estimated. It was not only that women enabled evangelists to establish a foothold in the family and the community, but that their activities ensured that religious values penetrated all aspects of everyday life in a way that institutionalised religion could not. Women's civilising influence was evident too in the combination of holy charity and biblical education so common in the nineteenth century. The social events over which they presided – bazaars, teas, sales and Sunday-school celebrations – tied the church or chapel closer to the community and established links which remain central to Ulster Protestant culture.

An over-concentration on the political aspects of Ulster religious history has diverted attention from less contentious aspects of its development. Personal, social and cultural values and the internal dynamics of religious faith, including the varieties of meanings and networks of relationships within which they are rooted, have fallen outside the mainstream of research. Women have too often been casualties of this historical bias. To incorporate their experiences and perceptions into this male-dominated history is to take an important step towards a more comprehensive understanding of the complexities of the past.

Notes

1 *Minutes of the Methodist Conferences in Ireland*, vol. 1, 1744–1819, p. 152.

2 D. Valenze, *Prophetic Sons and Daughters: Female Preaching and Popular Religion in Industrial England*, Princeton, NJ, 1985, and W. F. Swift, 'The women itinerant preachers of early Methodism', *Proceedings of the Wesley Historical Society*, 28, 1951–2, pp. 89–94; and 29, 1953–4, pp. 76–83.

3 See Northern Ireland Public Record Office (NIPRO), Ouseley Collection, CR6/3, letter from Zachariah Taft to Gideon Ouseley, 15 February 1823.

4 C. H. Crookshank, *History of Methodism in Ireland*, 3 vols, London, 1885–8, vol. 2, p. 153.

5 E. Thomas, *Irish Methodist Reminiscences: Memorials of the Life and Labour of the Late Reverend S. Nicholson*, London, 1889, p. 10.

6 D. N. Hempton, 'Methodism in Irish society: 1770–1830', Transactions of the Royal Historical Society, 5th series, 26, 1986, pp. 117–42.

7 Although dealing with a different profession and period, an interesting analysis on the gap between women's access to a profession, and equal opportunities within it, is provided in an essay by J. K. Conway, 'Politics, pedagogy and power', *Daedalus*, 1987, pp. 137–52.

8 H. Bingham, *The Life Story of Ann Preston*, Toronto, 1907, p. 33.

9   Crookshank, *History of Methodism*, vol. 2, p. 31.

10   Letters of Anne Lutton of Moira; a volume of original letters of 'Holy Anne' Lutton, *c.* 1810–1840. We wish to thank Mr J. Gamble for making this available from his private collection.

11   NIPRO, Ouseley Collection, CR6/3, Ouseley, 22 September 1802. See also D. N. Hempton, 'Gideon Ouseley: rural revivalist 1791–1839', *Studies in Church History*, 25, 1989, pp. 203–14.

12   O. Goodbody, *Guide to Irish Quaker Records 1654–1860*, Dublin, 1967, p. 4.

13   The best general assessment of women's involvement in voluntary religious agencies in this period is provided by F. Prochaska, *Women and Philanthropy in Nineteenth-Century England*, Oxford, 1980.

14   *Report of the Hibernian Bible Society*, 1822, Dublin, 1822.

15   *Religious Tract and Bible Society, 16th Report*, Dublin, 1830.

16   *24th Annual Report of the London Hibernian Society*, Dublin, 1830; TCD, see *Annual Reports of the Irish Society for Promoting the Education of the Native Irish through the Medium of their Own Language*, especially 1834 and 1836.

17   F. E. Bland, *How the Church Missionary Society Came to Ireland*, Dublin, 1935; RCB, HCMS, auxiliary letter book, Report of the Deputation to the North, 26 September 1820.

18   Prochaska, *Women and Philanthropy*.

19   W. D. Killen, *Memoir of John Edgar, DD, LLD*, Belfast, 1867, p. 249.

20   The printed reports of the Female Association for Promoting Christianity among the Women of the East are held in Presbyterian Church House, Belfast.

21   *Report of the Female Association, 1876*, Belfast, 1876.

22   *Report of the Female Association, 1877*, Belfast, 1877.

23   *Report of the Female Association, 1875*, Belfast, 1875.

24   *Report of the Debates which took place at the Two Meetings of the Ladies Auxiliary to the London Hibernian Society, held at Cork, 8th and 9th September, 1824*, Dublin, 1824.

25   *Belfast People's Magazine*, 1, 1847.

26   *Report of the Debates . . . at Cork . . .*, Dublin, 1824.

Chapter 17

Caitríona Clear

■   from **WALLS WITHIN WALLS: NUNS IN
NINETEENTH-CENTURY IRELAND**, in Chris Curtin,
Pauline Jackson and Barbara O'Connor (eds), *Gender in
Irish Society*, Galway, 1987, pp. 134–51

> The refinement of manners which naturally characterises ladies by birth
> and education is one of the striking features presented on entering
> convent schools after leaving a school of any other description.[1]

THE IMPRESSION WHICH WAS RECEIVED by Balmer, one of the
Powis Commissioners of 1870, and which is quoted above, was that nuns
came from comparatively privileged socio-economic backgrounds. Several
onlookers both secular and religious, Catholic and Protestant, made similar observations in this period. [. . .] A report on St Brigid's Orphanage, Dublin, in 1897,
mentioned that the Sisters of the Holy Faith, who ran the orphanage, were 'much
higher in social position and intelligence' than the nurses who ran other, similar
projects.[2] [. . .] There is also evidence that the convent was seen as an institution
which conferred a high social status on the entrant: 'The homely patronymic is
exchanged for the title of some long-dead and buried saint, and the daughter of a
publican ranks equally with the descendant of the Howards'.[3]

How accurate were these observations? Here, an attempt is made to determine the social background of some recruits to the religious life in the second half
of the nineteenth century in Ireland. Accompanying this is an attempt to define
the exact nature of the most obvious division of rank which existed in the majority
of Irish convents in this period: the distinction between choir nuns, the religious
who were employed in the work for which the congregation had been founded,
be it nursing, teaching or a combination of these, or other activities, and lay sisters,
who worked principally in the domestic sphere.

[. . . T]here are 'glaring gaps' in our knowledge about the socio-economic
status of the convent entrant and [. . .] we know virtually nothing about lay sisters
or dowries.[4] This is not surprising. Anybody who hopes to find lists (at diocesan
or at provincial level) of all the women who took vows in any years will be disap-
pointed. The Catholic directories for the period, though listing all the secular and
most of the regular clergy in the country, did not always list the total number of

women religious per diocese, never mind their names, and entry registers containing details about every woman who entered do not survive in every convent.[5] It is as if Catherine McAuley's recommendation to her sisters in religion to strive to be the most hidden and unknown[6] was taken to heart by many of those who had dealings, to a greater or lesser extent, with convents in nineteenth-century Ireland. [. . .]

Canon law stipulated that every woman bring a certain sum of money to the convent with her.[7] Amounts varied. Hardiman[8] reported that the women who entered the Presentation convent in Galway in the early nineteenth century had to bring £500 each with them. A list in the Galway Diocesan Archives, dated 26 December 1857 and detailing the size of dowry of each woman professed as a choir nun in the Galway Mercy convent between 1840 and 1857, shows that the average was £375, and the lowest sum was £200.[9] [. . .] Occasionally a postulant had a very large fortune; Jane Arthur, one of the famous Limerick Arthurs, entered a convent in England in 1836 with £22,000, and O'Riordan referred to two women of his acquaintance who brought £2,000 each to the convent with them.[10]

Catherine McAuley is credited with saying that she would never refuse a candidate for religion on the grounds that 'she had not got a bag of money'. Mother Teresa Ball, foundress of the IBVM or Loreto order in Ireland, 'never refused a postulant for lack of means'.[11] These remarks imply that impoverished candidates were somehow exceptional and more than this, the phrases 'a bag of money' and 'lack of means' seem to refer to an inability to raise a required sum, rather than inability to produce any money at all.

Several people to whom I spoke described lay sisters as 'those who had no dowries'. Yet two lay postulants to the Galway Mercy convent in the 1840s brought £50 each to the convent with them. It seems, however, that lay sisters did not always have to bring money with them; the Mercy rule stated[12] that a professed religious who was being dispensed from her vows, if she had not brought a dowry with her, had to be provided with money sufficient to maintain herself for a period of time. Perhaps the £50 paid by the two lay sisters mentioned was not a dowry at all, but a sort of down-payment?

[. . .] The women who entered in the capacity of lay sister in the years from 1850 to 1859 had an average valuation of 9s. 6d. on their dwellings of origin, and the equivalent for choir entrants in these years was £86. These figures apply only to the Mercy convent, as the register in the Good Shepherd convent did not begin till 1861. In the 1860s the homes of origin of lay postulants were valued at an average of £9. 4s., those of choir postulants at £69. In the following decade the homes of origin of the latter group were valued, on average, at £33, those of lay entrants at £9. The falling average valuation of the backgrounds of choir entrants indicates the growing popularity of the religious life among the less wealthy sector of the middle classes.

[. . .] The religious who worked at life-maintaining tasks such as cooking, cleaning and gardening, answering doors and fetching and carrying were, it seems, drawn largely from the artisan, small farming and labouring classes. Those who performed the work for which the convent had been established tended to come from decidedly wealthy backgrounds at the beginning of the period, but as the last quarter of the century approached, the daughters of civil servants, clerks and other white-collar workers, as well as those of 'comfortable', if not exactly wealthy, farmers entered in greater numbers. Typical was Bridget Fitzgibbon, the daughter of a clerk in Limerick city whose property was valued at £13, who entered the Good Shepherd in 1871.[13] The upper-middle classes continued to be represented; one example is Ethel Spillane, of the Limerick tobacco factory family, who entered the Mercy convent in 1892.[14]

Examining each convent in isolation helps us to determine the extent to which the particular features of each convent influenced the social composition of its recruits. The women who entered the Good Shepherd as lay postulants, for instance, tended, up to 1880 at any rate, to come from backgrounds which were better off than those of Mercy lay entrants in the same years. [. . .]

While both convents drew on the 'respectable' labouring classes (i.e. those who were not destitute, deviant or vagrant) for their lay sisters, it can be suggested that from 1861 to 1880 at least, the French convent tended to take its lay postulants from the upper echelons of the working classes. Does this imply that the Good Shepherd nuns operated a conscious policy of accepting only those candidates who came from what were obviously 'provident' and therefore, respectable backgrounds? All of the Mercy convents in the diocese of Limerick had everyday contact, through their national schools, with potential recruits to the lay sister ranks. The other convent did not have contact through its work with women who might want to enter, and lacking this familiarising, long-term acquaintance with potential recruits, had recourse to what it saw as outward signs of stability, which often depended upon a certain income level. And indeed, it could be that because many labouring-class women never came into contact with the Good Shepherd order as they did with the Mercy or the Presentation, it was only the more well-informed and literate at this social level – those who could buy and read Catholic periodicals and newspapers – who would have considered joining this order.

The comparative wealth of the Mercy choir novices between 1860 and 1879 is also striking. The ability of this convent to attract a larger number of women from very wealthy backgrounds must be attributed to the high visibility of this congregation, and to its secure, established position in Irish Catholic life. The superior of St Mary's convent stated in 1895 that thirty-three of the Sisters of Mercy in Limerick at that date (out of approximately sixty if she is referring to the city) were past pupils of Laurel Hill convent, a boarding and day school run by the Faithful Companions of Jesus (a French congregation) and a school whose prohibitive fees made it the preserve of the upper-middle classes.[15]

It could be argued that the Good Shepherd's field of activity dissuaded the very wealthy from entering this congregation, but this is unlikely, given first of all the willingness of women from this social stratum to teach, nurse and visit the very poor in the Mercy congregation, and thus to be exposed, to a far greater extent than in the Good Shepherd convent, to the shocks of what was virtually a different culture, without the 'protection', as it were, of the carceral system operated by the French nuns. It is also important to remember the extremely powerful mystique of the penitents' asylum in this period,[16] which no doubt attracted many women to the Irish Sisters of Charity, to the Sisters of Charity of the Refuge and, indeed, to several Mercy convents which ran 'Magdalen homes'.

[. . . H]istories, contemporary accounts, rule-books and other sources consistently fail to define the exact position of [lay sisters] in the convent, given also their unsung status in the triumphalist literature of post-famine Catholicism. The entry requirements of a lay postulant, according to the Mercy rules,[17] were a vocation, a good constitution, and an ordinary education. Some convents did not, it seems, demand literacy of their lay entrants. Martha Glynn, who was received into the Dominican convent in Galway in 1865, could not sign her name, and neither could Mary Rush, received into this convent in 1872, nor Mary Anne O'Brien, who began her novitiate here in 1878.[18] The first lay sister to be professed in this convent was Mary Cole who, prior to her entry in 1859, had been prioress of a tertiary chapter of the Dominican order in Westmeath and, as this would imply, was literate.[19]

A reason which was often advanced to explain the status of lay sisters rests on the argument that the class from which these sisters were drawn had not sufficient knowledge of Latin to enable them to recite office in choir.[20] It is hardly likely, given the curriculum of most female 'superior' or pay schools in Ireland at this period[21] that many middle-class women had more than a nodding acquaintance with the language either. [. . .] And there were instances of lay sisters who were well-educated enough to teach. Sr. Joseph Calasanctius Shannon, who died in the Presentation convent in Limerick in 1869 'although professed as a lay sister showed such talents for instruction that she was constantly employed in the schools'.[22] [. . .]

The Mercy Guide, although it offers a very comprehensive treatment of most aspects of the religious life, does not contain a section devoted exclusively to lay sisters. This could imply that no real difference between choir and lay religious existed in this congregation, or that lay sister status was taken so much for granted that no clarification was needed. A section devoted to the care of penitents, or reformed prostitutes, provides an insight. It states that if a choir nun is not available to supervise these women a 'prudent lay sister' will suffice. With regard to the Chapter of Faults, a weekly exercise in spoken confession and accusation, it stipulates that lay novices and lay sisters are to make their accusations in it first, then to retire before any choir nun opens her mouth.[23] The reference to a prudent lay sister implies that choir nuns were prudent by definition, lay sisters, by happy accident. The segregation which prevailed in the regular exercise in humility and self-abnegation suggests nothing other than a conscious intention not to allow the lay sisters to know the faults and failings of choir nuns, although the reverse did not apply. [. . .]

A contemporary authority described lay sisters as 'those who have a religious but no ecclesiastical vocation'. Spiritually lay sisters could be on a par with or surpass the highest ecclesiastic, but temporally and structurally they were, and would remain, at the bottom of the hierarchical ladder.[24] This category of religious always took simple vows, even in orders that had solemn vows.[25] They were without elective voice in several orders and congregations.[26]

An entry in the annals of the South Presentation in Cork in 1822 provides further clarification of the status of lay sister: 'Sr. Catherine Howlett pronounced her final vows today, in the quality of Lay Sister. The ceremonies were conducted in the order of second-class feasts, there being no choir sister professed with her.'[27]

[. . .] The designation 'second-class' to describe the celebrations accompanying Catherine Howlett's profession suggests a definite inferiority about the vocation of a lay sister. [. . .]

The divide does not appear to have narrowed with time. In 1882 the Presentation convent in Clondalkin specified that three of its professed religious were lay sisters[28] as did many other convents in this year. The women who performed the domestic work of the convent dressed in a distinctive way, up to the 1960s; in the Dominican order they wore a black scapular instead of the white one worn by choir nuns.[29] In the Mercy congregation they wore an apron and their habits were 'without train'[30] The Presentation lay sisters also wore aprons, and short veils. There were of course practical reasons for these modifications in dress – trains would have been cumbersome and awkward while scrubbing or gardening – but the similarity between lay sisters' regalia and the uniforms worn by domestic servants in big houses is hard to overlook. [. . .]

The spiritual duties of those who scrubbed and cooked were less onerous than those of the religious involved in other tasks. Most obviously they were not obliged to recite office in choir.[31] In the Mercy congregation choir novices were not allowed to take part in any of the external works (i.e. teaching, nursing) of the convent for at least a year, but lay novices were allowed to perform all the duties of lay sisters 'in a subordinate capacity', as long as these did not conflict with their spiritual duties, which were, it is implied, less time-consuming than those of choir novices.[32]

[. . .] Emphasis on the privileged social origin of choir nuns was often blended with an invocation of the traditional noblesse seen to be attached to ecclesiastical office. Catherine McAuley said,

> The demeanour of the sisters, before and after entering the convent, should be as that of one unexpectedly raised to the dignity of a queen, and who, elevated to so exalted a position, would feel bound to demean herself with a dignity becoming her exalted station.[33]

[. . .] Class-based values are displayed in her exhortation that the sisters' manner with seculars be governed by 'the rules of good breeding and religious politeness'.[34] A contemporary, herself a religious, commented with approval that the Mercy sisters practised among themselves 'the usages of good society', and that they took pains to preserve the 'ladylike refinement of manners and ideas' which they had brought with them from their homes.[35]

[. . .] A microcosm of the sex-based division of power and labour which existed in society as a whole prevailed in religious communities of women, and the fact that some lay sisters were involved in the 'external works' (teaching or nursing) of some convents did not change anything; like the women who were filtering into professions and other 'responsible' occupations in nineteenth-century Western society, their occupational promotion did not guarantee them a franchise in the communities which they served, nor a toehold upon the hierarchical ladder. [. . .] Virtually prohibited by 'birth', or socio-economic background, from holding executive position, lacking franchise, keeping in the background, and featuring only marginally, if at all, in histories, biographies and other accounts both contemporary and retrospective, lay sisters' position in the convents of the period was roughly analogous to that of women as a group in the larger society.

Notes

1   T. J. Walsh, *Nano Nagle and the Presentation Sisters*, Dublin, 1959, p. 225.

2   M. Gibbons, *Life of Margaret Aylward*, London, 1928, p. 192.

3   Unsigned, 'Convent boarding-schools for young ladies', *Fraser's Magazine*, 9, 1874, pp. 778–86.

4   T. Fahey, 'Female asceticism in the Catholic Church: a case study of nuns in Ireland in the nineteenth century', Ph.D. thesis, University of Illinois, 1981, pp. 61–2.

5   *Catholic Directory*, Dublin, 1864; *Guy's Munster Directory*, Cork, 1886; *Irish Catholic Directory*, Dublin, 1882, 1900.

6   Mercy congregation, *Maxims and Counsels of Mother Catherine McAuley*, Dublin, n.d., p. 121.

7   I. Fanfani and K. O'Rourke, *Canon Law for Religious Women*, Iowa, 1961, pp. 193–40.

8   J. Hardiman, *History of Galway*, Dublin, Galway [1820], new edn 1958, p. 278.

9   Galway Diocesan Office, List of monies received at the profession of sisters in St Vincent's Mercy convent, Galway, 1840–57.

10 A Loreto Sister, *Joyful Mother of Children: Mother Mary Frances Teresa Ball*, Dublin, 1961, p. 169; M. O'Riordan, *Catholicity and Progress In Ireland*, St Louis, 1905, p. 371.

11 Mercy congregation, n.d., *Maxims and Counsels*, p. 9; A Loreto Sister, *Joyful Mother*, 1961, p. 115.

12 Mercy congregation, *Rules and Constitutions of the Religious Called Sisters of Mercy*, Rome, 1926, pp. 22–4.

13 Good Shepherd convent, Clare St., Limerick, Register of women received into the convent 1861 to 1900.

14 St Mary's Mercy convent, Limerick, Register of entrants 1850–1900.

15 Faithful Companions of Jesus convent, Laurel Hill, Limerick, Ms. record of events in the year 1895: *Irish Catholic Directory*, 1900, pp. 174–5, and advertisement section.

16 cf. Thomas Burke, OP, *Ireland's Vindication: Refutation of Froude and Other Lectures Historical, Literary and Religious*, London, n.d., *c.*1872, p. 21; Anon., 'The Magdalens of High Park', *Irish Rosary*, 1, 1897, pp. 176–84, 179.

17 Mercy congregation, *Rules and Constitutions*, p. 93.

18 Register of receptions to the Dominican convent, Taylor's Hill, Galway, 1859–78.

19 Typewritten history of the Dominican convent, Taylor's Hill, Galway compiled from the annals by Mother M. Bernard Heuston in 1949, p. 102.

20 W. Addis and T. Arnold, *A Catholic Dictionary*, London, 1884, p. 507.

21 G. O'Flynn, 'Some aspects of the education of Irish women throughout the years', *Capuchin Annual*, 1977, pp. 164–79.

22 Presentation convent, Sexton St., Limerick, Annals 1837 to the present day.

23 Mercy congregation, *A Guide for the Religious Called Sisters of Mercy*, Limerick, 1866, pp. 63, 233–4.

24   Addis and Arnold, *Catholic Dictionary* p. 507.

25   *New Catholic Encyclopaedia*, 15 vols, Washington DC, 1966, XIV, pp. 756–8.

26   Fanfani and O'Rourke, *Canon Law*, pp. 79–80; also several oral testimonies.

27   South Presentation convent, Douglas St., Cork, typewritten compilation of annals 1802–25 for internal distribution, 1981, ii, p. 27.

28   *Irish Catholic Directory*, 1882, p. 110.

29   Sr. M. Rose, DCG, Sr. M. Pierre, MCI, the late Sr. Mary Patrick, IHC, provided these details.

30   Mercy congregation, *Rules and Constitutions*, p. 94.

31   Addis and Arnold, *Catholic Dictionary*, p. 507.

32   Mercy congregation, *Rules and Constitutions*, p. 28.

33   Mercy congregation, *Maxims and Counsels*, p. 8.

34   Ibid., pp. 27, 80.

35   A Member of the Order of Mercy, *Leaves from the Annals of the Sisters of Mercy*, New York, 1881, p. 244.

Chapter 18

J. J. Lee

■ from **WOMEN AND THE CHURCH SINCE THE FAMINE**, in Margaret MacCurtain and Donnchadh Ó Corrain (eds), *Women in Irish Society: The Historical Dimension*, Dublin, 1978, pp. 37–45

T HE GREAT FAMINE DRASTICALLY WEAKENED the position of women in Irish society. Before the famine women's economic contribution was so essential to the family economy that they enjoyed considerable independence. Growing factory competition was, it is true, sapping the strength of domestic industry, but as late as 1841 women accounted for more than half the total non-agricultural labour force. Women also played an active role in agriculture itself, and shared most of the normal male responsibilities.

The famine helped change this situation in three main ways. First, it delivered a crippling blow to domestic industry. The number of spinners of wool, cotton and linen fell about 75 per cent between 1841 and 1851. The main source of independent income enjoyed by women all but vanished. Only in the Belfast region, where linen became a factory industry, did opportunities for female employment significantly increase. Second, the famine permitted a marked shift from tillage to livestock, and agriculture became less labour intensive. Women were now less necessary about the farm. In the major sector where they remained important, dairying, they were gradually superseded as milk came to be sent increasingly to creameries in the twentieth century. Domestic service became the only major employment left for women except in the North. By 1926 about 60 per cent of women employed outside agriculture in the six counties were engaged as domestic servants, compared with about 30 per cent in 1841. Third, the proportion of agricultural labourers to farmers, and of smaller farmers to stronger farmers, fell sharply. As women had probably enjoyed greater economic equality among the poorer orders than among the wealthier, this in itself sufficed to tilt the balance of economic power within the family in the male direction.

On the other hand, the woman's functions in the home changed significantly. Before the famine many women did not have to know much about cooking. The potato pot demanded no great culinary pretensions. The spread of stoves and ranges, and the greater variety of diet, meant that women had to spend far more time cooking after the famine than before. As the clothes and utensils the family possessed increased, the wife had to spend more time cleaning and scouring. Making the bed and washing the sheets was a simple matter in many cases before the famine, when the bed was often a pile of straw on the floor. Pre-famine women did not spend most of their day isolated in the kitchen, if only because more than half the houses had no separate kitchen in which to spend it. However much work pre-famine women had to do, it did not include a great deal of housework in the narrow sense.

The deterioration in the economic status of women affected their marriage prospects. Before the famine a wife's earnings in domestic industry and her contribution to agricultural labour made marriage a viable proposition for the hardy but poor youth. He would rely on the combined efforts of his wife and himself to eke out a modest subsistence. This became less and less the case after the famine, and helped to reduce the possibility of young people establishing independent households without the support of their parents. This loss of the woman's economic independence made her much more vulnerable to male economic dominance. It helped explain the growing importance of the dowry after the famine. As the wife made a lesser economic contribution in current terms to the household, the amount of capital she brought with her assumed greater importance. Because the daughter had little to bring except the dowry she got from her father her marriage prospects now depended more completely on him and she had to become more subservient to his wishes. The relative independence that daughters had enjoyed in choosing a mate before the famine diminished.

Partly as a result of this, the marriage rate fell. By 1926 about 25 per cent of women remained unmarried aged forty-five, compared with about 10 per cent before the famine. In addition, as parents lived longer, sons had to wait longer to inherit their farms and to marry. The age gap between husbands and wives widened. Before the famine about 20 per cent of husbands were ten years older than their wives. By the early twentieth century the proportion had climbed to about 50 per cent. Women increasingly married, when they married at all, men distinctly older than themselves. This tended to enhance the authority of the husband, who could claim to be much more experienced than his wife. This age gap further reinforced the husband's control, which was growing in any event because he was now generally the sole earner in the family.

The proportion of women who remained unmarried was exceptionally high by international standards. And it was high despite the fact that a relatively large number of women emigrated in search of the chance to start a family that their society denied to them. Only about one-third of emigrants from Europe as a whole between 1850 and 1950 were women. But in Ireland the proportion reached about 50 per cent. This deviation from the European pattern reflects the hopelessness of the girl's marriage prospects in Ireland. Farmers would not normally dower two daughters. That would dissipate their savings, and drag the family down in the social scale. Marriage might be a sacrament, but for the farmer the marriage contract was essentially a commercial transaction, and it devalued the family currency to put two daughters on the marriage market. A society dominated by strong farmers, and providing little female employment, inevitably denied most of its children the chance of rearing a family in the country. It was therefore crucial to maintain the economic dominance of the new order that all thoughts of marriage in Ireland should be banished from the minds of the majority of Irish youth. Temptation must not be placed in their way. Sex, therefore, must be denounced as a satanic snare, in even what had been its most innocent pre-famine manifestations. Sex posed a far more subversive threat than the landlord to the security and status of the family. Boys and girls must be kept apart at all costs.

Economic circumstances therefore conspired to make Ireland an increasingly male-dominated society after the famine. The churches, and particularly the Catholic Church, whose members were disproportionately affected, could not escape the implications. The rise of the strong farmer coincided with the growth of clerical power. The Irish churches in general, but especially the Catholic Church, underwent an organisational overhaul in the generation after 1850. In the Catholic case this is particularly associated with the guiding genius of the great Cardinal Paul Cullen. Cullen himself, who combined a good mind with great common sense, was not quite as preoccupied with sex as some of his subordinates and successors. However, he greatly improved the administrative efficiency of the Catholic Church. The number of churches, the number of clergy, the number of devotions, the frequency of the sacraments, not least confession, increased spectacularly in his lifetime. The Church was able to preach its doctrines in detail for perhaps the first time in Irish history to the mass of the people just at the moment when the new image of woman, and the new public obsession with sex, was gaining the ascendancy. In addition, the spread of literacy permitted a rapid growth in the number of publications, religious as well as general, and provided yet another means of effective indoctrination. The proportion of clergy to laity also began to rise dramatically after the famine. In 1840 there was one Catholic priest to about 3,500 lay people. In 1960 there was one to every 600. The proportion of priests increased about six-fold. The proportion of nuns rose even faster. There was one nun to about every 7,000 Catholics in 1841, compared with one to about 400 a century later. The growing numbers of Catholic clergy were drawn disproportionately from what Fr. Guinan, author of the popular and revealing *Priest and People in Doon* (Dublin, 1903), called 'The respectable and fairly comfortable class of the tenant farmers'. Inevitably, therefore, the clergy instinctively shared the farmers' attitudes.

[. . .] It is one of the ironies of the intellectual history of modern Ireland that at a period when Catholic propagandists lovingly portrayed everybody as out-of-step except our Paddy, and when they were prone to denounce England as decadent, they imbibed unconsciously, as their Protestant brothers did more consciously, the prudish values of Victorian middle-class morality, which simultaneously idealised and repressed women. Pre-famine Irish society was renowned for its chastity, but prudery was conspicuously absent. As the Irish language declined, however, and Gaelic values were eroded, prudery seeped through Irish society, and came close to being equated with morality itself. [. . .]

It is not surprising that the agricultural labourers succumbed to the farmers' image of women. The labourers had often been suspicious of farmers' values before the famine. But if the strong farmers did well out of the famine, the labourers were broken. Their numbers declined rapidly, and their general defeatism as a beaten race sapped their resistance to the mental dominance of the stronger farmers. The success of the farmers in capturing the towns for their values was more striking.

Belfast may have provided a partial exception, if only because Belfast working-class women enjoyed a somewhat greater economic independence than their southern sisters, due to the linen industry, which, however horrific its employment conditions, did at least put some money in the girls' pockets.

Rural values infiltrated the other towns through two agencies. First, the bulk of urban clergy appeared to have been recruited from the country, and were educated in seminaries dominated by the strong farmer ethos. Second, the educational system came increasingly under clerical influence. Before the famine much education was independent of the churches. After the famine, the spread of clerical authority coincided with the spread of the educational system. Perhaps more importantly, the status of the teacher changed. In 1841 two-thirds of teachers were men, compared with only one-third a century later. [. . .] Before the famine the schoolmaster often provided an alternative source of intellectual authority to the clergyman. This became less and less the case after the famine partly because of the growth in the number of female teachers, who commanded less general authority in the community than male teachers, and partly because the churches captured not only the schools but the teachers. The hedge schoolmasters had not generally been systematically trained. The teacher training colleges which began to be established after 1870 were strongly influenced by the churches. There was little danger of any deviation from prevailing orthodoxy among minds drilled in those institutions. [. . .]

It is ironic that at a moment when educational opportunities increased for Irish women, the educational system began to be more systematically used to indoctrinate them into adopting as self-images the prevailing male image of woman. Literacy, for all its ultimate emancipatory potential, became in the short term another instrument for stifling independent thought. Dutiful woman teachers, including many dedicated nuns, taught girls obedience, docility and resignation to the role assigned to them by a male providence, until the more gullible came to believe that the role was a law of universal nature and not simply the product of a peculiar and transient set of local circumstances. Female marriage patterns helped to consolidate the grip of the new orthodoxy on women themselves. Before the famine widows and spinsters aged over forty-five accounted for about one-sixth of the women in the country. A century later their proportion had doubled to about one-third, and these women were presumably liable to be more conservative, more prone to cling to the new conventional certainties as the main prop of their psychological security.

Nuns themselves were not exempt from the general image of women that became prevalent in Irish society after the famine. In a narrower sense, of course, female religious orders provided one of the few opportunities for able women to realise their talents in leadership roles, even if some of their male brethren may have conveyed the impression that nuns should be neither seen nor heard. But the desexualisation of women in general had its counterpart in the depersonalisation of nuns in particular in the Irish imagination. Nuns were de-humanised in public images to a far greater extent than priests. Priests feature fairly prominently in modern Irish writing, nuns hardly at all, except in the orgiastic ecstasies of the Belfast Protestant yellow press. [. . .]

It would be a gross distortion to imply that the clergies were the conscious agents of materialistic man in post-famine Ireland. They patently were not. Even the lunatic fringe working out their personal neuroses on courting couples with the blackthorn stick are subjects more for the psychiatrist than for the historian. But the clergies shared something of the capacity for delusion of the society from which they sprang. Otherwise they could scarcely have failed to perceive that the idolatrous self-image of Ireland as a beacon of spiritual light in a world deluged in a materialistic sea was a convenient piece of self-deception indulged by a society that counted every step to the altar to the last avaricious farthing. The innumerable acts of charity of generations of individual clergy, and of sympathetic societies like the Legion of Mary, cannot disguise the fact that the individual problems they sought to alleviate were often the products of the system their teaching sanctioned. The real tragedy for women in post-famine Ireland lay in the conflict between the viciousness of the system and the kindness of the individuals operating it.

The gentle Fr. Guinan provides an opposite example. He was deeply disturbed at the fate worse than death that awaited what he called the poor, sheepish unsuspecting country girl in America. 'How happy, in comparison', he went on 'and how blessed would have been the lot of an Irish girl, the poor betrayed victim of hellish agencies of vice, had she remained at home and passed her days in the poverty, aye and wretchedness, of a mud wall cabin – a wife and mother, mayhap – her path in life smoothened by the blessed influences of religion and domestic peace until it ended at a green old age in the calm, peaceful repose of God's just.' But of course the reason that the poor country girl had emigrated was that she saw no chance of becoming wife and mother in the blessed island that so stridently trumpeted its devotion to the idea of the family. Fr. Guinan felt deeply for the victims of emigration. He couldn't see that it was the values of the society he cherished that condemned these girls to emigration.

The same delusion can be detected in the work of Fr. Michael O'Riordan, the learned and kindly rector of the Irish College in Rome who claimed that 'genuine Irish Catholic girls are never short of proposals to share a home with them'. But that is precisely what many genuine Irish Catholic girls, and many genuine Irish Protestant girls as well, were short of in Ireland – proposals. Genuine Christianity provided little competition for a full purse on the marriage market.

It took the churches a generation to adapt to the changes in the status of women that followed the Great Famine. There were even then some older priests unable to grasp that the traditional society they inherited had passed away. But the Catholic Church, at least, was fortunate in that the rapidly rising number of clergy meant that a high proportion of them were young and adaptable to the changing circumstances.

[. . . I]ndustrialisation and urbanisation, whose pace has so greatly accelerated since the 1950s, have created new opportunities for women and spread new attitudes among men. The farmer has gradually lost his grip on Irish values. If two-thirds of working women outside agriculture were employed in domestic service in 1926, that proportion has dwindled to almost nothing a half century later. More girls are going into occupations that give them some chance for independent thinking. The majority of working women are no longer confined to jobs that largely deprive them of the use of their minds. Inside marriage the age gaps between husbands and wives are closing once more and genuine partnership is becoming possible for a bigger number of couples.

[. . .] Institutions do of course develop their own rigidities, and delays inevitably occur. But in historical perspective it is not the rigidity of the churches, but their receptivity to change, that is now most striking. [. . .] The wheel is coming full circle, as women begin once more to enjoy something of the economic independence many of them knew before the famine. Men are adapting, however reluctantly, to the implications of this change, and the clerical image of woman, like the male image of woman in general, is being refurbished accordingly. The past [nineteenth] century may soon come to be seen as no more than a sharp but temporary deviation from the main course of the history of women in Ireland.

Further reading

C. M. Arensberg and S. T. Kimball, *Family and Community in Ireland*, Cambridge, Mass., 1940, 2nd edn, 1968.

K. H. Connell, *Irish Peasant Society*, Oxford, 1968.

S. J. Connolly, 'Catholicism and social discipline in pre-famine Ireland', *Irish Economic and Social History*, IV, 1977, pp. 74–6.

D. Fennell (ed.), *The Changing Face of Catholic Ireland*, London, 1968.

J. Guinan, *Priest and People in Doon*, Dublin, 1903, 6th edn, 1925.

D. S. Hannan and L. A. Katsiaouni, *Traditional Families?*, Dublin, 1977.

S. G. Kelly, *Teaching in the City*, Dublin, 1970.

R. E. Kennedy, *The Irish: Emigration, Marriage and Fertility*, Berkeley, 1973.

M. O'Riordan, *Catholicity and Progress in Ireland*, London, 1905.

N. H. Youssef, *Women and Work in Developing Societies*, Berkeley, 1974.

Chapter 19

Gráinne M. Blair

■   from 'EQUAL SINNERS': IRISH WOMEN
UTILISING THE SALVATION ARMY RESCUE
NETWORK FOR BRITAIN AND IRELAND IN THE
NINETEENTH CENTURY, in Margaret Kelleher and James
H. Murphy (eds), *Gender Perspectives in Nineteenth-Century
Ireland: Public and Private Spheres*, Dublin, 1997, pp. 179–92

[. . .]

WOMEN WERE CONTINUALLY INVOLVED as leading mission-
aries and administrators for the developing Salvation Army programmes.
Salvationist women raised and administered the necessary funds for the Women's
Social Services which operated independently from the rest of the Army. Women
were also involved in the evangelical revival that spread across the Army's British
Isles Territory. Caroline Reynolds was one of those women who, according to the
War Cry of 4 September 1886, joined what was known as 'The Female Band' – a
company of Whitechapel soldiers who went about to different parts of London
and caused 'a great sensation in London'.[1] It was Caroline Reynolds who undertook the 'invasion' of Ireland, arriving in 1880; in the next twenty-eight months
she opened sixteen stations, beginning in Belfast and Derry. By 31 May 1888,
when the first corps in Dublin was set up in South Richmond Street, there were
twenty-eight corps already established in Ulster. Although Ireland was part of the
British empire, local customs and beliefs were different, to say the least, and unfortunately the Salvationists were not well prepared. As Captain Reynolds woefully
remarked in 1886:

> No one will ever know what we went through. The Army colours
> given for Ireland had a green corner with the harp and no crown. We
> did not know that this was treason. Then we had orange hymn books.
> The Orangemen gloried in that, and the Catholics were wild at it!
> There were always crowds of Roman Catholics in our open-air meet-
> ings. They won't stand songs about fighting, but anything about the
> Cross or the Blood they will listen to.[2]

Once Belfast was better established, Major Reynolds moved on to Derry where, as was the norm in establishing Corps elsewhere, she initially faced strong opposition, with five days of riots. On their first afternoon there, they had no people to join in the hymns and she tells how they had 'only sung one verse when young men came running from all sides – regular Fenians! I thought, here's a beautiful lot of people to get saved!'[3] Undaunted the Salvationists held a meeting, and afterwards the police escorted them to a safe house. Despite the local difficulties, by the time the General visited Belfast in October 1886, 10,000 people were present at the meeting. Two years later, Catherine Booth saw 1,500 soldiers on the march.

In 1887, 'The Irish Rescue Home' was situated in 63 Great George Street in Belfast, described as 'a locality in which abound the class of girls we are seeking to save'. In order to offset the expenses incurred by the rescue home, the Salvationists, as was common with other homes, began to take in some work. In Belfast this was 'the top-sewing of linen and handkerchiefs for one manufacturer, and the finishing of shirts for another'. Fulton's warerooms and laundry, located in Fountaine Street, provided the home with sewing and also provided employment to three of the women when they left the rescue home.[4] The poverty of the women is clear from the Salvationists' request for cast-off clothing for the girls to wear as 'most of the girls came in barefooted, with a shawl over their heads'.[5] Major Adelaide Cox tells us that by 1889

> Two hundred and fifty-five cases had been admitted into the [Belfast] Home, a large proportion of which have been successfully dealt with, many have been sent into situations, and others – long-lost daughters – have been taken home to their parents.[6]

Opposition to the newly formed Salvation Army came in many forms in the nineteenth century, both in Ireland and England. [. . .] As was common worldwide, these early Salvationists were attacked physically and verbally, with whatever came to hand, and so it was in Dublin. A 1901 edition of the *War Cry* describes Dublin as a city 'whose women are said to be treated with a courtesy unsurpassed in any other part of the world – strange to say, the sight of a woman wearing an Army bonnet in the streets acts upon the crowd like a red rag to an infuriated bull'.[7]

In the case of Ireland, both in Derry and in Dublin, their respectability was not doubted, just the Army's 'corybantic religion'. Belfast, on the other hand, welcomed the sight of these 'respectable warriors'. Ireland in the nineteenth century became polarised between Catholics and Protestants through religious consolidation, socio-economic, political and regional separation. Evangelicals were anathema to the re-establishing Catholic Church.[8] So to the majority of Catholics in Ireland the Salvation Army may have symbolised the oppressor, the British Protestant proselytising overlord. However, that did not stop some Catholic and other religious groups recognising the innate goodness and equality that the Army espoused. The strength of opposition to the Army in Dublin was fuelled no doubt by fear and ignorance as to the real nature of their work, at a time when the

Catholic Church was trying to establish its own charities and warning against proselytism. Catholics appeared frightened that their children would be 'captured in
the war for souls', a 'battle' well-established in Ireland before the Salvation Army
entered the fray.[9] The Army in contrast described themselves in the following
words:

> We have no politics, and therefore cannot enter into discussion or
> arouse enmity . . . on that point. We do not contend with other reli-
> gious bodies or attack their creeds. We are not a sect, but an Army
> of peace, whose one duty is to preach the full, free, uttermost salva-
> tion of Jesus Christ to the souls of the people and to care for their
> bodies. We are aggressive against the devil and sin in all shapes and
> garbs, and that aggression should appeal to the militant spirit of the
> Irish. We are full of fire and life, so are they. Our religion is plain,
> practical, happy and bubbling over with songs.[10]

However, some ranks in Dublin were unable to wear their uniforms in public.
One woman was advised not to wear her bonnet publicly by the Captain. 'Not a
bit of it!' replied the girl, staunchly, as the *War Cry* of 13 July 1901 reported: 'I
have always worn my bonnet and I shall continue to do so. I am not going back
on my principle.'[11] This principled soldier was followed on her first Saturday night
in Dublin by

> a howling crowd of men, women and children [. . .] The following
> Sunday evening, however, a gang of rough lads were waiting about for
> her; they followed her through the streets, hustling and pushing her,
> while respectably-dressed men and women encouraged them, and
> hurled their hisses and maledictions at the bonnetted Salvation lassie.
> The ensuing battle by the crowd for her bonnet failed, but the onward
> rush of the crowd drove the defenceless girl's head through the glass
> panel of the door, [of her Mistress's home] and soon her face was
> bleeding profusely. The mob then turned its attention to smashing the
> windows of the house and continued this little entertainment until
> dispersed by the police.[12]

[. . .] Who were the 233 Irish women who used the Salvation Army rescue
network in Ireland and Britain between 1886 and 1892? The majority were born
or lived in Ulster, and worked in either domestic service or the textile industry,
possibly both. Eleven came from Cork and thirty-five were born in Dublin or its
environs. A few came from a rural background. [. . . F]or seventy-two women
Ulster was their point of entry, and Dublin for thirty-eight others. Most of them
were unattached and aged between fourteen and twenty-nine when they became
involved with the Salvation Army. The majority of these women stated that they
had lost their parents and partners through death and desertion. They came because
they were homeless, sick or pregnant, in debt, afraid or at risk. Many of them
had travelled a lot, a few to places as far away as New York, Canada or France,

others all over Ireland and Britain. They spent, on average, four months in an Army refuge. They used other institutions like hospitals and refuges frequently. For all of these women life was hard, society unwelcoming.

Twenty per cent of the 233 Irish women in the British Isles Territory were recorded by the Salvationists as having 'fallen' due to 'bad company'. One hundred and seventy-one women were single or engaged, and pregnancy was not a major cause of entry to the network as 57 per cent of the single women aged between fourteen and thirty-nine had never given birth. It is often assumed that rescue work in the nineteenth century was particularly designed for pregnant unmarried women, and that women who entered such rescue networks did so due to pregnancy. In fact the highest attributed factor for entry to the Army's British Isles Territory rescue network was 'women at risk', recorded as 18 per cent.

Since the Salvation Army in Ireland was more established in Ulster between 1886 and 1892 than in any other part of Ireland, it is not surprising that the majority of Irish women were from that area. This would also have influenced their employment opportunities, as this was the one area in Ireland in the late nineteenth century where employment prospects were good, even if the wages were not. Although categorisation of social class was in its infancy in the 1880s, the 1881 Census attempted a division of the population into six different social class categories. Using that categorisation and from the information available, it does not appear that the women in this study initially came from very poor working-class backgrounds.[13] [. . .]

Depending on the individual case of the woman passing through the Salvationist rescue network, it became apparent that not all women were suitable for domestic service, and so some other form of alternative employment had to be found. In England bookbinding was operating in Devonshire House, Hackney and in Whitechapel by 1888. This was considered appropriate employment as 'it is sheltered, it is fairly paid, it is quickly learned, and it requires a concentration of thought and attention which is an invaluable shield and discipline'.[14] The *Deliverer* shows that knitting, text washing, upholstery and needlework were all industries undertaken within the rescue homes.[15] Laundry work was undertaken in 1891. [. . .]

A detailed examination of the 233 Irish women cited in this study reveals that 16 per cent or thirty-eight women stayed for a period of four months in the Army's rescue network throughout the British Isles Territory. Overall, 192 women or 82 per cent were recorded as staying between one and ten months. Only 6 per cent remained within the rescue network for a period between fourteen months and under three years. In general, these were women who entered the network early in their pregnancy, and stayed until a situation could be found for them and arrangements made for their child. Others in this category were women who were particularly ill and needed to convalesce, or were unsuitable for employment outside the network, and chose to work and live with the Salvationists.

Records also show that 56 per cent (131) of the Irish women were admitted to non-Salvation 'refuges', on a total of 208 occasions. Women who stayed in these other refuges were destitute, homeless, estranged from their families or orphaned, some syphilitic, institutionalised, pregnant or otherwise at risk, and for the most part were considered unrespectable or 'fallen' in one way or another.

The Salvationists offered a different type of 'refuge', trying to give a 'fresh start' to many:

> For the methods of The Salvation Army are essentially movement, life, activity – light and colour and noise – the exchange of destructive excitements for these which are, at all events, harmless, when even not life-giving. And for women who have lived in the lurid glare and wild uproar of vice, this is better than the gloomy retribution of penance and penitence. [. . .][16]

One particular type of 'refuge' used frequently was Magdalen asylums. Women were committed to these asylums for a variety of reasons. Many women stayed in these places for two or three years and even longer, until pronounced 'fit to attain their proper station in life'. In contrast, Irish women stayed in the Salvation rescue network from a few days to over two years, and were much freer within these institutions, bringing their children and friends with them, allowed to leave to get their belongings unaccompanied, and in general treated as an equal adult woman.[17] Yet, despite the harshness of the regime of many of the non-Salvationist refuges, many women had no choice but to avail themselves of these particular institutions. A visitor to the Army's women's shelter in Hanbury Street emphasises this difference, describing how the rollicking and rousing evening service, accompanied with banjos, tambourines and general noise often struck a right chord:

> the conscience vibrates in unison with the appeal, outcast sinners rise redeemed as penitent Magdalens. For such as these The Salvation Army has ever a glad welcome . . . and, we venture to add, a more rational way of dealing with them than is to be found in the strict seclusion and dull monotony of many penitential homes.[18]

The personal contact that the Salvationist rescue network provided to Irish women was also in marked contrast to many other institutions at that time. The Salvationists understood the lack of self-esteem in the women who presented themselves for help. Society judged harshly women who had 'fallen' and expected them to continue in the 'fall'; the women themselves defined themselves as 'bad' and 'evil' and could see no way out of the downward trend. As Florence Booth observed,

> Now she is expected to be good; and, as a rule she is good. Considering the shattered nerves, the habits of drinking, the craving for excitement, the restlessness of mind and body with which a women [sic] who has been for any length of time leading a sinful life comes to our homes, we could sometimes wonder ourselves as pronouncedly as they do others at the large percentage who have been permanently reclaimed therein.[19]

The Salvation Army presented an opportunity for these Irish women to attain 'respectability', by becoming a soldier or even through a personal commitment to the Army's ethos. It provided shelter, training and retraining, employment, personal development and a new support network of friends and a larger family group, if requested, thus responding to the perceived needs of the 'congregation' they were helping. Yet the Salvationists' primary task was to evangelise the masses, and the women's social work was a method of doing this. This work involved a clear recognition of the economic inequalities and the vulnerability of all women. Similarities did exist between other rescue societies of the time and the Army; in particular, the Salvationist belief that fornication outside a legal union was sinful reinforced contemporary whore/madonna dichotomies. A significant difference however, was their belief that everyone was entitled to help, no matter how black the sin; in fact as far as the Salvationists were concerned, the blacker the better, as the saving would be all the greater.

The nature of the Salvationist work with women, as I have examined it, shows clearly their genuine belief in their ability to identify with the Irish women that they were helping. In 1865 the *Wesleyan Times* described Catherine Booth in the following words: 'She identified herself with them as a sinner, saying that if they supposed her better than they, it was a mistake, as all sinners were sinners against God.'[20] Within this philosophy these women were equal with their helpers; in this the Salvation Army had something unique to offer the women it strove to save.

Notes

1   *War Cry*, 4 September 1886, p. 4.
2   Ibid.
3   Ibid.
4   Final Reports of the Salvation Army Receiving House Statements, Country Book I, 1887–1890.
5   *War Cry*, 26 February 1887, p. 6.
6   *Deliverer*, 15 September 1889, p. 27.
7   *War Cry*, 13 July 1901, p. 12.
8   K. Theodore Hoppen, *Ireland since 1800: Conflict and Conformity*, London and New York, 1989.
9   Jacintha Prunty, 'The Geography of Poverty, Dublin 1850–1900: The Social Mission of the Church, with Particular Reference to Margaret Aylward and Co-workers', unpublished Ph.D. thesis, Geography Dept, University College Dublin, 1992; Joseph Robbins, *The Lost Children: A Study of Charity Children in Ireland, 1700–1900*, Dublin, 1987; Desmond Bowen, *Souperism: Myth or Reality, a Study in Souperism*, Cork, 1970.
10   *All the World*, September 1902, p. 471.
11   *War Cry*, 13 July 1901, p. 12.
12   Ibid.
13   Report of the Census of Ireland, 1881; Table 2 in Gráinne Blair, '"Equal sinners", Irish Women utilising the Salvation Army rescue network for Ireland and Britain in the nineteenth century: an analytic portrait', unpublished MA thesis, Women's Studies, University College Dublin, 1995, p. 63.
14   *All The World*, February 1888, pp. 64–5; Jenty Fairbanks, *Booth's Boots: Social Services Beginnings in the Salvation Army*, London, 1983, p. 105.

15 *Deliverer*, September 1891, p. 45; January 1892, p. 120; August 1891, p. 24; October 1891, p. 56. [. . .]
16 *Deliverer*, September 1891, p. 45.
17 Fairbanks, *Booth's Boots*, p. 9.
18 *Deliverer*, September 1891, p. 45.
19 *A Brief Review of the First Year's Work*, London, 1891, p. 117.
20 *Wesleyan Times*, 27 March 1865.

Chapter 20

Margaret MacCurtain

■ from **GODLY BURDEN: CATHOLIC SISTERHOODS IN TWENTIETH-CENTURY IRELAND**, in Anthony Bradley and Maryann Gialanella Valiulis (eds), *Gender and Sexuality in Modern Ireland*, Amherst, 1997, pp. 245–56

B Y 1 9 0 0 T H E R E W E R E J U S T O V E R 8,000 nuns and thirty-five female religious orders in Ireland. There were 368 convents. More than half of the high-walled stone buildings that became a feature of twentieth-century towns and cities were Mercy and Presentation foundations that had stemmed from the modest beginnings of Catherine McAuley's vision and Nano Nagle's aspirations to teach poor children – even before Catholic Emancipation had been won in 1829. The second half of the nineteenth century witnessed a dramatic growth in the number of women who entered convents: from 1,552 in the 1851 Census to 8,031 in 1901.[1] Invitations had come steadily from Catholic bishops to superiors of religious orders to establish convents in their dioceses and to offer educational facilities to girls of all ages.

The terms 'sister' and 'nun' have distinct meanings in canon law but there is a wide practice of employing them interchangeably. The sisterhoods in this essay signify what canon law recognised as 'active orders' in the twentieth century, becoming 'apostolic orders' in 1967 with the Decree on Religious Life issued by the Second Vatican Council. The problem of jurisdiction, that is, whether the religious orders were governed directly from the Vatican or by the local bishop, had been resolved by the beginning of the twentieth century in favour of the local bishop. Enclosure within the convent precincts and supervision of the convent *horarium*, as well as visitation, were potential areas of tension between bishops and the sisterhoods prior to the Second Vatican Council.

The centralisation of the Catholic Church became concrete with the Dogma of Papal Infallibility in 1870 at the First Vatican Council. As well as increasing church bureaucracy, it strengthened the control of the bishop and parish priest. 'The Church,' wrote Pope Pius X, 'is essentially an unequal society, comprising two categories of persons, the Pastors and the flock.' Such was the climate into which the sisterhoods settled uneasily in 1900, desperately needed as auxiliaries by bishops, possessing an ill-defined status as sisterhoods with simple vows, yet bearing the burden of enclosure and, in some orders with medieval origins, the uncertainty of not knowing whether the sisters were in simple or solemn vows. The encroachment of the bishop's jurisdiction over the movements of sisters was further augmented by the Code of Canon Law promulgated in 1917.

There was no decrease in the number of entrants to Irish convents [. . .] They continued to multiply and to find outlets for ministry throughout the world. The explanation lies partially in the missionary enterprise that marks church activity in the first half of the twentieth century. In that unprecedented growth Belgium and Ireland were at the fore. [. . . T]he aftermath of the Easter Rising [was] a time of intense idealism in which the founding of the Maynooth Mission to China and that of the Columban Sisters to the 'Far East' took place.[2] It was a period when young people searched for outlets for a heroic life because they were disillusioned by the misplaced ardour of war. The missionary movement, as it expressed itself in Irish Catholic life, provided young people with an opportunity in the decades after the civil war of 1922–3 to turn away from the troubling dilemma of legitimised physical force. It was an age when devotional Catholicism peaked. The popes, Pius XI and Pius XII, vigorously advocated a style of religious observance and practice that combined expressions of piety in the context of church-based devotions. The establishment of new religious feasts – in particular the cult of Mary – and the encouragement of pilgrimages to her shrines received papal approval. Novenas such as the Miraculous Medal, the Nine First Fridays, and sodalities were assiduously promoted at parish level. The culmination of this highly charged, emotional Catholicism was the promulgation in 1950 of the dogma of Mary's assumption into heaven, followed in 1954 (the year decreed by Pius XII as 'the Marian year') by an epidemic of shrine-building all over Ireland. The 1950s were the high point of female religious vocations in twentieth-century Ireland. The 1941 census revealed that one out of every four hundred women was entering a convent and admissions increased in the following decade. So great was the prestige of the sisterhoods in Ireland by the mid-century that in 1949 a lecturer from England at the annual Conference of Convent Secondary Schools in Ireland declared to the assembly: 'It is wonderful to see the power you have in education. In fact the Nuns have all the power to guide and control education policy. You have the Department of Education in the hollow of your hand.'[3]

Behind the success and triumphalism of the mid-century lay the larger issue of what constituted work and ministry for the sisterhoods. In the previous century the convent was subsidised by dowries. [. . .] By the end of the nineteenth century the dowry as asset had been augmented by the boarding school. Religious communities established fee-paying boarding schools to provide room and board for students who lived far away and whose parents sincerely desired a formative Catholic environment for the education of their daughters. The decision by the government to hand over the Poor Law Union hospitals, the so-called Workhouse Hospitals, to the care of the Sisters of Mercy from the 1860s onward, was decisive and significant in involving sisters in the work of the State.

The emergence of the secondary school was a major development in what constituted the ministry of the convent. The Intermediate Act (1878) was a milestone in girls' schooling, allowing girls a state qualification to enter civil service appointments and prepare for matriculation into the universities. Single sex or separate schools for boys and girls along denominational lines set the pattern for twentieth-century state schooling in Ireland. By 1922 all churches, and the Jewish community, had well-established claims on the State. A mutually beneficial relationship was hammered out between the British Ministry of Education and the Stormont government of Northern Ireland, and between the Free State and the church schools. For the Free State with its largely Catholic population the gain was financial and ideological. A considerable number of day-to-day expenses were borne by religious orders. Because the system of education had inherited the single sex structure from the previous era, girls' education was largely in the hands of the nuns for the next decades. Moreover, the Catholic school developed qualities the state desired in its citizens: orderliness, discipline, obedience, self-control. The involvement of the sisterhoods, and the larger church investment in education, added to the political legitimacy of the educational system as it evolved in the Dublin civil service over the next decades.

The background of this alliance between the convents and the state enables scrutiny of the policy-makers in the convents. The first university degrees were awarded [to women] in the 1890s, and, ironically, Ireland had little acceptable work for these graduates. Quite a number of them entered religious life, and the flow continued steadily and in increasing numbers until the 1940s, when the rule of enclosure was relaxed to allow sisters to attend university classes and take examinations. Remarkable women, born in the 1870s, became a pioneering graduate élite, tutored in womens' colleges funded by religious orders such as the Loretos, Ursulines, and Dominicans. [. . .] A substantial number joined religious orders after the Civil War and claimed membership in Cumann na mBan while at university. [. . .]

One situation in convent life that was not addressed until the mid-century was the status of the lay sister. Lay sisters are present in records from the abbeys and monasteries of the Middle Ages, when it was customary for wealthy women who entered the cloister to bring their serving women with them, or, if they were very young, their nurses. There is no evidence that there was such a division in the small groups of Irish nuns who came together in dwelling houses during the eighteenth century, when convents and Catholic schools were forbidden to function by state law. With the resurgence of religious life for women in nineteenth-century Ireland the lay sisters became a visible structure within the convent. They entered without dowry, coming from small farming families or artisan backgrounds. They were responsible for support tasks in the convent: cooking, laundering, working in the farm, cleaning the school and dormitories. They led a hidden life. They possessed no vote in community affairs and they did not elect to the leadership of the community; nor were they eligible for election as superior.

Yet the lay sisters were not perceived as domestic servants in an age when Dublin had fifty servants for every thousand women. They had a freedom to converse with men on the farm, to supervise the entrance door as portresses, and to attend the sick. [. . .] Convent life with its rhythm, its security, and its sense of space was a desirable option for girls without dowry. What is perplexing is that the two-tiered system remained in existence in Ireland long after it was abolished in the new world of America and Australia. The anomaly of the Irish twentieth-century lay sister contributed to the stratification of Irish society for many decades. Hierarchy within the convent reflected public life in twentieth-century Ireland.

From the mid-nineteenth century, Protestant missionaries had taken the lead in sending thousands of missionaries to Asia: doctors, catechists, leaders of mission stations in far-off places like outer Mongolia or deepest Africa. Early in 1912 the Maryknoll Missionary Sisters were founded in the United States by an Irish-American woman, Mollie Rogers. A decade later the Columban Missionary Sisterhood was founded by Frances Moloney, a widow. In 1924 Mary Ryan founded the Holy Rosary Sisters of Killashandra for mission in Africa. In 1902, previous to these endeavours, Teresa Keaney had gone to equatorial Africa, and gradually it became clear to her that the resources of Catholic church missions in issues of disease and health care were inadequate. Thereafter, she crusaded tirelessly for hospital training, including midwifery certification. Finally she established her own sisterhood, the Franciscan Missionaries to Africa, and opened a midwifery training school in Uganda.[4] [. . . P]rofessional qualification in surgery and obstetrics, Rome's 'forbidden skills,' enshrined in the 1917 Code of Canon Law, [forbade] Sisters to take studies in midwifery, obstetrics, and all branches of medicine, including surgery and gynaecology. The struggle to win recognition from the great medical schools was complicated by the necessity to lobby the papacy, and the Roman curia. Pope Benedict XV remained impervious. The capitulation to a claimant demand on the part of missionary bishops and heads of religious orders occurred in 1936, when Pius XI issued Canon 489: Maternity Training for Missionary Sisters.

The Medical Missionaries of Mary, founded by Marie Martin in 1936, were, possibly, the most innovative of the Irish missionary orders of women in twentieth-century Ireland. Her institute was devoted to health care and her sisters studied all branches of medicine and qualified as surgeons. Their example was quickly followed by other missionary groups. An examination of the politics of the religious women's campaign for medical training reveals the adventurous dimension of the religious calling in decades that were perceived as dehumanising to sisters working in Irish orphanages and boarding schools. [. . .]

There were two areas in the daily lives of sisters where the burden of religion sat heavily on their shoulders. The first was the Code of Canon Law as it applied to women religious. By 1900 apostolic activity as a legitimate exercise of a convent's mission had been acknowledged both by Rome and by local bishops. There was recognition that travel, dress, and the strict laws of enclosure needed modernisation. The 1917 Code of Canon Law set, for decades to come, the limits of autonomy for women religious: weekly confession, daily Eucharist, set hours for prayer including meditation. Laws of fast and abstinence were strictly enforced in convents during Lent and Advent and each Friday of the year. The practice of religious life became a process of fulfilling a series of obligations. Catholicism, until the Second Vatican Council, was a religion of authority concealed by the beauty of the liturgical revolution, which revitalised Gregorian chant and brought ritual into the lives of ordinary church-goers. It was an age of pageantry and ritual; the liturgical plainchant of the choir office became an art form in convent culture and drew an appreciative audience to the solemn liturgies of Holy Week, Easter, and Christmas. It took its toll on the health of the sisters already overburdened in classroom and hospital ward. [. . .]

The image of the nun in mid-century Ireland (and elsewhere) was that of a docile and submissive figure, clad in a black or white or blue sweep of garment with a medieval headdress, who rarely raised her voice or eyes. Yet these same women were major players in Church–State relations below the official level of the Catholic hierarchy. Owners and matrons of the main hospital system in the country, they were entrusted by the State with the State's industrial schools and orphanages and with the reponsibility of implementing the State's fragile and largely underdeveloped welfare policy.[5]

One canon of the 1917 Code is frequently overlooked: Catholics were forbidden to attend schools open to non-Catholics. That stricture was brought to bear in the negotiations between the Catholic hierarchy and the Free State Department of Education in 1924, formally recognising Catholic schools as state schools. Salary scales were implemented, capitation and building grants were agreed upon. Examining convent accounts,[6] it is evident that, initially, the relief was great: the burden of teaching extracurricular subjects, such as music, singing, voice projection – for necessary revenue – was lifted. Then, in 1929, came Pope Pius XI's encyclical, The Christian Education of Youth, which put a seal of approval on the ministry for educating the young at school and college level. Thus, far from discouraging sisters from acquiring professional qualifications, Pius XI urged the heads of religious orders to qualify sisters for the schools and colleges he advocated. It should have been the beginning of the modernisation of the Irish sister. She now attended university or hospital as a student (wherever possible one with a Catholic ethos). If unable to study by day because of other work, she studied by night and during weekends. Summer schools were not offered in the Ireland of that period. It was in truth an age of 'eternal verities'. The sisterhoods represented an eternity on earth: clothes, ways of thinking, rules were changeless. The imposition of cloister and the frequent canonical and episcopal strictures on its enforcement placed women religious in Ireland in a culturally rigid role. Impossible burdens of work and unrealistic asceticisms dried up human affectivity in the increasingly younger aspirant to religious life, who moved from the institutionalised boarding school into the structured novitiate.

In 1950 Pope Pius XII, concerned with evidence that the level of professional excellence among many of the sisters was far below that of their lay counterparts, summoned an international congress of superior generals to Rome and exhorted them to educate their subjects on a par with their lay colleagues. Inspired by his mandate, the 1950s was a decade of summer schools in theology, scriptural studies, and the updating of subjects taught at school level. Sisters began to take higher degrees and lectureships at third level. On the eve of the Second Vatican Council, the sisterhoods had organised themselves into confederations and were talking among themselves, comparing experiences and inviting sisters from other religious orders to address them. The isolation was breaking down. One of the lightning conductors was the development of the theology and spirituality of religious life. The Pontifical Institute of Regina Mundi was set up in Rome by directive of Pius XII in 1954 to offer three-year religious courses for women, both lay and religious, and those who enrolled returned to positions of responsibility within novitiates.[7]

They brought back a new concept of the mission of religious orders, one that placed emphasis on vowed poverty as a way of witnessing and serving the needy in society. Celibacy was valued in its ability to give greater freedom of time and energies to those in need. Obedience was interpreted as listening to the gospel values and to the overall mission of the Church. Thus it can be argued that the renewal of religious life anticipated the mandates of Vatican Two. The change that seemed so gradual in the first sixty years of the twentieth century was unthreatening to Rome and to convent structures. Popes had encouraged it. In the earlier part of the century the Irish State and the Stormont Government in Northern Ireland had facilitated Church–State relationships in granting recognition to the apostolic ministries of teaching and social welfare, as well as bestowing positions of responsibility on sisters, without examining their professional qualifications. The Vatican had, in turn, granted dispensations, for the professionalisation of the sisters, which seemed harmless enough, such as permission to travel singly, to discard the religious garb if studying medicine, to absent oneself from the common table and even common prayer. Too late it was perceived that removal of the canon concerning cloister was a structural change of such magnitude that it would affect all elements of religious life in the convent in twentieth-century Ireland.

There were other factors certainly; change was in the air in the early 1960s, but the demands of professional work standards and the obligations of conventual living set in a nineteenth-century mould were to prove incompatible. [. . .] By stopping on the threshold of the post-Vatican Two era there is a completion to the narrative. What happened next belongs to a new Ireland and a questioning Catholicism.

Notes

1   Tony Fahey, 'Nuns in the Catholic Church in Ireland in the nineteenth century', in Mary Cullen (ed.), *Girls Don't Do Honours: Irish Women in Education in the Nineteenth and Twentieth Centuries*, Dublin, 1987, p. 7. Data for years 1851 and 1901, 'Tables of occupation,' Census of Population of Ireland.

2   Edmund Hogan, *The Irish Missionary Movement: A Historical Survey, 1830–1980*, Dublin, 1992, pp. 95–7.

3   Report of Conference of Secondary Schools in Ireland 1949 (52 in Archives Education Secretariat, Conference of Religious of Ireland, Milltown Park, Dublin).

4   Hogan, *Irish Missionary Movement*, pp. 114–16.

5   Sheila Lunney, 'Institutional solutions to a social problem: childcare in Ireland 1869–1950,' MA thesis, University College Dublin, 1995, publication forthcoming.

6   The Conference of Religious of Ireland was founded in 1961 as the Conference of Major Superiors. For some years it was a loosely knit group meeting periodically. From the beginning, one of its main tasks was to bring the managerial and ownership structures of the complex school systems of the Catholic religious orders under its jurisdiction.

7   Patricia Wittberg, *The Rise and Decline of Catholic Religious Orders*, Albany, 1994, p. 211.

Chapter 21

Maryann Valiulis

■ from **NEITHER FEMINIST NOR FLAPPER: THE ECCLESIASTICAL CONSTRUCTION OF THE IDEAL IRISH WOMAN**, in Mary O'Dowd and Sabine Wichert (eds), *Chattel, Servant or Citizen? Women's Status in Church, State and Society*, Belfast, 1995, pp. 168–78

IN THE EARLY YEARS OF THE FREE STATE, after the turmoil and turbulence of the Anglo–Irish War of Independence and the Civil War, there was an ongoing debate between political and ecclesiastical authorities on the one hand, and middle-class feminists on the other, over women's relationship to, and role in, the new State.

Irish feminists maintained that they were full citizens of the State, that they had a right to inclusion within the body politic on the same terms as men. This, they argued, was guaranteed in the Constitution, and was, moreover, a right which women had earned during the revolutionary struggle. They also contended that, as women, they had a special contribution to make to the political life of the State.

Political and ecclesiastical leaders argued that women needed to be returned to their rightful position within the home, a position some had vacated during the revolutionary struggle. Returning women to the home, these authorities declared, was essential to the stability of the family, the State, and a Catholic society. Public duties simply drew women away from their proper domestic sphere and gave them access to an arena in which they neither belonged nor were needed.

This conflict over women's roles was a theme in Irish society throughout the years of the Free State. Respective governments brought in gendered legislation which restricted women's access to the public sphere and increasingly curtailed their freedom.[1] Ecclesiastical leaders sanctioned and legitimated the political restrictions.

In advocating and supporting – indeed applauding – restrictive gender legislation, Catholic leaders constructed a particular identity for women. [. . .] In fact, the construction of the ideal Irish Catholic woman, which church leaders claimed was in keeping with the tradition of the ancient Gaelic State, in reality took its lead more from papal encyclicals than from the early Irish annals.

[. . . T]he dominant political belief was that the proper function of women was motherhood, that their place was in the home, tending to the needs of their husband and children – from Kevin O'Higgins's assertion that the natural and normal role for women was that of bearers of children and keepers of the home and only abnormal women thought otherwise[2] to de Valera's 1937 Constitution which clearly situated women in the home.

[. . .] Ecclesiastical discourse of the period of the 1920s and 1930s – that is, the Lenten pastorals, the popular Catholic press, more scholarly Catholic writing, the propaganda of various Catholic lay organisations – all supported, legitimised and gave moral sanction to this image of women. Drawing heavily from the papal encyclicals of the period, especially *Casti connubi* published late in 1930, and from the long tradition of the subordination of women in Catholic teachings, Catholic leaders denied women a public identity, casting them solely in terms of domesticity. [. . .]

The ideal Irish Catholic woman was pure and good, with a particular appreciation for the beautiful, the pleasing. Implicit in this statement was a reiteration of the belief in woman as the angel in the house who creates a haven to which men can retreat after their sordid dealings in the world of political and economic power. This public arena wherein political and economic power resided was no place for women, ecclesiastical discourse maintained. Any attempt by women to leave their domestic confines would wreak havoc not only on the home but on the nation as well. As one Catholic publication noted, woman has but one vocation:

> the one for which nature had admirably suited her . . . that of wife and mother. The woman's duties in this regard especially that of bringing up the children, are of such far-reaching importance for the nation and the race, that the need of safeguarding them must outweigh almost every other consideration.[3]

Such beliefs certainly made the feminist demand for full citizenship seem particularly threatening. The feminist view, said some in the Catholic Church, lays 'claim to equality which is foreign to her [woman's] nature',[4] and which is based on a 'new (unchristian) conception of society'.[5] Ecclesiastical leaders saw women's citizenship as fraught with danger. Some within the Catholic Church believed that women should not have even been granted the vote because it was:

> inconsistent with the Christian ideal of the intimate union between husband and wife that they should exercise the political franchise as distinct units, and be thus enabled by law even to take opposite sides on public issues.[6]

Nor should they participate in other aspects of public life. During the debate over the issue of jury service in the 1920s, church leaders argued that to suggest:

> that married women should be called upon for the duties of jurors is manifestly inconsistent with their home duties; and that any women be eligible to act as jurors in certain types of criminal cases is contrary to the Christian ideal of female modesty. Hence it is desirable that women be exempted from that duty.[7]

According to church teachings, those who desired a public identity for women were offering nothing but false liberty, an exaggerated and distorted notion of equality of rights.[8]

It was not only political duties which posed a threat to women's continued domesticity. There were economic snares as well. Ignoring the fact that most Irish women worked because they were obliged to out of economic necessity, church leaders proclaimed it:

> the duty of a Christian State to remedy, by prudent legislation, the abuses which have driven an excessive number of women into industrial employment outside the home . . . In a Christian State women should be excluded even by law from occupations unbecoming or dangerous to female modesty. The employment of wives or mothers in factories or outside their own household should be strictly limited by legislation. Girls should not be employed away from their homes or in work other than domestic until they have reached a sufficiently mature age, so that they be not exposed too soon to external dangers to their modesty; and that they have sufficient time before leaving home to become acquainted with household work.[9]

Political and economic power were thus to be left in the hands of men.

But the Catholic Church was concerned with more than just a glorification of motherhood, a sanctification of the cult of domesticity. Throughout the 1920s, there were other clearly articulated themes prevalent in ecclesiastical discourse: the pursuit of pleasure, the evils of modern dress, modern dance, the cinema, and indecent literature. Quite often, the bishops, for example, would thunder about the 'lure of exotic dances, extravagance and immodesty in dress, and the craze for hectic pleasures of every kind'[10] – all of which they believed were destroying traditional Irish Catholic life.

Women were central to this discourse – as symbols of the nation, as innocent victims of modern trends, and as purveyors of immorality. This level of argument was clearly anti-emancipationist, seeing in the stereotypical flapper of the period the incarnation of immorality. The flapper was juxtaposed to the young girl who was innocent and vulnerable. Ecclesiastical discourse thus defined women in the traditional Madonna/Eve split – a dualism which is an integral part of Catholic teaching.

Women were associated with both national identity and the moral health of the nation. Ecclesiastical discourse explicitly tied together nationalism and Catholicism, arguing that a return to Catholic standards would bring about the return of a traditional Gaelic nation.

According to the bishops, what was at stake in this discussion was the very self-definition of the Irish people. To many in the Church, one fundamental basic characteristic of Irish society, of Irish national being, was purity.[11] Purity was primarily cast as a woman's responsibility, a woman's crowning glory. Women were thus critical to Irish self-definition and any rejection of traditional standards of purity endangered Ireland's definition of self. [. . .]

If there were any doubt about who had to bear responsibility for this state of affairs, societies like the Catholic Truth Society made it abundantly clear who was to blame:

> The women of Ireland, heretofore, renowned for their virtue and honour, go about furnished with the paint-pot, the lip-stick . . . and many of them have acquired the habit of intemperance, perhaps one of the sequels to their lately adopted vogue of smoking. A so-called dress performance or dance today showed some of our Irish girls in such scanty drapery as could only be exceeded in the slave markets of pagan countries.[12]

[. . .] Purity was, therefore, a primary characteristic of the ideal Irish women. [. . .] It also was a virtue which was being threatened by revealing fashions, suggestive dances, and the like: 'The cult of sex is everywhere. Sex is blazoned on our fashion plates, palpitates in our novels, revels in our ball-rooms [. . .]'[13]

Purity and modesty, however, were not simply about sexual behaviour. There were implications for cultural nationalism as well, especially as regards fashion and dance. The bishops regularly exhorted mothers to dress their daughters in Irish fabrics — heavy, solid tweeds which covered rather than draped the body and in 'an Irish standard of dress instead of imitating those foreign importations which offend Christian refinement'.[14] Similarly, the bishops exhorted their flocks to engage in traditional Irish dances which were not sexually provocative and which had the added virtue that they could not be danced for long hours at a time.[15] Why, the bishops asked, 'should this ancient Catholic nation copy and ape what is worst in the foreigner?'[16]

To women then fell the onerous responsibility for the moral and cultural life of the country — leaving men free, not surprisingly, to pursue political and economic power. But there was a problem. Women seemed to be failing in this role. What was particularly appalling to ecclesiastical leaders was that in Catholic Ireland, which they believed had a history of noble and virtuous mothers, there were now to be found mothers:

> who shirked or neglected their duty to their children . . . There were mothers who preferred the fashionable and crowded thoroughfare to their own quiet home; there were mothers who preferred talking on a platform or in a council chamber to chatting with their children in the nursery [. . .][17]

To these mothers, the bishops said:

> Do not forget that you are Irish mothers; do not forget your glorious traditions . . . Appear seldom on the promenade, and sit oftener by the cradles; come down from the platform and attend to the cot; talk less with your gossipers, pray more with your child.[18]

[. . .] But it would be misleading to think that the bishops were only concerned about sexual morality and Gaelic resuscitation. [. . .] What the prelates, the priests, the propagandists were also concerned about was the possibility for emancipation inherent in these modern amusements and the levelling effect which these modern amusements had, on women in particular, and the population in general. Modern dances, for example, were ones in which anyone who could pay the price of admission was free to attend. Modern dress defied hierarchy and did not signify one's place in the class structure, as did nineteenth-century fashion. [. . .]

Objections to the cinema, the pictures, were equally complex. Certainly, some films offended Catholic sexual morality. But ecclesiastical objection also centred on the fact that the cinema was noted throughout Europe as a very female pastime and the movie theatre as a female public space. Not only did the Church object to public spaces for women, they particularly objected to those which were uncensored, unchaperoned, unprotected. Equally significant, these films vividly portrayed alluring lifestyles, which according to religious leaders left young women 'sick with discontent at the grim contrast presented by the realities of their own drab lives'.[19] Thus young women were venturing out in a 'public space' only to be morally corrupted and culturally dissatisfied.

This complexity of concerns was demonstrated in the 1934 controversy surrounding the decision of the National Athletic and Cycling Association to allow women to participate in the same athletic meetings as men. [. . .] One of the first into the dispute was Dr McQuaid, then president of Blackrock College. McQuaid sent a letter of protest to the Athletic Association, characterising their decision as 'uncatholic and un-Irish' and stating unequivocally 'that no boy from my college will take part in any athletic meeting controlled by your Organisation, at which women will compete, *no matter what attire they may adopt*.'[20] (emphasis added.) [. . .]

McQuaid's sentiments were echoed by others in the community. Some on the athletic board supported his objections, but for quite different reasons. For example, one member said that 'men members of the association had been disgruntled because women members who had won medals had set themselves up to be as good as the men'.[21] Under attack from McQuaid and others, the council eventually rescinded its original position and concluded that if women wanted an athletic association, they should form it themselves.

[. . .] Overall, the construction of the ideal Irish woman revealed much about Catholic ecclesiastical leaders in particular and Irish society in general. First, the picture that ecclesiastical discourse constructs – pure, modest, deferential, respectful of hierarchy, unassuming, content with one's station in life – represents the ideal of a pre-modern society. In societies that have modernised, the emphasis is on equality of opportunity with merit superseding birth, by a decline of deference based on hereditary status, by the creation of political consciousness, and by the growth of functional specialisation. The ideal that the bishops were advocating reinforced the attributes that were antithetical to a modern or modernising society.

Historically, the Catholic Church saw the forces of modernisation as a threat to its power and influence – as evidenced in a number of papal encyclicals.[22] In this instance, the Irish Catholic bishops chose women as the group with which to make their stand not simply against the modern world, as is often said, but against the forces of modernisation. Because they were primarily defined in domestic, private terms, because the Church believed women were more malleable with their 'more emotional temperament and . . . weaker personality', their 'natural gifts of sympathy and love', their 'keener sensitiveness', their 'special aptitude to promote the happiness of domestic life', Church leaders identified women with a pre-modern way of life. The ideal Irish woman thus represented a bulwark against modernisation. [. . .]

Women's lives clearly transcended the single domestic dimension of the ideal constructed by ecclesiastical discourse. The reality was that increasing numbers of women worked outside the home. A significant number of women never married. Women continued to emigrate in increasing numbers. Women were exploring their sexuality, were having children outside of marriage. Women were going to dances, wearing imported fashions and going to films – often enough for the complaint to be heard that they were never at home. Women were agitating for political rights, demanding a public identity. In essence, women were modern actors in a modernising society. Thus, the Church's construction of womanhood was, on one level, a response to women's changing lifestyle: a statement of disapproval, an acknowledgment that what they defined as traditional Irish Catholic culture and traditional Irish Catholic virtues were indeed under attack.

[. . .] Ecclesiastical discourse on the ideal woman gave an important moral justification to political restrictions against women. For example, because women were not supposed to work outside the home, the government need not have any qualms about restricting women's right to the highest levels of the Civil Service, or of giving the Minister for Industry and Commerce the power to limit the number of women in any given industry. Because women had no power to claim political rights and a public identity, women were effectively denied the right to serve on juries. Because bearing children was the primary and defining function of women, women were denied any access to birth-control information. Thus Irish ecclesiastical discourse about the ideal woman had very direct and very real consequences for women in the Irish Free State.

[. . . W]hen viewed through the lens of gender ideology, Irish ecclesiastical discourse emerges not as a unique and isolated phenomenon, but, more accurately, as a part of a general conservative movement throughout Europe. [. . .]

The ideal Irish woman then – the self-sacrificing mother whose world was bound by the confines of her home, a woman who was pure, modest, who valued traditional culture, especially that of dress and dance, a woman who inculcated these virtues in her daughters and nationalist ideology in her sons, a woman who knew and accepted her place in society – served the purposes of the ruling Irish male élite. Political and ecclesiastical leaders sought to re-establish gender boundaries and hierarchy after the promise of equality and the experience of freedom of the revolutionary period. [. . .] Neither feminist nor flapper, the ideal woman as constructed by Catholic ecclesiastical leaders stood as a potent discursive symbol of European womanhood in the inter-war years.

Notes

1   In 1924 and 1927, the Cosgrave government brought in legislation to restrict women's right to serve on juries; in 1925, women's right to sit for all examinations in the Civil Service was curtailed; in 1932, compulsory retirement was introduced for married women teachers and eventually applied to the entire Civil Service; in 1935, the government assumed the right to limit the employment of women in any given industry; in 1937, the constitution defined women's role in the State exclusively in terms of the hearth and home.

2   See the *Dáil Debates*, vol. 18, on the 1927 Juries Bill for Kevin O'Higgins's statement.

3   *Irish Monthly*, 1925.

4   W. P. Mac Donagh, 'The position of women in modern life', *Irish Monthly*, June 1939.

5   Edward Cahill, SJ, 'Notes on Christian sociology,', *Irish Monthly*, December 1924.

6   Ibid., 'Social status of women', *Irish Monthly*, January 1925.

7   Ibid.

8   *Cork Examiner*, 26 January 1931.

9   Cahill, 'Notes on Christian sociology'.

10   Editorial, *The Irish Catholic*, 5 March 1927.

11   *Irish Monthly*, November 1925.

12   *Irish Independent*, 13 October 1926.

13   *Irish Monthly*, March 1926.

14   *Cork Examiner*, 28 February 1927.

15   Ibid., 30 November 1925.

16   *Irish Independent*, 2 December 1924.

17   Ibid., 25 October 1924.

18   Ibid.

19   *Irish Monthly*, February 1925.

20   Letter from Dr McQuaid to Honourable Secretary of the National Athletic and Cycling Association, 6 February 1934 (Dublin Diocesan Archives, McQuaid Papers, General Correspondence, 1933–1937).

21   *Irish Press*, 12 March 1934.

22   See for example Pope Pius IX's Syllabus of Errors, issued in 1864.

PART FIVE

Emigration

EMIGRATION TOUCHED MANY WOMEN'S and men's lives in nine-teenth- and twentieth-century Ireland. But for much of this period, in numerical terms, female emigration surpassed that of male. Between 1800 and 1922 approx-imately 4 million women left Ireland.[1] Irish women travelled to many parts of the world, but in particular the United States, Britain, Australia, New Zealand and Canada were favoured destinations. In addition, another distinctive feature of Irish migration was the large number of young single women who left the country as opposed to those who formed part of a familial group. Many of these women were undoweried and hence unable to find a partner and make the so-called, and by now infamous, 'match'. Thus emigration could been seen as a relatively attractive prospect, offering an alternative to the limited prospects awaiting those who chose to stay at home.

Attention should also be paid to the significance of extended family networks in the countries in which women settled. For those leaving the country, family and friendship networks acted as a guide in a strange environment, giving much needed emotional and financial support. With this support many women settled into a life of relative prosperity. Less, however, is currently known of those Irish women who struggled to cope in a new land, who experienced mental illness or turned to crime and prostitution.

The impact of emigration was felt not only by those who actually left their country of birth but also by those whom they left behind, who had to cope with losing daughters, sons, sisters, brothers, friends and loved ones. In addition to this emotional aspect, emigration was of considerable economic and demographic impor-tance. Although for some women emigration may have been an escape route from restrictive family control, for others keeping in contact with their families was highly desirable and they continued to financially support their relatives at home.

Furthermore the exodus of women from rural Ireland was especially noticeable, and had repercussions in, demographic and marital patterns. Thus emigration is a key factor in understanding the history of late modern Ireland.

Note

1   See Donald Harman Akenson, *The Irish Diaspora: A Primer*, Belfast and Toronto, 1996, p. 159.

Suggestions for further reading

Pauline Jackson, 'Women in nineteenth-century Irish emigration', *International Migration Review*, 18/4, 1984.

Robert E. Kennedy, Jnr., *The Irish: Emigration, Marriage and Fertility*, Berkeley, 1973.

Trevor McClaughlin (ed.), *Irish Women in Colonial Australia*, St Leonards, NSW, 1998.

Dympna MacLoughlin, *Women, Subsistence and Emigration, 1840–70*, Dublin, 2000.

Janet Nolan, *Ourselves Alone: Women's Emigration from Ireland, 1885–1920*, Lexington, 1989.

Ide O'Carroll, *Models for Movers: Irish Women's Emigration to America*, Dublin, 1990.

Patrick O'Sullivan (ed.), *Irish Women and Irish Migration: The Irish World Wide*, vol. 4, London, 1995.

Chapter 22

Donald Harman Akenson

■ from **WOMEN AND THE IRISH DIASPORA:**
THE GREAT UNKNOWN, chapter 7 of *The Irish Diaspora:*
A Primer, Toronto and Belfast, 1996, pp. 157–87

[. . .]

EVERYTHING THAT WE KNOW ABOUT the history of Irish women
in the diaspora revolves around one central set of facts. One-half of the great
Irish diaspora was female. Between the Act of Union of 1800 and the independence of southern Ireland in 1922, about 4 million Irish females left the homeland.
Those who were not minor children did not merely leave but chose to leave. That
is crucial. Each made a conscious decision as a result of weighing alternative futures.
Those who, after assessing the alternatives, chose to stay in Ireland were just as
much involved in choosing their own futures as were those who left. [. . .]

Until roughly the middle of the twentieth century, the economic base of Irish
society, as well as the chief social unit, was not a factory, not a multi-owned
corporation, but the family-operated farm. This congruence of the main social unit
and the main economic unit of society meant that all of the important decisions
of a woman's life – whether or not to marry, whether to take a job as a domestic
servant, whether to accept employ as a farm worker, whether or not to emigrate
– were made with the family as the backdrop of the decision. [. . .]

It has been aptly remarked that one of the great paradoxes of post-famine
Ireland is that while the commercial and cultural systems were being modernised,
the fundamental familial-economic structure was becoming increasingly archaic.[1]
Facing this set of contradictory forces, a woman's options were limited, but she
had more choices open to her than might at first appear. For most women, the
most advantageous position was to enter a rural marriage. A woman thus became
a junior partner in an enterprise whose two primary goals were production and
reproduction. Each was important: a childless marriage was considered a failure.
There were strong traditions (admittedly hard to document in detail) of childless
women in pre-famine Ireland being 'sent back' to their fathers.

A woman who did not become part of a match could choose to emigrate from
her home. For many, 'emigration' was within Ireland, a move to Belfast or Dublin,

where they might work as domestic servants or, if lucky, find places in the needle trades or in a textile factory.[2] (Many of the others who did not leave the home region found employment in service with doctors, lawyers, or better-off farm families.) Emigration could be to Liverpool, Glasgow, or London; or to the far side of the world. [. . .]

Female emigration only came to exceed male emigration in the 1890s just when, for the first time, it became obvious that about half the women in the most marriageable age group were not finding a match. Emigration for tens of thousands of women was not a terrible fate but a safety net, for 'even the humblest husband or job abroad was better than no husband and no job at home'.[3]

[. . .] There are five main periods of female emigration from Ireland but, unhappily, only on one of them do we have much information. The first period is from the end of the Napoleonic War until the famine, spanning 1815–45. The data for that era are fragmentary, but it is clear that the bulk of the long-distance migration (that is, excluding Great Britain), was in the form of family groups or childless married couples. A reasonable estimate (really, an educated guess) is that unmarried women of adult age comprised somewhat less than one-half of the outflow of Irish females before the famine.[4] The second period, 1846–51, encompasses the famine and is a time of great confusion. The exodus swamped the record-keeping system. Not until 1 May 1851 was a reasonable system of counting emigrants developed, and then it had to be recalibrated, in 1853. The great historical loss is that we really know very little of what happened in the years 1846–51. Women left in the hundreds of thousands, but whether they were married or single, young or old, is unknown. A third period, 1851–76, was the classical era of Irish emigration. Unlike the years of the famine exodus, when everything was whirl and there was no obvious continuity with anything that either had come before or would come after, the period 1851–75 blended into the fourth era, 1876–1920. The chief difference between the two is that in the earlier period males almost always outnumbered females in the emigrant flow, whereas in the late Victorian era and in the early twentieth century, females were apt to be the majority. Finally, after 1920, the character of female emigration changed considerably, most of it now being to Great Britain rather than to distant locations. Only from the last quarter of the nineteenth century to 1920 do we have good information on the basic matters of Irish female migration: good record-keeping on most matters started in 1876 but, after the partition of Ireland in 1920, the quality of emigration records declined to pre-1875 levels.

Using the period of good data, 1876–1920, as a window on the entire history of female emigration from Ireland, it appears that there were six distinct sorts of emigrants, and that each of these categories represents a quite distinct strategy of migration. Each strategy uses emigration as a part of the life-cycle, but in ways very different from each of the others. [. . .]

Group 1, the smallest, consisted of widows who had dependent children accompanying them. This was not an insignificant group because [. . .] post-famine marriages involved a considerable age gap between men and women so that widowhood was a common experience. In the cases of women emigrating with children, it was not their widowhood that was unusual, but that it had come to them sooner than expected, while their children were still dependants. A very rough estimate (based on the Vogel sample for New Zealand for 1876, the only full sample we have)[5] is that widows with dependent children made up slightly more than 1.5 per cent of Irish female emigrants. In most cases these were women above thirty years of age.

Group 2 consisted of married women who had a husband and children accompanying them. If the Vogel sample is at all representative, these were mature women, on average in their early thirties. We can estimate such women as being between 11 and 12 per cent of total female emigration.[6] These women were individuals who had begun marriage in the dominant marital pattern of the time – engaging in a match, creating a family economic unit, and having children – but for whom life for some reason became less satisfactory than they thought it would be elsewhere. These people were not necessarily the failures of Irish society. Some failures, yes, but, this group must also have included the persons whose lives were going well but who had bigger ambitions than Ireland could satisfy.

Group 3, although also consisting of married women, was very different. It comprised women who were accompanied on their journey by their spouses, but who had no dependent children. Again, using the Vogel sample as our guide, we see that they made up perhaps 7 per cent of the Irish female emigrants. In the usual case they were younger than married women who emigrated with children. Probably most were still in their twenties.[7] The key thing here is that these women, although married, cannot be automatically assumed to have been part of the full-blown traditional Irish family pattern. Some may have been so, having contracted traditional matches, and then, with husbands, deciding to emigrate. But for others, marriage and then emigration soon after being married, represented an alternative to the traditional match. Young persons with minimal resources were free to marry, so long as they then quickly escaped Ireland. But whatever the individual background, these women who emigrated with spouses, but without children, were adopting what was perhaps the most effective emigration strategy. They left home accompanied by an insurance policy. Unlike single migrants, and unlike couples with dependent children, women (and men) in childless marriages usually had someone in employment to fall back on when themselves sick or unemployed. Crucially, in such a marriage, each partner usually was able to work. A childless couple was highly mobile geographically, and was eagerly sought by farm managers, hotel keepers, and a range of employers who needed both female and male skills in their businesses. As long as the couple postponed pregnancy, women who emigrated in this fashion were the most advantaged among female emigrants.

Group 4 was made up of dependent unmarried females; most of these were below the marriageable age. These mostly were girls who travelled to a New World with their mothers and fathers, or with at least one parent. In a small, but still noticeable minority of cases, young dependent girls emigrated with older brothers and sisters. A few of young age (as young as age seven, in records that I have seen) emigrated alone, being in essence shipped overseas to family or relatives who had emigrated earlier.

Our historical problem is that we lack direct data on female dependants. The problem becomes more complicated when one realises that although most dependent single females were young girls, there were significant numbers of mature women who emigrated in family groups as dependants. One finds 'spinsters' in their thirties and forties being carried as family dependants, and on occasion I have encountered an old aunt in her seventies being brought along. The best way to estimate this large, but disparate, group of female single dependants is to use age categories. We can assume as a base for our estimate that virtually all girls under fifteen were dependants. They comprised 15.6 per cent of all female emigrants from Ireland in the decade 1871–80.[8] [. . .] In total, a very rough estimate is that 21 per cent of the Irish female migrants in the later 1870s were unmarried, but were dependent upon families for their support. These individuals would not have to encounter the fundamental, and fundamentally traumatic, foundation of the Irish social system, the match, but they were hardly free spirits: they were emigrating as dependent upon other family members, persons whose own values and behaviour had been formed in the Old Country.

Group 5 in many ways is the most interesting. It consisted of non-dependent females who were of marriageable age, but who emigrated as unmarried women. These women should have found emigration emancipating, for they were leaving behind the archaism of the Irish countryside and were not doing so in the company of their parents. On the other hand, they were taking greater risks than married women or single women who emigrated as family dependants. The key here is that they were of marriageable age and could look forward in the usual instance to forming a family in the new land, and (perhaps) under new rules. If one sets for statistical purposes the end of the marriageable age bracket as thirty-five years, then it appears that slightly over half (50.5 per cent) of the Irish female migrants in the 1870s were unmarried, non-dependent, and marriageable.

Group 6 is numerically much smaller and represents an entirely different life course. These were women who had not married in Ireland and who, for the most part, were now past the age at which marriage was likely: over thirty-five. They had either been family dependants at home or had been employed as domestics, farm servants, or in the needle trades, and now for whatever reasons were seeking a better life. Some few of them might marry in the New World, but most would not. Moreover (given nineteenth-century dietary conditions), they were in, or at least approaching, an age when child bearing was unlikely. This group, comprising about 8.5 per cent of female emigrants in the 1870s, probably faced the most uncertain future of any group. Unskilled, single, most of them could look forward to supporting themselves for the rest of their lives by hard labour in a strange land.[9] [. . .]

Five distinct time periods. Six distinct groups of women. Six major destinations. This divides Irish female emigrants, 4 million or more of them, into 180 separate cells, each representing a distinct form of female experience within the Irish diaspora. And that is just the beginning.

[. . .] There was nothing charitable or disinterested about the way the British colonies and the USA facilitated Irish female immigration. All of the nations to which the Irish migrated (with the exception of Great Britain itself) were in the midst of seizing large tracts of land and resources from native peoples, and they needed increased population, agricultural and industrial growth and, if possible, civil order. That various governments actively wanted Irish women is clear from a whole range of governmental policies. These ranged from the active importation of women (Australia, New Zealand and South Africa) to the facilitation of banks and telegraph companies in transmitting 'remittances' home and in the forwarding of prepaid tickets from migrants in Canada and the USA to potential migrants in the Irish homeland. [. . .]

Of course it is offensive to modern ears to encounter concepts such as importing women, or as taking them as part of some male's emigration gear, but, in hundreds of thousands of instances that was the historical reality. All historical realities have more than one side, however, and what from one perspective was simply good governmental policy (encouraging Irish men to import their own wives) from another perspective was family loyalty and continuity. Thus, it was reported to be common practice in the pre-famine years for husbands to migrate first with the hope of saving enough money in the New Land to bring out their wives[10] and, indeed the pattern has not disappeared at the present day.

But this financing of female emigration by private means was not limited to men who supported their spouses. Brothers frequently financed their sisters' migration. Just how extensive Irish self-financing of emigration was indicated by the magnitude of remittances sent from North America to Ireland. Studies done for the years 1848 and 1868 indicate that enough prepaid passages were sent back to the British Isles from United Kingdom emigrants to bring out three-quarters of all British and Irish emigrants to North America.[11] The proportion sent by Irish persons must have been at least as large, for studies elsewhere (in Australia and New Zealand, for example) indicate that the Irish over-participated in such arrangements. [. . .]

Before they married, what did the Irish emigrant women do in their new homeland? In every country and (one strongly suspects) in every period of diaspora history from 1815 to 1920, the most common occupation of single Irish women was domestic service, either in a city or on a farmstead. This pattern reached its peak in the USA, where the Irish-born female population was the most urban of any in the world. There a majority of Irish women who were in full-time employment were in service. [. . .]

Generally, Irish women migrants were successfully integrated into the economies of their new homelands. However, long-distance migration is an unsettling process. [. . . T]he Irish as a migrant group had a high degree of mental illness compared to groups from other countries, and the women's mental hospitalisation rate was as high as was the men's. That was human wastage, and so too was the proportion of single Irish women who turned to crime [. . .] In her study of women in Port Phillip and Victoria, Australia, 1840–60, Sharon Morgan found that Irish-born women constituted almost half of the female prison population at the end of the 1850s; this was at a time when the Irish-born were roughly 15 per cent of the total population and about one-quarter of the foreign-born. Public drunkenness was the most common offence committed by Irish immigrant women and vagrancy the second. The former offence was not totally incompatible with economic productivity, but the latter is an indication of economic failure. Petty crimes such as minor thefts and prostitution were the other most common offences. Heavy crime was not frequent.[12] Even when one makes compensation for the loading of the justice system against immigrants, it is clear that a real problem existed in Australia. This suggests a matter that should be researched in all societies that received single Irish women in significant numbers: what happened to those who neither married nor found a decent job? [. . .]

Given that most Irish women (both immigrants and second and subsequent generations) married, and given the attitude towards birth control that ran through all religious denominations until at least the 1920s, it was inevitable that the great majority of Irish women procreated. In what degree (what was the average completed family size?) remains to be discovered, but there is no doubt that generations of Irish migrant women did what nineteenth- and early twentieth-century governments wanted them to do: helped to breed an indigenous white population.

A very touchy problem for contemporary Irish men and women (as well as for some modern historians) is the matter of endogamy – meaning, 'Did the Irish immigrants marry their own kind?' and 'Did Catholics marry Catholics, or did they step outside of the faith?' This latter possibility worried everyone, Catholics and Protestants alike. [. . .] Migrants were frequently at great pains to assure family at home that the new spouse was acceptable, and this was especially true when they married, as the Irish migrants frequently did, outside of their own group.[13] [. . .]

There is a second, less emotionally sensitive form of 'mixed marriage', namely a union in which an Irish person married a non-Irish one (this would not necessarily mean that they were of different religious faiths, just different ethnic groups). [. . .] T]here undeniably was a good deal of leakage in the Irish community, by intermarriage with persons of various other ethnic groups. [. . .]

Thus, whether or not emigration was a big step towards emancipation for most Irish migrant women, or merely the method by which they obtained in a New World what they could not have in the old – a husband and family – is something we cannot know. The great danger for us as modern observers is to draw simple correlations based on modern assumptions – such as the idea that the unmarried non-dependent women were emancipated from their Irish past, but that the ones who married and had children were not. We have already seen that most of the seemingly independent single female migrants were helped by family members and that there were non-patriarchal family networks made up of brothers, sisters, cousins, within which it was possible for many of them to spend their entire lives. Economic independence and the abandonment of social and cultural networks derived from the Old World were not at all the same thing.

Conversely, many of the Irish migrant women who married actually lived very independent lives, quite emancipated from the restrictive aspects of Irish culture, while enjoying its considerable good points.

Notes

1   David Fitzpatrick, 'The modernisation of the Irish female', in Patrick O'Flanagan, Paul Ferguson and Kevin Whelan (eds), *Rural Ireland 1600–1900: Modernisation and Change*, Cork, 1987, pp. 162–3.

2   On women's life in the Belfast textile industry, see Betty Messenger, *Picking Up the Linen Threads: A Study in Industrial Folklore*, Belfast, 1975.

3   David Fitzpatrick, '"A share of the honeycomb": education, emigration and Irishwomen', *Continuity and Change*, 2/1, 1986, p. 225.

4   [. . .] See William Forbes Adams, *Ireland and the Irish Emigration to the New World from 1815 to the Famine*, New Haven, 1932. [. . .]

5   Widows with children made up 1.7 per cent of the Vogel sample in 1876. See D. H. Akenson, *Half the World From Home: Perspectives on the Irish in New Zealand, 1860–1950*, Wellington, 1990. [. . .]

6   See ibid., pp. 45–6, for Vogel sample.

7   Ibid.

8   N. H. Carrier and J. R. Jeffery, *External Migration. A Study of the Available Statistics, 1815–1920*, London, 1953, Table K(1), p. 106.

9   The distribution of the unmarried non-dependent females (59 per cent of the total female outflow) as between those of marriage age and those over that age is done by using the age-data for female emigrants, found in Carrier and Jeffery, *External Migration*, Table K(1), p. 106.

10   [. . .] David Fitzpatrick, 'Emigration, 1801–79', in W. E. Vaughan (ed.), *A New History of Ireland*, vol. V, *Ireland under the Union, I, 1801–70*, Oxford, 1989, p. 601.

11   Ibid., citing the work of Arnold Schrier.

12   Sharon Morgan, 'Irish women in Port Phillip and Victoria, 1840–60', in Oliver MacDonagh and W. F. Mandie (eds), *Irish-Australian Studies*, Canberra, 1989, pp. 240–5.

13   David Fitzpatrick, '"That beloved country, that no place else resembles": connotations of Irishness in Irish-Australian letters, 1841–1915', *Irish Historical Studies*, 27, November 1991, pp. 334–5.

Chapter 23

Trevor McClaughlin

■ from *BAREFOOT AND PREGNANT?*
IRISH FAMINE ORPHANS IN AUSTRALIA,
Melbourne, 1991

S OLID DETAILED RESEARCH ON THE SUBJECT of Irish female
migration to Australia has not yet been done, a state of affairs which needs
some rectifying considering the relatively large numbers of Irish women who came
here and their alleged influence on the position of women in Australian society.
That approximately one-third of the female convict population came directly from
Ireland is well known. Less well known are the transfusions of Irish female blood
arranged from time to time by the British government, the girls from foundling
hospitals in Cork and Dublin in the 1830s, the famine victims of 1848–50 or the
'excessive' numbers of single females assisted to Victoria and South Australia during
the 1850s, for example. [. . .]

The young women who landed at Adelaide (more than 600 of them),
Melbourne (circa 1,200) and Sydney (circa 2,300) were victims of the Great Famine
and had been selected from among the inmates of Irish workhouses by government officials. [. . .] But their reception in Australia was not as warm as they would
have wished.

Critics of the [1848–50] orphan emigration scheme were not slow to voice their
disapproval of the young women in the most deprecatory terms. The young women
in the immigration depot in Adelaide were described as 'dirty brutes'. An official of
the Childrens' Apprenticeship Board referred to the 'extreme filthiness and unimag-
inable indelicacy of some of these workhouse girls', while the Melbourne *Argus*
slandered them as 'the most stupid, the most ignorant, the most useless and the most
unmanageable set of beings that ever cursed a country by their presence'. [. . .]

Single female immigrants to Australia were too often looked down upon by
religious leaders and members of the upper- and middle-class public in both Britain
and Australia for much of the nineteenth century. [. . .] The hostility of the early
days towards convicts and the paupers of the 1830s for example, was to forge
images and condition attitudes towards later female migrants, not least the famine
orphans from Irish workhouses. Virtuous single women just did not emigrate to
such a distant country as Australia 'without natural protectors'. Ergo, those who

did could not have been really virtuous. George Hall put it to a South Australian parliamentary enquiry in 1856 that one 'never could expect to derive girls of good character from such a source' as Irish Poor Law Unions. [. . .]

Between October 1848 and August 1850, over 4,000 female orphans arrived in Australia from Irish workhouses as part of Earl Grey's pauper immigration scheme. Famine and poverty in Ireland had driven the young women to the dreary walls of the workhouse. Earl Grey, the British Secretary of State for the Colonies in Lord John Russell's Whig government, thought he could solve Australia's problems of a shortage of labour and an imbalance of the sexes by alleviating the overcrowding in Ireland's famine-filled workhouses. But the free passage he provided for female orphans and his underhand attempt to renew transportation so angered Australian colonists that they rose in opposition to this squandering of their land funds on such unwelcome migrants.

Colonial criticism of the female orphan scheme, starting with the scandal over the orphans who arrived by the first vessel, the *Earl Grey*, rose to such a crescendo that the scheme was brought to an end by 1850 – but not before the Orphan Immigration Depot in Adelaide had been likened to a 'Government Brothel' or John Dunmore Lang had called Earl Grey and the Lord Lieutenant of Ireland 'dupes of an artful female Jesuit' who sought 'to Romanise the Australian colonies'. In Melbourne, the orphans were at the centre of a political furore in the city council and in mass meetings organised by Bishop Goold, reports of which pervaded the Melbourne press throughout the first six months of 1850. In Sydney, as in Melbourne and Adelaide, the arrival of female orphans was a signal for anti-Irish and anti-Roman Catholic elements in the community to give free rein to their prejudice. [. . .]

There were a number of other things preventing a warm welcome being given to the female orphans when they arrived in Australia. Never far from public view was the bad press given the thousand or so young women who had come to Hobart and Sydney, from foundling hospitals and poorhouses in Ireland and England, in the 1830s. Few people were well-disposed towards the new scheme, not least because prejudice and selective memory had condemned all the young women with the bad reputation of a few. 'Cargoes of juvenile prostitutes' were how they were remembered. 'Red Rovers', after the name of the vessel carrying young women from a Cork foundling hospital in 1832, had become a term of abuse applied indiscriminately to prostitutes. Female Irish orphans were thus erroneously equated with prostitutes in the public mind.

Of more immediate relevance were the scandals and rumours surrounding the *Hyderabad*, the *Subraon* and the *Fairlie*, ships which carried single females to Sydney in the months before the arrival of the *Earl Grey* in October 1848. The female domestic servants of the *Hyderabad* were reported as 'extremely ignorant of their callings' and [it was said] that some of them had 'fallen into bad courses'. Five of the women by the *Fairlie* were reputedly 'women of most abandoned character', 'a constant source of trouble and annoyance' to the ship's surgeon, associating with the ship's crew, causing fights and uproar, when they were sent below, singing 'indecent and filthy songs'.

The scandal over the *Subraon* was particularly appropriate for at its centre were 'young, unprotected and friendless girls from a foundling institution in Dublin'.

These twelve young women [. . .] had been included among the government-assisted migrants on board the *Subraon* as an experiment to see if they would be welcomed by the colonial authorities. [. . .]

A number of the girls – Emma Smith, Dorcas Newman, Martha McGee, Augusta Cooper and Alicia Ashbridge – were enticed by a promise of wages to act as servants for the captain, Mr J. P. Mills, and the ship's officers, Mr J. Hill, Mr Cawardine and Mr Day. Once in the officers' cabins, they were plied with drink and became intoxicated, on more than one occasion. The consequences were disastrous for young Dolly Newman, who had been represented to the Board of Enquiry as 'a very interesting young girl, and a great favourite in the institution from which she was sent'. Her distress at being hoisted to the top of the main-mast, by a rope tied round her middle, early in the voyage, her love affair with the chief mate, James Hill, 'upon whom she waited', her attempted abortion and subsequent miscarriage and death, shortly after the vessel arrived in Sydney, were all described in fulsome detail at the Board of Enquiry.

The scandal, gossip and rumour associated with the single female migrants who arrived by the *Fairlie* and the *Subraon* did little for the first boatload of female orphans by the *Earl Grey*. [. . .] The young women of the *Earl Grey* were from the destitute class of Irish society. They were adolescents orphaned by the Great Famine who in desperation, in those terrible times, had turned to the local Poor Law Union for charity. It was there, in the workhouses of Belfast and Banbridge, Armagh and Antrim, Downpatrick and Dungannon, that they were offered a chance to escape to a new and apparently prosperous land. Reports of conditions in Australia, in Irish newspapers, painted a glowing and attractive picture of life in the Antipodes: of colonists wanting females as domestic servants at high . . . wages. Australia was a land where, above all, food was in plentiful supply. It was a land whose prospects were infinitely more enticing than the hunger and despair around them.

From northern Irish workhouse records the impoverished state of these young women is clearly evident. Their condition, when they entered the workhouse, was recorded in admission and discharge registers, some of which have survived: Cathy Fox, a fifteen-year-old, of no fixed address, was without employment and described as 'thinly clothed and hungry' when she entered Armagh workhouse in July 1847; Annie and Jane Hunter were 'thinly clothed and destitute' and Catherine Conway, a servant girl, was 'in a starving condition'. [. . .] But they were not all famine victims. A number of them had been abandoned by their parents or had come into the workhouse as part of a family group, consisting of widowed mother and depen-dent children. In April 1842, for example; shortly after Armagh workhouse first opened and a number of years before the famine struck, Rose Devlin, a 39-year-old widow came in with her three children, nine-year-old Margaret, Patrick, six and Bernard, four. After four months' stay, she and her children left, only to re-enter three months later. But this time, her fourth child, twelve-year-old Sarah Anne, came with her. On at least nine different occasions throughout the 1840s this little Devlin family group re-entered Armagh workhouse, sometimes for as short a period as one month, at others for as long as six or ten months until in June 1848, two of their number, Sarah Anne and Margaret, set sail for New South Wales on board the *Earl Grey*.

The fragile, single-parent Devlin family [. . .] were caught, as were so many others, in what economists like to call 'the poverty trap'. [. . . F]ew of them had any real experience of domestic service, still less of the domestic service expected by the middle class or 'bunyip aristocracy' of colonial Australia. [. . .]

Though not clearly formulated or acknowledged by every government official, the view existed that the female orphans were, to use a modern term, wards of the State. These young women were orphans not so much because their parents were dead as because their parents were unable to look after them. [. . .] Into the breach came the State. The Boards of Guardians of the various Poor Law Unions in Ireland, as indeed, the Guardians appointed in Melbourne, Adelaide and Sydney, were appointed *in loco parentis*. [. . .]

In the first instance, the Irish Government, through its Poor Law Unions, provided each young woman with an outfit for the voyage: 'six shifts – two flannel petticoats – six pair stockings – two pair shoes – two gowns . . .', perhaps the first outfit she had ever owned. It also arranged for her conveyance to Plymouth, the port of embarkation. [. . .] Once at Plymouth and during their 122 days at sea on the *Earl Grey*, the young women became the responsibility of the English Government viz. the Colonial Land and Emigration Commissioners. [. . .]

Government responsibility for and regulation of the orphans' lives persisted during their early years in Australia. [. . .] Under the direction of the Imperial Government, an Orphan Committee was established, composed of both local lay and clerical dignitaries, with Merewether [the Immigration Agent in Sydney] as chairman. Similar committees were established in Melbourne and Adelaide. [. . .]

The Orphan Committee also decided the young womens' immediate fate for it dictated the terms on which they could be hired as domestic servants. Those under seventeen years of age were to be apprenticed at fixed rates of wages. Fourteen-year-olds would earn seven pounds per annum, fifteen-years-olds, eight pounds, sixteen-year-olds, nine pounds and those who were still apprentices at seventeen, ten pounds. The other orphans were to be hired under ordinary agreements, only by people approved by the committee and at a rate of ten pounds per annum, payable monthly in cash. Merewether and the committee were aware that these rates were below current rates for female servants and that the orphans' appearance in the market would reduce the wages of female servants throughout the colony. In this, they were united in upholding the interests of their class. [. . .]

In folk memory, the female orphan ships have been remembered as 'bride ships'. But it is clear that the Australian guardians of the young women insisted on finding them employment as domestic servants and gave their consent to marriage only after careful scrutiny of a formal application. In fact consent was given readily. From 254 reconstituted families of the orphans in Australia, we know that they married early, at the tender age of nineteen years, on average, and that 60 per cent of them married within three years of their disembarkation. Similar figures apply to the *Earl Grey* orphans, fifty-four of whose families have been reconstituted. Seventy-seven per cent of these married within three years of their arrival. [. . .]

The Sydney Orphan Committee, under the vigorous and busy chairmanship of Merewether, controlled more than the employment and marriage of the young women. They were their moral guardians as well. Shortly after their arrival, Sarah Ann and Margaret Devlin were employed as servants by Thomas Small Junior, a substantial landowner of Clarence River, in northern New South Wales [. . .] Arriving at the Small property they would have been required to fulfil the terms of their agreement. In return for full board and lodging, wages and training in domestic service, they would have cooked, washed and sewed, swept out the house, worked in the yard, fetched water, taken clothes, perhaps to the river, to wash them and leave them to dry on rocks and bushes. Before long, however, young Margaret was in trouble: she was seduced by William Small, son of her employer, by whom she became pregnant.

Once Merewether and the Orphan Committee became aware of this fact, they brought her back to Sydney and placed her in the Parramatta Invalid Establishment to have her child. Lengthy negotiations were entered into, whereby some form of allowance for the child and its mother was asked of William. Since he was slow to reply, an appeal was made to his father, Thomas, threatening legal proceedings. After two years of negotiation it seems that, in the end, they settled for a lump sum payment of fifty pounds. Margaret's guardians, the Orphan Committee, had at least offered her some protection. They arranged for her confinement, placed her son William in the Protestant Orphan Institution in Sydney and extracted from William Small some reparation. How much of this money Margaret received is unknown. [. . .]

Records of the numerous cases of cancelled indentures and agreements between master and servant may be interpreted in a number of ways. People's expectations were undoubtedly contaminated by the scandal surrounding the *Subraon* and the *Earl Grey*. [. . .] However, indentures cancelled on grounds of the orphans' absconding, insolence, misconduct, negligence or disobedience are not simply evidence of the orphans being 'improper women', 'unsuited to the needs of the Colony'. Such evidence might also reflect the young women's resistance to being treated as drudges by masters 'too lately got up in the world'. [. . .]

Undoubtedly, too, both master and servant tried to work 'the system'. The protection offered the young women by colonial officials encouraged employers to complain the more. Masters thought they could return their unruly servants [. . .] forgetting that they were already compensated for the orphans' ignorance of domestic service by the low wages they paid. Masters' dissatisfaction was also fuelled by the bad press the young women received. 'They had been swept from the streets into the workhouse and thence to New South Wales', they were 'Irish orphans, workhouse sweepings', 'hordes of useless trollops', 'ignorant useless creatures', a drain upon the public purse who threatened to bring about a Popish ascendancy in New South Wales and Victoria. [. . .] In turn, the young women, hearing of better conditions elsewhere (higher wages, a kinder master or mistress) knew full well that insolence or neglect of their duties was the means of terminating their employment. [. . .] It was a gamble many were willing to take.

The question of how well the orphans turned out is not easily answered. Exaggerated stories of their incapacity and immorality, of their prostitution, drunkenness and theft, had a political purpose, viz. to bring Earl Grey's pauper immigration scheme to an end, as quickly as possible. [. . .] Sadly, some of the female orphans committed suicide, and some did become prostitutes, drunken derelicts and thieves. But that is not to say that they were so before they arrived, or that these dramatic and in the end, exceptional cases were typical of the female orphans as a whole. [. . .]

Although some died tragically and others stayed beyond respectable society, the Irish female orphans had an honourable history in Australia as pioneer women, as 'little Irish mothers' and as women of strength, courage and endurance. [. . .] Such women were pioneer women but it should be remembered that bush life was hard, lonely, even brutal and unremittingly cruel. Giving birth to children every two years, raising them in a two-roomed wattle and daub hut, on poor quality land, was scarcely better than life in the insanitary and cramped living conditions of working-class Sydney, Brisbane or Melbourne, where other orphans had settled.

Yet, despite the hardships which many of them endured, they became part of the expansion of Australia's cities and the 'push into the bush'. They were women who made a remarkable contribution to the natural increase of Australia's population. Like Sarah Ann and Margaret Devlin they became founders of large extended families. Their children were instilled with their ambitions, hopes and values. Their descendants enjoyed opportunities unheard-of in Ireland. Although much maligned, the female orphans literally became mothers to the Australian character. [. . .]

Chapter 24

Hasia R. Diner

■   from **THE SEARCH FOR BREAD: PATTERNS OF FEMALE MIGRATION**, Chapter 2 of *Erin's Daughters in America: Irish Immigrant Women in the Nineteenth Century*, Baltimore and London, 1983, pp. 30–42

[. . .]

BEGINNING IN THE EARLY NINETEENTH CENTURY, the exodus from Ireland to the United States amounted to a virtual tidal wave of human beings leaving one home and seeking another. That more than half of these immigrants were women, that the migration constituted basically a mass female movement, did not escape the notice of observers on either side of the Atlantic. No other major group of immigrants in American history contained so many women. Among the Germans, a group that arrived over the same span of years as the Irish, the women made up 41 per cent of the total immigrant population, whereas among the Irish, women accounted for 52.9 per cent. [. . .] The only large foreign-born immigrant population where men and women came in roughly equal numbers were Jews, yet even here men still outnumbered women slightly. Furthermore, a goodly proportion of the new Jewish arrivals were children, indicating that a large number of the immigrants were married and had brought their young with them. The Irish immigrants were primarily still single women and men. Only about 5 per cent of all Irish immigrants were children, as compared with 28 per cent of all Jewish immigrants.[1]

Why did the Irish male–female ratios differ so fundamentally from those of other groups? What was there about the Irish and their culture to create this particular pattern? Irish female immigration patterns had been distinctive even before the famine, yet it was only afterwards, with the emergence of the modern Irish family structure, that the Irish became so unique, so dramatically female in the migratory habits. As that family form became universalised in Ireland, the intensity of the female exodus became more pronounced. Thus, by the early twentieth century, when the family in Ireland had really hardened into its characteristic form, the number of women leaving swelled to even greater proportions. Women made up about 53.8 per cent of all immigrants in 1900, as compared to 35 per cent in the 1830s.

Immigration during the famine differed considerably from the exodus of the Irish before it and contrasted sharply with what would happen afterward. Sheer numbers make the famine a pivotal event in immigration history, although it was hardly typical. From 1821 to 1850 about one million Irish came to the United States. Of that million, 120,000 of them account for only two years, 1845 and 1846. In the eight years between 1847 and 1854, the worst years of the famine and those following immediately thereafter, over one and a quarter million had made their way to the United States. Another three million immigrated in the half century between 1851 and 1901. Those who migrated during and just after the famine, more than those before or those afterward, represented the landless and the poor, who just could not remain at home. During the famine married couples with children immigrated more readily than they had before and certainly than they would later, emphasising the aberrant nature of the immigration of the famine years. Thus, during the famine one sees less clearly the true trends of the Irish movement to the United States and its essentially young, unmarried, female component.[2]

The real impact of the famine on migration came from the traumatic shock waves it sent through Irish society, which accelerated the rearrangement of family life and which caused many young Irish men and particularly Irish women to immigrate. Looking at Irish immigration figures in the decade afterward provides a much more profound sense of how the society sought to cope with newly evolving land and family forms. For one thing, age became a more important factor and fewer children emigrated, stressing that single people were leaving. Between 1850 and 1887 over 66 per cent of all immigrants fell between the ages of fifteen and thirty-five. In the last decades of the nineteenth century, from 1880 to 1897, a mere 7.9 per cent clustered below the age of fifteen, while a slightly more substantial 9.0 per cent exceeded thirty-five years of age. From 1852 to 1921 the median age for all male immigrants was 22.5, whereas for women it was 21.2, younger than the median age of marriage. In the twenty-three years from 1887 to the century's end, married people constituted only slightly more than 16 per cent of all those who arrived in the United States.

This differs sharply with Irish immigration to Britain, where many more children went as well as many more older people, presumably those less able to work. This suggests that when entire families were compelled to leave they could not afford the longer, more expensive trip across the Atlantic. Immigrants to Britain were also committing themselves to a less permanent move, and statistics indicate that the Irish who did not choose America were more likely to return to Ireland.[3]

Other than the very poor, the Irish who immigrated as single men and women did so because of their unfavourable place in the family land arrangements of the Irish countryside. Despite seasonal fluctuations, occasional dips in the number of immigrants, and regional variations, the movement of women out of Ireland continued unabated through the end of the century. Even during the years when prospects dimmed for men in the United States, as during the American depressions of 1873 and 1893, the migration of Irish women continued unchecked. In fact, during these periods the percentage of young women among the arrivals from Ireland mushroomed. Between 1861 and 1870, 21.1 per cent of all migrants were women between the ages of fifteen and twenty-four and 23.3 per cent were men of those ages. In the years 1871 through to 1880 men and women of these ages arrived in exactly equal proportion. From 1881 through to 1890, 30 per cent were women and 27.4 per cent men, and from 1891 until the end of the century 35.4 per cent were women and 24.5 per cent men.

Thus the percentage and the absolute number of female immigrants from Ireland rose in direct proportion to the hardening of family lines and the circumscribing of opportunities for women in Ireland. Women did not predominate among Irish newcomers to Britain until the 1890s, whereas among those Irish who chose to cast their lot in Australia, men and women came in equal numbers until 1911 and then women took the lead.

The preponderantly female emigration originated primarily from Munster and Connaught, the most rural provinces. The more urban areas like Ulster (home of Belfast) and Leinster (which included Dublin) offered greater employment options to women. In Ulster, women still made money through a variety of home-based industries, and therefore they did not have as much reason to leave.

During the last half of the nineteenth century, the emigration became increasingly composed of women as it came to be increasingly centred in the western agricultural areas. Although in 1882 the emigration from all of Ireland had grown two-and-a-half times since 1878, it had grown three times from County Clare and four times from Kerry and Leitrim. In Galway it increased four-and-a-half times, whereas the exodus from Mayo was seven times larger and from Sligo nine times greater than at the end of the 1870s. The female emigration from these western districts originated in environments so scarred by the famine and now so committed to the single-inheritance system that excess children, particularly daughters for whom no resources could be expended and for whom no alternatives existed, left in droves, depopulating – and defeminising – rural Ireland.[4]

From the point of view of those who remained in Ireland, the large number of women, 'the flower of the population', who left their homes to try their luck in the United States meant that Irish life, particularly in agricultural areas, became increasingly dominated by males. Irish observers during the migration, particularly in the last decades of the century, panicked at the prospect that the migration had reduced 'that element of the population which furnishes the natural increase of any people'. The censuses of 1861, 1871, 1881, and 1891 confirmed that the population was dwindling, and especially its female portion. For example, 1,542 men and 1,365 women lived in the Aran Islands in 1891; 20 years earlier, men had outnumbered women by 27. Even the non-farming areas felt the sting of the female exodus. By the 1880s it had become impossible to find young women in places like Donegal who would work in domestic service in Ireland. A *Times* reporter noted that serving girls were 'scarcer everyday' as the lure of America captured them, since they left as soon as they had saved up the needed money.[5] [. . .]

Each emigrant must have had her own story on how she came to the decision to leave Ireland. Yet certain patterns did emerge. Much of the immediate famine exodus, for example, constituted a flight from hunger, a migration of desperation. *Illustrated London* in 1849 told about Bridget O'Donnell of the seaside town of Kilrush, about to have a baby, whose husband had abandoned her with two children, with no resources of any kind, and on the verge of eviction from her four-and-a-half acres of bog. She left for America, pushed out by overwhelming circumstances.[6]

After the famine, however, emigrants tended to flee less from actual hunger and disease, although they still intensively yearned to leave. One American who visited Ireland in the early 1850s noted, 'There is nothing unnatural in the desire of the unfortunate Irish to abandon their cheerless and damp cottages, to crawl inch by inch, while they have yet a little strength, from the graves which apparently yawn for their bodies.'[7]

During the famine and in its immediate aftermath, several agencies assisted Irish men and women to emigrate. For example, in the 1860s approximately 6,500 (out of 900,000) immigrants had their passage paid by the Poor Law Guardians. Some landlords, their consciences apparently pricked by the harrowing scenes of starvation and disease, helped their tenants leave. They may also have reasoned that the money for the passage was an excellent investment, since it facilitated the consolidation of holdings needed to shift the land from tillage to grazing. Occasionally the Irish Prison Board, even as late as the 1870s, released well-behaved convicts on the condition that they leave Ireland for either the United Kingdom, for other parts of the British empire, or for the United States.

Some immigration schemes were aimed primarily at women. For example, women, who constituted most of the inmates of the Irish workhouses, were assisted to leave but only in modest numbers. In 1850, 2,847 women left the workhouses for America courtesy of the Poor Law Guardians. In the first years of the 1850s Vere Foster, an English philanthropist, organised the Irish Pioneer Immigration Fund and a Women's Protective Immigration Society to finance the migration of thousands of young women to Canada and the United States from the poor counties of the west of Ireland. The emigrants were to be selected on the basis of 'their excellence of character and industrious habits'. Similarly, in the 1860s a Female Middle Class Immigration Society, organised by Maria Rye, sought to promote the successful immigration of young, educated Irish women, particularly to Australia.[8]

Organised schemes to assist emigrants never accounted for more than a fraction of those who left. Many more came over because relatives already in the United States had sent them the money. Vast numbers of emigrants left through the generosity of their sisters, brothers, and friends, which suggests that the movement was a positive and enthusiastic one. [. . .]

Women actively promoted migration and travelled along what might be seen as female chains. They made the trips together, they helped finance one another, and they met and greeted one another. Although they certainly assisted male kin as well, particularly brothers, the primary emphasis focused on their sisters and other female relatives. Journeying to the United States to a sister, an aunt, or a friend became the typical pattern for Irish migrant women.[9] In 1897 the St Vincent de Paul Society in Boston surveyed Irish female arrivals and found that out of 2,945 that year only 76 were not met by 'friends'.[10] In 1907 a survey of foreign arrivals in Boston uncovered that of the Irish women, 106 came to join relatives, seven came with relatives, one came with a friend, and yet another had a friend to meet her. A grand total of two came to marry. In terms of passage money, two had their passages paid by husbands and forty-six were aided by older relatives. Seventy of the women had raised the money themselves, and 120 had been financed by 'relatives of the same generation', most likely brothers or sisters, and none by fiancés.[11] [. . .]

The migrations did not always occur without problems or disruptions and occasionally the colleen arrived with no one to greet her. All of the Irish-American newspapers, like those in most immigrant communities, ran columns for people attempting to locate missing friends and relatives. In the 1870s the *Irish World*, a New York-based paper, reported a roughly equal number of men and women as 'missing' [. . .] Usually sisters or brothers sought one another out, with sisters looking for sisters most often and then brothers looking for sisters. Similar grim listings of the lost and the lonely appeared in the Boston *Pilot* as well as the other Irish newspapers, and again demonstrated the female bonds and ties between siblings.[12] [. . .]

Whether they had migrated alone or with a sister, whether they left Ireland in the company of parents or children, or friends, the overwhelming majority of the Irish consciously eschewed rural life in the United States and became urban dwellers. For one thing, it took money to venture far beyond the port of arrival, and to leave New York, Boston, or Philadelphia to farm required more capital than most Irish had with them. Also, Irish newcomers harboured very negative sentiments about the agricultural life. Since they had left Ireland precisely because of the limited – or, more accurately – shrinking opportunities of farm life, they showed no eagerness for it in the United States. That the migration was so heavily female and single also helps explain the apathy of the Irish for rural living [in the United States]. Most importantly, farming involved a family effort – an effort in which husband, wife, and children laboured together – an undertaking totally inappropriate for the single women who comprised so large a portion of the immigrants.

On the other hand, the cities and industrial towns of the North and the urban Middle West offered economic opportunities for women and men. For unskilled hands, factory and millwork, domestic service, and the physical labour of public work projects were the prizes to be had in the cities. In 1860 the Irish had already so engulfed urban America as to be the single largest immigrant group in Boston, New York, and Philadelphia and the second largest in Baltimore and Cincinnati. In 1869 they also predominated in Providence, New Haven, Albany, and Pittsburgh and occupied the rank of second most numerous in Buffalo, Milwaukee, Chicago, and St Louis. Substantial Irish communities exploded in size across the last half of the nineteenth century in San Francisco, Omaha, Memphis, New Orleans, Cleveland, Detroit, and Denver. The Irish showed up in large numbers wherever workers were needed. In milltowns like Lawrence, Lowell, and Pawtucket, Irish women appeared, too, making many of these Gaelic communities predominantly female as well as providing Americans with the largest ethnic group of domestic servants.[13] [. . .]

Because women outnumbered men as migrants and as new Americans they played a strikingly significant role in the economic life of Irish America as well as in the creation of informal networks that linked Irish America to the homeland. [. . .]

What effect did the preponderance of women as migrants have on the economic, social, and cultural patterns of Irish America? The kinds of family the Irish carved out in America as well as the work patterns, educational achievements, and sense of self of Irish women all need to be examined in light of the female-dominated migration.

Just because women surpassed men in number does not necessarily imply that women achieved greater power and authority in the formalised institutions of their communities. Just because more Irish women than men had chosen to migrate to the United States does not necessarily mean that equal or even greater resources and services in the communities went to them. Just because the 'typical' immigrant was a young, single woman does not mean that women's actions were fully autonomous. In fact, it may have been that the older, Irish traditions of gender antagonism and segmentation plus the numerical insecurity of Irish males in the United States caused them to cling to power in formal institutions even longer and more tenaciously than if they had not been so outnumbered.

More importantly, Irish women immigrated in huge numbers to the United States because of the greater opportunities that awaited them. Irish women migrated not as depressed survivors of famine, but in the main they made the journey with optimism, in a forward-looking assessment that in America they could achieve a status that they never could have at home.

Notes

1 US Immigration Commission, *Statistical Review of Immigration, 1820–1910: Distribution of Immigration, 1850–1900*, Washington, DC, 1911; John R. Commons, *Races and Immigrants in America*, New York, 1907, p. 122.

2 Frances Morehouse, 'Irish migration of the 'forties', *American Historical Review*, 33, 1928, pp. 579–92; S. H. Cousens, 'Emigration and demographic change in Ireland, 1851–1861', *Economic History Review*, 14/2, 1961, pp. 275–88; Gerard Shaughnessy, 'A century of Catholic growth in the United States: 1820–1920', Ph.D. dissertation, Catholic University of America, 1922; S. H. Cousens, 'The regional pattern of emigration during the Irish Famine, 1846–1851', *Institute of British Geographers, Transactions and Papers*, 27, 1960, pp. 119–34.

3 Maldwyn Alan Jones, 'The background of emigration from Great Britain in the nineteenth century', *Perspectives in American History*, 7, 1973, pp. 3–92; James Meehan, 'Some features of Irish emigration', *International Labour Review*, 69/2, 1954, pp. 128–39.

4 Cousens, 'Regional Pattern', p. 309; Meehan, 'Irish emigration'; John Archer Jackson, *The Irish in Britain*, London, 1963, p. 18; 'The Irish in America', *Westminster Review*, 129, 1888, pp. 713–32.

5 Census data in Robert E. Kennedy, *The Irish*, Berkeley and Los Angeles, 1973, pp. 67–8, 77–8. The *Times*, London, quoted in Richard J. Kelly, 'Emigration and its consequences', *New Ireland Review*, 21/5, 1904, pp. 257–67. [. . .]

6 Quoted in Edith Abbott, *Historical Aspects of Immigration*, Chicago, 1926, pp. 662–3.

7 Ibid.

8 Robert F. Clokey, 'Irish emigration from workhouses', *Journal of the Statistical and Social Inquiry Society of Ireland*, 25, 1863, pp. 416–35; Robert Ernst, *Immigrant Life in New York City: 1825–1863*, New York, 1949, p. 243; R. Denny Urlin, 'Remarks on the middle class (female) emigration society', *Journal of the Statistical and Social Inquiry Society of Ireland*, 25, 1863, pp. 439–46.

9   Brendan MacAodha, 'Letters from America,' *Ulster Folklife*, 3/1, 1957, pp. 64–9; 'Irish Poor Laws and Irish emigration,' *Quarterly Review*, 157/314, 1884, pp. 440–72; 'An Irish emigrant's letter,' *Living Age*, 32, 1852, p. 422. [. . .]

10   Quoted in Franklin E. Fitzpatrick, 'Irish immigration into New York, from 1865 to 1880', Master's thesis, Catholic University of America, 1948, p. 42.

11   'Immigrant women and girls in Boston: a report', 1907, box 7, folder 49, WEIU Papers.

12   *Boston Pilot*, 1850–3; I.W., 1870–7.

13   Kennedy, *The Irish*, pp. 66–85; Frederick A. Bushee, 'The growth of the population of Boston', *Quarterly Publications of the American Statistical Association*, 7/46, 1899, pp. 239–74.

Chapter 25

Sharon Lambert

■   from IRISH WOMEN'S EMIGRATION TO
ENGLAND 1922–1960: THE LENGTHENING
OF FAMILY TIES, in Alan Hayes and Diane Urquhart
(eds), *Female Experiences: Essays in Irish Women's
History*, Dublin, 2000

I T IS NOT JUST THE ATTITUDES of the host community which determine how far immigrants are assimilated into that society; they also bring with
them values and traditions from their original country. Women coming to England
from Southern Ireland after 1922 left a climate of post-colonialism in which Irish
cultural identity was emphasised as being distinctly not British, or more specifically not English.[1] [. . .] Using oral evidence from the life histories of forty Irish
women who were living in Lancashire between 1922 and 1960, this paper inves-
tigates how Irish women coped with the apparent contradictory forces of family
duty and leaving home, and Irish patriotism and settling in England.[2] An argument
is developed that, rather than escaping from increasing family ties and responsibilities, Irish women in England were motivated to keep in close contact with their
original homes in Ireland. The cultural climate of newly independent Ireland generally ensured that emigrants to England left with a desire to uphold their Irish
identity in the country from which Ireland had only recently gained independence.
Indeed it seems that as an Irish woman's identity was defined by her role within
the family she was less likely to sever family ties than to adopt strategies of maintaining them from a distance.

In the first forty years after partition, the new Irish State pursued successive
policies which emphasised not only its political but also its economic, spiritual and
cultural independence from its colonial past. Gaelic sports, music, dancing and
language and the Catholic faith were vigorously promoted as examples of a distinctly
Irish national identity. Attempts at economic self-sufficiency during this period can
be seen as another example of the Irish State ideologically distancing itself from
Britain, its main trading partner. [. . .] Of all the ideologies of independent Ireland,
women's lives were most affected by the idealisation of the family and their roles
became increasingly circumscribed to caring for the family within the home. [. . .]

During this period . . . hundreds of thousands of Irish women were leaving
their family homes and emigrating. Between 1926 and 1951 about 52,000 women
left Southern Ireland for the United States and a further 180,000 went to Britain.[3]

Another irony is that it was also during this period of post-independence, when official rhetoric was promoting all things Irish and denigrating all things British, that Britain replaced the USA as the main destination of Irish emigrants by 1929. Maura, for example, reluctantly left her home on a small farm in Co. Roscommon to find work in Lancashire in 1945 when she was eighteen. She saw the absurdity of the idealisation of rural Ireland, combined with anti-English rhetoric, when the mass-exportation of people across the Irish Sea was continuing: 'They taught us to hate England and then they sent us here!'

In explaining the high rate of female emigration to Britain in the 1940s and 1950s, O'Carroll has suggested that: 'Essential to this move was a desire to distance themselves from control by family and patriarchal society.'[4] However, given the strength of the family ideal in Irish culture it is likely that a complete rejection of family ties after emigration was, at the very least, difficult for most Irish women. [. . .]

All the women in this study either offered unprompted information or were asked specifically about their reasons for emigrating from Ireland. Economic reasons were most often cited as the impetus for emigration, especially amongst women from poorer rural backgrounds, where labouring on the family farm or domestic service were usually the only local employment alternatives. Small family-farm incomes were unable to sustain all offspring as they left school. Indeed, women who worked on the farm expressed an awareness of being a financial burden on the family and a sense of prolonged childhood as they had to ask for money to buy new clothes or go to dances. Only two women, however, said that they emigrated in order to distance themselves from what they perceived to be excessive parental control. One was Maeve, who was born into a wealthy family in Co. Tipperary in 1917 [. . .]

> I wanted to come to England, I didn't want to try for a job in Ireland. Well frankly I wanted to get away from home because my mother was one of those, you never had very much freedom. I never had very much freedom growing up, being the only girl she was strict with me. [. . .]

The economic situation of her family and her order in the family were important factors in determining whether or not a woman emigrated. Lena was one of eight children born to a small farmer and his wife in Co. Galway in 1930. She left school at fourteen and worked on the family farm until she emigrated to England at the age of fifteen and a half, with the assistance of an agency which arranged employment for her as a child-minder in London. [. . .] Lena saw emigration as a necessary family obligation, since the remittances from older siblings enabled her younger brothers and sisters to receive a secondary education:

> All my family used to send money to my mother. They needed it in this country [Ireland] then. But every family, all the children who went in the forties and fifties, did the same thing. They went to help the younger children and to educate them. Yeah, we did, we educated them.

Several respondents also noted that their younger brothers or sisters progressed to secondary education whereas they and their older emigrant siblings did not. Economically assisting their family, rather than themselves, was a common motivation for Irish women's emigration.

The strength of the family ideal in Irish society meant that the behaviour of individual members reflected upon the reputation of the whole family. Indeed, upholding the good name of the family was an important motivation for conforming to socially acceptable behaviour. A strict moral climate prevailed in the post-independence years, where sin was exclusively equated with sex.[5] Without exception, respondents to this case study reported that the greatest shame they could have brought upon their families in Ireland was to have had an illegitimate child. [. . .]

The taboo on sex outside of marriage was so strong that even discussing it was forbidden in most Irish families. It would appear that most girls were not even prepared for the onset of their periods. Only two respondents were told about them, one by her mother and the other by a female cousin.[6] The overwhelming memories of the rest of the women were of being shocked and frightened when their first period occurred and feeling ashamed by the secrecy of the monthly rituals of soaking and washing soiled cloths and towels which had to be kept hidden from male family members. Given this taboo, it is perhaps not surprising that most women reported that they were ignorant of sexual matters during their youth. [. . .]

A pattern of female family members colluding to conceal unmarried women's pregnancies is evident in several of the life histories. Lily, who was born in Athlone in 1929, had lived in Morecambe for two years when she arranged the marriage of her pregnant sister and provided a home for the young couple. Her story is significant because it illustrates that Protestants [she was Baptist] were as keen to hide family indiscretions as Catholics:

> My mother wrote to me and she said: 'I'm sending her over, arrange a wedding!' It was a bit of a rush wedding. They came over here because it might not have been the right thing for people to know at home . . . The child was born here but they didn't like it here and they went home. They didn't go back to Athlone . . . they got a job outside Wicklow.

The young couple had not wanted to emigrate, or even leave Athlone, but they did so in order to protect the reputations of their families. The circumstances of Lily's own emigration in 1950, when she was twenty-one, also highlight how emigration was often undertaken less for individual than for family needs. At this time, Lily had a good job in a shop and she was very happy living in Athlone. In her life history she revealed that neither she nor her sisters were allowed to date Catholic boys when they were young but there were comparatively few Protestants in the town and her family were related to a lot of them. She had no intention of emigrating but was forced to do so by her mother when she became friendly with a male cousin. Her mother also wanted Lily to move near to two of her uncles who had lost contact with the family in Athlone:

> I was friendly with a cousin at home [. . .] I didn't think there was
> anything wrong with it but quite suddenly I was told: 'You're not to
> go over there anymore.' I think my mother saw what was coming and
> decided it was time I was shipped out. She had two reasons, that was
> one, and the other one was to find out what her brothers were doing
> [. . .] In those days you had to be obedient to what your parents said
> [. . .]

The emigrant women in this study left Southern Ireland for various economic or
social reasons but, whatever the basic cause was, it usually concerned the emigrant's
family as much as herself individually. It has been shown that some women even
emigrated involuntarily in order to fulfil their families' expectations. Family
networks were also the most important means of arranging and maintaining emigration. It was, however, only in the area of concealing a pregnancy that the familial
network became gendered. In other instances women were as likely to have their
emigration arranged by, or to go and stay with, male relatives as female. Moreover
most women went to live in areas where they had relatives. It seems therefore
that female emigration from Ireland cannot be simply explained as a conscious
rejection of family duties since family involvement and networks were crucial to
the emigration process. [. . .]

The importance of familial ties is also demonstrated by the efforts which women
made to maintain contact with their Irish homes and families after emigration.
Telephones were not easily accessible to working-class people in Ireland or England
during the period of this study. Letters, therefore, remained the cheapest and most
utilised form of communication between the two countries. [. . .] The nature of
the letters which passed between women and their relatives in Ireland shows a
pattern of transmitting only good news wherever possible:

> Oh you always wrote, always. But you never told the bad things
> [. . .] It didn't matter how bad you were, you'd suffer in silence, you'd
> pretend everything was splendid. Me mother would write great big
> long letters. And she'd tell you about everybody you knew: where they
> were, if they were home, the children that were born. She'd tell you
> about the animals and all the news from there. That was your lifeline.
> She didn't tell us anything bad. Yet there must've been bad things
> mustn't there? But she never did tell us them. (Joan, b. 1915, Co.
> Mayo)

[. . .] An over-positive image was often portrayed in letters from both sides of the
Irish Sea. Female emigrants consciously cultivated an optimistic view of their lives
abroad, partly for their own self-esteem and also to alleviate their parents' anxiety.

[. . .] By the middle of the twentieth century the sending of parcels and money
was a well-established tradition amongst Irish emigrants. The importance of
emigrants' remittances to the Irish economy was noted by the Commission on
Emigration and other Population Problems, which conducted a major survey
between 1948 and 1954.[7] It seems that many Irish families relied on money and
parcels sent from their offspring abroad. [. . .]

The greater proximity of Britain than the previously favoured emigrant destination of the USA, and improved and cheaper sea passages, made visits home more accessible to Irish emigrants in the mid-twentieth century than at any previous time. [. . .] Apart from proximity and affordability, social factors also determined whether or not women visited their families in Ireland. [. . .] Overwhelmingly though, Ireland was the usual holiday destination of the women interviewed and most of them spoke of 'going home' as often as they could afford to. Single working women, especially nurses who did not have to take fixed holidays, were often able to accrue their leave entitlements and have extended summer holidays in Ireland. There was also a labour shortage in post-war Britain and when the National Health Service was founded in 1948 some health authorities used subsidised travel home as an incentive to recruit Irish women into nursing. [. . .]

Having children, rather than getting married, was the point in women's life-cycles which most affected their ability to visit Ireland. The expense of taking the whole family over appears to be the main reason why some Irish women went home less often after they became mothers. [. . .] A desire to acquaint their children with their relations in Ireland and their Irish cultural inheritance was often expressed by mothers, but ironically some could not afford to travel back to Ireland as frequently once they had children.

Women also made visits to Ireland for reasons other than holidays. Caring for old or infirm family members was a significant reason for emigrant women to return, sometimes for lengthy periods. [. . .] Childbirth provided another reason for some women to return to their family in Ireland [. . .]

> My daughters were both born in Ireland and I think it was really important for me that they were born there. They were Irish you see. (Eileen, b. 1927, Co. Wexford)

[. . .] The death of parents was another life-cycle stage which affected women's pattern of visiting Ireland. Some women continued to visit but expressed regret that things had changed whilst for others, especially if all their brothers and sisters had emigrated, it marked the end of 'going home':

> There's nothing there, you know, after my father and mother died, the nostalgia, it was terrible. They were such happy days that we had there and it's all gone; finished! No, I never wanted to go back. (Mary, b. 1917, Co. Mayo)

In conclusion, significant contact was maintained between emigrant women in Lancashire and their families in Ireland. [. . .] The less affluent women of the study expressed a desire to have returned home more often if they had been able to afford it. Some women also returned home to give birth. Life-cycle stages affected the frequency of visits to Ireland, especially motherhood, when ironically a desire to aquaint children with their Irish families and cultural inheritance was often accompanied by increased financial restraints. Female emigrants also took on the responsibility of caring for family members in Ireland and it seems that they were more likely to return home for this task than Irish men. But it was the death

of parents and siblings in Ireland which often signified a change in the pattern
of visits.

[. . .] The experiences of Irish emigrant women in Lancashire between 1922
and 1960 contradict the conclusions of O'Carroll's research on female emigration
to America in which she stated: 'Irish women turned their backs on Ireland', and
'the rejection of family life was a major theme in the story of Irish emigrants to
the USA'.[8] Conversely, it is argued here that the family often played an extensive
role in the female emigration process and some women even emigrated against
their own personal wishes in order to enhance the economy or protect the reputation of their family. Furthermore, existing family networks were an important
feature of emigrant women's destinations. Although some women undoubtedly
used emigration as a means to escape from family ties, there is more evidence
to suggest that emigration was often their only means of fulfilling family obligations. [. . .]

One explanation for the continuance of traditional family ties after emigration
can be found in the cultural climate of post-colonial Ireland. [. . .] A woman's
perception of Irishness was increasingly associated with her role within the family
and the home. [. . .] These women had no problems with their national identity:
they were Irish emigrant women who happened to live in England. [. . .]

The familial contact which was maintained by Irish emigrant women has
implications for challenging the accepted notion of the assimilation of Irish women
in twentieth-century Britain.[9] Lennon *et al.*'s pioneering oral study of Irish
women in Britain found that 'none of the women who emigrated from Ireland
considered herself to have assimilated' but they also observed that 'women face
greater pressures to adapt to British society than men, because of their family
role and responsibilities'.[10] [. . .] Whilst Irish women's comparative invisibility in
Britain has been taken to mean that they asserted their Irishness less readily than
Irish men, their absence from the male-dominated Irish public spheres of clubs,
pubs and associations could also be evidence of a continuance of Irish patriarchal
culture after emigration. Irish emigrant women were maintaining their Irish iden-
tities within their families and, by their extensive links with their family homes in
Ireland, they were transmitting an Irish cultural identity to their children.

Notes

1   'Southern Ireland' is commonly used to refer to the twenty-six counties that are
    now independent from Britain [. . . I]t provides a convenient name for the
    geographical area in any time period [. . .] The women studied here all emigrated
    from Southern Ireland.

2   [. . .] Oral life-histories were used in this research to address new themes which
    were relevant to Irish emigrant women's lives. The main themes of the thesis
    were family, religion and sexuality. [. . .]

3   Pauric Travers, 'Emigration and gender: the case of Ireland, 1922–60', in Mary
    O'Dowd and Sabine Wichert (eds), *Chattel, Servant or Citizen: Women's Status in
    Church, State and Society*, Belfast, 1995, p. 190.

4   Ide O'Carroll, *Models for Movers: Irish Women's Emigration to America*, Dublin, 1990,

p. 12. Although in this instance she was discussing Irish emigrants to Britain, O'Carroll's source of evidence for her book is Irish women in America.

5   See J. J. Lee, *Ireland 1912–1985: Politics and Society*, Cambridge, 1989, pp. 158–9, for details of how far Irish censorship legislation and Roman Catholic Church pronouncements were concerned with sexual immorality.

6   Barbara, b. 1935, Co. Donegal and Siobhan, b. 1938, Co. Donegal.

7   *Reports of the Commission on Emigration and other Population Problems 1948–1954*, Dublin, 1956, [Pr. 2541] Para. 313.

8   O'Carroll, *Models for Movers*, p. 145.

9   This assumption is identified by Mary Lennon, Marie McAdam and Joanne O'Brien, *Across the Water: Irish Women's Lives in Britain*, London, 1988, p. 15.

10   Ibid., pp. 15–16.

PART SIX

Work

THE WORLD OF WORK IS OFTEN cited as the area where the separate spheres of men and women are most apparent. Certainly there were clear boundaries between what was considered to be male or female work. This was apparent within the home, in the workplace and in the unpaid philanthropic work which was performed by an increasing number of women in the course of the nineteenth century. In the home, women's work usually centred on the house and its immediate environs. In the workplace, women's work, for instance in textile production, was generally categorised as less skilled than work performed by men. Furthermore, many female philanthropists worked on single-sex committees, striving to help members of their own sex who were in need of assistance.

However, investigation into women's paid and unpaid labour in Ireland in the nineteenth and early twentieth centuries highlights that our assumptions of what constitutes 'women's work' have been somewhat one-dimensional. Indeed, the work conducted by women was not as restrictive as one might first imagine. Theirs was a valuable and diverse role, defined by a crucial combination of acceptability and ability, in terms of the tasks women were physically able to perform. It was a woman who, for example, took responsibility for day-to-day domestic tasks, for child-bearing and child-rearing. Women also controlled most of the household budget and tended crops when their husbands left to work as seasonal migrant harvesters. Women's work in the household was clearly of considerable economic importance, but her position was affected by her marital status, age and whether she resided in her own, or in her in-laws' home. Indeed the latter could lead to serious tussles for power amongst the women of a household. Certainly the idea of women in the home being in an unenviable position of dependency, subservience and powerlessness needs to be addressed. Similarly the position of an employee cannot always be equated with powerlessness. For instance, good, experienced domestic servants were difficult to find. Thus it was possible for a servant to swing the weight of favour in her direction by threatening to resign from service. But this element of power should not be generalised. In essence each employer and employee had a unique personal relationship where conditions and expectations varied.

Textile production, agriculture and domestic service were major employers of women in nineteenth- and early twentieth-century Ireland. Yet, common to all these areas was the low level of female trade-union organisation. The development of women's involvement in the trade union movement fluctuated for a number of reasons. Their apparent reluctance to subscribe to a union needs to be addressed in terms of women's attitude to paid work. For many it was a stopgap between school and marriage, a temporary and transitory period in their lives. For others it was economic necessity which drove them out to work in a time of economic hardship. Women were largely excluded from the better-paid areas of skilled work and their wages generally amounted to between half and two-thirds of male wage rates. Women were, therefore, unwilling and in many cases, unable, to pay trade-union subscription fees from their already meagre wages. There were also practical limits, as many working women were already struggling to balance paid employ with domestic responsibilities. This left women with little time and in many cases an apparent lack of impetus to join a union. But we also need to assess this issue from a male perspective as there was a clear reluctance on the part of union officials to admit women into their echelons. Fears were certainly widespread regarding women's potential for undercutting men's wages. In addition to this, the belief that a woman's place was in the home was another consideration. With this background, even though the opportunities for female employment expanded, moves towards equality in terms of equal pay and promotional opportunities have been slow. Resilience was the key in changing the ethos of women's work from being of secondary importance, not only to the work of men, but also to what was seen, until comparatively recently, as women's true vocation – domesticity.

Suggestions for further reading

Joanna Bourke, *Husbandry to Housewifery: Women, Economic Change and Housewifery in Ireland, 1890–1914*, Oxford, 1993.

Caitríona Clear, *Women of the House: Women's Household Work in Ireland, 1922–61*, Dublin, 2000.

Brenda Collins, 'The organisation of sewing outwork in late nineteenth-century Ulster', in Maxine Berg (ed.), *Markets and Manufacture in Early Industrial Europe*, London, 1991.

Mona Hearn, *Below Stairs: Domestic Service Remembered in Dublin and Beyond, 1880–1922*, Dublin, 1993.

Mary Jones, *These Obstreperous Lassies: A History of the Irish Women Workers' Union*, Dublin, 1988.

Betty Messenger, *Picking up the Linen Threads: Life in Ulster's Mills*, Belfast, 1988.

Margaret Neill, 'Homeworkers in Ulster, 1850–1911', in Janice Holmes and Diane Urquhart (eds), *Coming into the Light: The Work, Politics and Religion of Women in Ulster, 1840–1940*, Belfast, 1984.

Eoin O'Leary, 'The Irish National Teachers' Organisation and the marriage bar for women national teachers, 1933–1958', *Saothar*, 12, 1987.

Pauline Scanlon, *The Irish Nurse: A Study of Nursing in Ireland: History and Education, 1718–1981*, Manorhamilton, 1991.

Chapter 26

Mary E. Daly

■ from WOMEN IN THE IRISH WORKFORCE
FROM PRE-INDUSTRIAL TO MODERN TIMES,
Saothar, 7, 1981, pp. 74–82

[. . .]

THE IRISH ECONOMY OF THE eighteenth century was predominantly
a peasant economy with a high volume of domestic production of food and
other necessities. Both agriculture and industry tended to be organised on the basis
of the household. All household members, male and female, contributed towards
family income if not incapacitated by extreme youth, old age or disability. There
were traditional women's chores, mostly those carried out within the house, such
as spinning or making butter, or those requiring less physical strength such as
weeding crops, but the distinction between male and female spheres of work was
not, as commonly in modern households, between non-income generating and
income-earning activities. In fact in many pre-famine Irish households, the woman
by her spinning provided the family's cash income while the husband through
farming concentrated on providing the food. During the late seventeenth and eighteenth centuries Irish women experienced increasing opportunities to earn money
with the expansion of the butter trade and the spread of the domestic linen industry.
Domestic textiles increased the earning capacity of both women and young men
and permitted them to marry at an early age and form households regardless of
parental approval. The spread of domestic textiles and the increased earning power
of young women was therefore a factor in the frequency of early marriages in pre-
famine Ireland and made an important contribution to Ireland's population increase.
The areas which displayed the greatest density of population and the earliest
marriages in 1841 were those with a strong domestic textile industry.[1]

This ability to earn money did not inevitably give women a greater status in
the community. In the majority of cases, women's earnings were used to pay the
family rent[2] and a woman's money was regarded as benefiting her family, either
her parent's family or that formed with a husband. Some of a woman's earnings
was generally used as pin money. Thus Isaac Weld writes of a parish in Co.
Roscommon in the early 1830s.

The people dress in a style far superior to the line of life in which they are placed, particularly the females who are fond of show, and comply with modern fashions as far as they can afford it. They are able to indulge in this propensity by their industry in spinning and weaving coarse linens; these they bring to market, and when disposed of, they purchase ornamented clothing with a part of the profit.[3]

The days of luxury for the young women of Roscommon were, however, short-lived. The spread of the factory system gradually eroded traditional domestic industries and the impact fell disproportionately on women, because much of the early Industrial Revolution concentrated on textiles. The 1841 Census counted over 600,000 textile and clothing workers, many of these living in the west of Ireland. By 1841 many had already lost much of their income and this trend accelerated in the following decades. In Britain the decline of domestic textile employment was compensated by the emergence of factory employment. In Ireland, however, this did not happen to any extent outside of north-east Ulster. Post-famine Ireland experienced a massive industrial decline and in 1891 manufacturing industry employed only 17 per cent of the workforce compared with 27 per cent in 1841.[4] The brunt of this fall in industrial employment was borne by women.

By the end of the nineteenth century the pre-famine economic structure through which women working in the home were able to contribute to family earnings survived only among the craft workers of the congested districts, and in the outworking clothing industry which was predominately located in north-west Ulster. It is perhaps no coincidence that these areas where women still made a cash contribution to the family income were areas which resisted the tendency towards later marriages. Margaret Irwin, author of a report on women outworkers in Ulster noted, in 1909: 'Marrying a skilled shirtmaker is for the casual labourer the equivalent of what marrying an heiress may be in another rank of life.'[5]

Declining opportunities in domestic clothing and textiles were not compensated to any great extent by growing job opportunities in other areas. The Industrial Revolution did open some types of work to women, such as shoe-making where the sewing machine and the division of the process into simple repetitive tasks gave rise to jobs for women as finishers. The printing industry, or rather its book-binding division, marks another industry where women in the nineteenth century penetrated what had previously been a male-dominated trade.

Factory work nevertheless employed only a minority of women. The largest numbers were employed in domestic service, or in agriculture. Opportunities in these areas, however, failed to compensate for the loss of industrial jobs. The proportion of women who were recorded in the census as occupied fell steadily from 29 per cent in 1861 to 19.5 per cent in 1911 and the 1861 level has never been regained.[6]

The census returns, however, are an inadequate representation of the role of women in the economy. Older daughters prematurely removed from school to assist their mothers in the home, or the many unmarried women who acted as unpaid servants to parents or brothers are all excluded from the number of domestic servants.

The economic role of women in agriculture is similarly under-recorded as only women farmers or wage-earning farm labourers are recorded. The sons of farmers were regarded by nineteenth-century census officials as productive workers, farmers' daughters were not. But if men and women are counted on the same basis, approximately one-third of the agricultural workforce in 1871 was in fact women. The largest single group were farmers' wives.[7] Within agriculture it would appear that women's duties became more strictly defined and more restricted in the post-famine period. Women labourers and the wives of labourers and small farmers carried out certain field duties in the pre-famine decades, particularly at times of peak demand such as harvest. The steady decline of tillage in the years after the famine reduced total labouring needs, and in consequence the involvement of women in field work. By the end of the century, women's field work appears to have been restricted to remote parts of the west of Ireland, where tillage still remained of relatively greater importance and where the numbers of available men may have been reduced by seasonal migration. Women in these areas were also used as beasts of burden, carrying turf and stones,[8] something not found in more developed areas at this stage. By the 1930s, the account of Arensberg and Kimball suggests that women's duties were strictly limited to home and farmyard and involved the care of calves, pigs, hens, and dairying duties.[9]

The spread of creameries in the closing decades of the century meant the removal of yet a further process from the domestic to the industrial sphere, where machines and men tended to supplant women. [. . .] The creameries sharply reduced the responsibility of such women with the disappearance of large-scale domestic butter manufacture.

The occupations open to women in post-famine agriculture dwindled as did their marriage prospects. In response the number of women within the agricultural community fell much more sharply than did the number of men. By 1912 they accounted for approximately one-fifth of the total, compared to one-third in 1871.[10] Paradoxically the decline in the number of women was most rapid in the more prosperous areas of the east and south-east. Until the 1950s the proportion of women remained highest on the small farms in the west of Ireland.[11] This suggests that the changing post-famine economy and changing attitudes within the female population are central to this evolution, rather than the harsh economic conditions which undoubtedly prevailed.

With the Industrial Revolution, the prospects of women in urban Ireland to play an active role in the family economy without leaving home were seriously limited, but many managed to make a useful contribution. Once again it is probable that the census underestimates their involvement. Many opened huckster shops or engaged in street selling. Others assisted husbands or fathers in running public houses, grocery shops or other types of retail business. Some did industrial work at home, as part of an outwork system such as the rosary beads industry or in a more informal fashion. The 1891 Census records 13,600 women engaged in dressmaking in Dublin, yet the 1895 Factory and Workshop returns reported only 4,300 women in such employment.[12] The sweated clothing industry was very uncommon in Dublin at this time so that we must conclude that the majority of women not counted by the factory returns worked on their own account, making clothes or doing repairs for neighbours or more prosperous families and trying in the process to eke out a living.

Another source of income which many found compatible with domestic duties was care of lodgers, or work as washerwomen or charwomen. [. . .] Few married women regularly left their home to do outside work unless their husband was disabled or chronically ill and unable to provide a regular wage.

While many women, married and unmarried, contributed substantially to family income, such involvement did not bring any increased status. Because prosperous middle- and upper-class women very consciously contributed neither to family income, nor to household chores, the role of women who worked, particularly those who earned an income, tended to be downgraded; the woman of leisure who devoted herself to accomplishments, or failing that, was a full-time homemaker, became the ideal for many. Such ideals gradually permeated Irish society. By the time of the famine it seems improbable that wives of comfortable farmers would have worked in the fields. By the end of the century, an income-earning wife was probably only acceptable among the lower reaches of the working classes and among farm labourers. [. . .]

The low status accorded to women's work had far-reaching implications. The majority of women worked out of necessity rather than as a means of self-fulfilment. The majority were transitory rather than permanent members of the labour force, working in their youth, or in times of need and returning to home life if circumstances improved. The report on Ulster's outworking clothing industry noted that the number of women working fluctuated sharply, reflecting male earning prospects. In times of recession women flocked to outworking, driving prices down.[13] Women in the workforce proved more vulnerable than men. A higher proportion were young girls; in 1881 over 40 per cent of the Dublin-occupied women were under twenty-five years of age. Many of the remainder were older women, such as widows or those with incapacitated husbands. Their vulnerability and rapid turnover made them difficult to organise. One consequence was that women's work was generally classified as unskilled or semi-skilled, even though many of the tasks which they carried out in linen mills or with the sewing machine required considerable expertise. Pressure of necessity, plus the need to supplement family incomes, as opposed to earning the total income, meant that women frequently took jobs at extremely low wages. By doing this they laid themselves open to exploitation by employers and incurred the wrath of male workers by driving down wages, which further convinced many men that the proper place for women was in the home.

During the nineteenth century women occasionally broke into areas of employment previously the preserve of men, but they did so only as part of a process of declining status and reduced skill level in the job. For women to break into properly organised skilled jobs was utterly impossible. In most of Ireland skilled jobs were under serious threat. Many Dublin trades restricted recruitment of apprentices to sons of skilled workers; the number of skilled jobs in many trades was contracting.[14] Women therefore had no prospects of entry, partly because of scarcity of jobs, but also because their work was becoming synonymous with low status, low wage occupations, precisely the things which the trades wished to avoid.

At the beginning of [the twentieth] century, therefore, the majority of women worked in poorly paid, exclusively female occupations. The largest numbers worked either as domestic servants or in agriculture. Those in industry were almost totally concentrated in textiles, clothing and food, where they held jobs which were exclusive to women. The process of change proved extremely slow. Domestic service, though in decline, remained the largest single source of women's jobs in the Republic of Ireland until the 1950s. [. . .] The women's share of the industrial workforce rose from 20 per cent in 1926 to 22.4 per cent in 1936, largely as the result of the new light industries established under protection, but by 1961 this share had only increased to 23 per cent. Women's industrial jobs continued to have a low skill content and remained concentrated in exclusively female areas. In 1926, 62 per cent of women industrial workers in the Irish Free State were employed in the clothing and textile sectors with a further 23 per cent employed in food, drink and tobacco. By 1961 clothing and textiles still predominated with 54 per cent of the industrial workforce, again followed by food, drink and tobacco with 22 per cent. The only new areas which had emerged were in light pharmaceuticals, such as soap and toiletries and the assembly of light electrical appliances.

The majority of the female workforce remained transitory. In 1926, 86 per cent of the women employed in industry were single and 46 per cent of all workers were under twenty-five years. The workforce in 1971 was even younger, with 63 per cent aged under twenty-five, though the proportion of single women had declined somewhat. [. . .]

Many [. . .] female trade unionists saw married women in the labour force as a social evil brought about by inadequate male wages and felt that the solution was to remove married women from the workforce by paying a higher wage to married, as opposed to single men.[15] This tendency to view women workers, not as individuals but as members of a family unit is expressed as late as 1953, when an equal pay resolution proposed at the annual conference of the TUC (Trades Union Congress) was supported by the IWWU (Irish Women Workers Union) with the rider, that they wished to 'debar the young married woman and the single girl from equal pay'.[16] On the question of equal access to work for single and married women there was a strong belief among rank and file women trade union members that priority should be given to employing widows and single women. [. . .]

The factors which altered the attitudes and aspirations of women in the Irish workforce are complex and can only be vaguely sketched in this paper. Economic growth with the consequent rise in living standards, and the example of international feminist movements are all key influences. Of major importance also is the transformation of traditional Irish society. Many of the changes first became obvious during the 1960s and it is in this decade that the female membership in the trade union movement shows a significant growth and there is a simultaneous increasing interest in equal pay and promotion possibilities.[17] [. . .]

The initiative for these moves, and the rising trade union enrolment came on the whole from women who had a higher level of education and held better-paid jobs. They were frequently white-collar workers, many of them in the public service, and most important, they frequently worked in close proximity to men. Thus the basis existed for analysing comparative pay levels and promotion possibilities, a process which was more difficult in the more traditional areas of female employment.

The expansion of white-collar female employment was a consequence of the improved economic conditions of the 1960s. However there is some evidence to suggest that the attitudes of Irish women had undergone a subtle change prior to this decade, during the much-maligned 1950s. This decade is crucial to any analysis of Irish society as it marks the decay and near collapse of the demographic system established in the post-famine period. For the first time Irish farmers, in large numbers, found themselves without potential wives as women left rural Ireland, particularly the western counties, in unprecedented numbers. Emigration had always been a common experience for Irish rural women, to a greater extent than in any other European country, but until the 1950s there had remained a substantial surplus of potential wives for Irish farmers. During the post-war years, however, Irish women increasingly refused to accept the subservient status and material poverty which was the lot of many farmers' wives, and their emigration threatened the very survival of countless family farms. This same period also marks the disappearance of domestic servants as a regular member of most middle-class homes. Girls chose emigration to England rather than accept this menial occupation. The belated disappearance of domestic servants and the absence of farmers' wives may seem minor changes, but they suggest that many women no longer found traditional Irish living conditions and the status which they afforded tolerable. The rising emigration of young women meant that they were placing their personal interest above those of family and society: a change from a family-based value system to one that gave greater weight to the woman as an individual. Only when women viewed themselves as individuals, rather than as members of a family unit, could they think in terms of careers, equal pay, promotion, or jobs available to all on a basis solely of merit.

[. . . T]he role of women in the workforce and attitudes towards their participation and their overall status are not matters which can be viewed in a vacuum. They closely reflect changes which are taking place in society as a whole. It is also salutary to reflect that the story of Irish women has not been one of continuous progress. There is no evidence of any significant progress for the overwhelming majority of Irish women between 1850 and 1950. A small minority gained access to higher education and challenging careers. The remainder benefited from rising literacy levels, better life expectancy and new technology such as electricity. These were benefits specific not to women as a whole, however, and cannot be seen as marking any advance in women's relative status in society. Changes in Irish politics, such as the achievement of independence and the granting of women's suffrage are equally of little relevance. The relationship between gaining the vote and economic and social gains for women has proved negligible, not only in Ireland, but in all western democracies.

Notes

1   Eric Almquist, 'Mayo and beyond: land, domestic industry and rural transformation in the Irish West', thesis abstract, *Irish Economic and Social History*, V, 1978, p. 71.
2   James McParland, *Statistical Survey of County Donegal*, Dublin, 1832, p. 90.
3   Isaac Weld, *Statistical Survey of County Roscommon*, Dublin, 1832, p. 489.

4   Charles Booth, 'The occupations of the people of Ireland', in W. P. Coyne (ed.), *Ireland Industrial and Agricultural*, Dublin, 1902.

5   M. H. Irwin, *Home Working in Ireland, Report of an Inquiry with an Introductory Sketch of the Anti-Sweating Movement*, Belfast, 1909.

6   Irish Transport and General Workers' Union (ITGWU), *Equality for Women*, Dublin, 1980, p. 6. The ITGWU analysis is based on the 1977 Labour Force Survey, CSO, Dublin, and shows that 288,300 women work in the Republic, comprising 28 per cent of the total workforce. The EEC average is 36 per cent.

7   Wives ranged from approximately 40 per cent of women in agriculture in the various counties of Leinster to 75 per cent in Leitrim and Mayo.

8   Charles R. Browne, 'The ethnography of Garumna and Lettermullen', *Proceedings of the Royal Irish Academy*, XXI, 1898–1900, pp. 251–2.

9   Conrad Arensberg and Solon T. Kimball, *Family and Community in Ireland*, Harvard, 1940, pp. 48–9.

10 This is based on calculations comparing the 1871 Census returns, the only ones to give a full profile of women in agriculture, with the *1912 Agricultural Statistics*, which provide the next complete figures for women in agriculture. A full analysis of these figures was presented in my paper 'Women in Irish agriculture', read to the Graduate Seminar in Economic and Social History, Trinity College, Dublin, November, 1980.

11 D. Hannan, *Displacement and Development in Irish Rural Community*, ESRI Paper, no. 96, Dublin, 1979, p. 48.

12 Annual return of persons employed in factories and workshops, 1895, *Annual Report of the Chief Inspector of Factories and Workshops for the Year 1896–1897*, C8561, pp. 153–340.

13 Irwin, *Home Working*.

14 B. McDonnell, 'The Dublin Labour Movement, 1894–1907', Ph.D. thesis, National University of Ireland, University College, Dublin, 1979, p. 57.

15 For greater detail on these issues see Mary E. Daly, 'Women, work and trade unionism', in Margaret MacCurtain and Donncha O'Corrain (eds), *Women in Irish Society: The Historical Dimension*, Dublin, 1978.

16 *ITUC Annual Report, 1953–4*.

17 It could be argued that the extension of female membership was part of a general drive by white-collar unions, reflecting their growing militancy and awareness. The question of women's participation in their trade union, as opposed to their simple membership, is a point of gathering debate both at ICTU (Irish Congress of Trade Unions) and constituent union level, see ITGWU, *Equality for Women*, Part Two.

Chapter 27

Maria Luddy

■ from **CONCLUSION** in *Women and Philanthropy in Nineteenth-Century Ireland*, Cambridge, 1995, pp. 214–18

WHETHER IT WAS HOUSE VISITATION, instituting an orphanage or school, working in prisons, refuges or workhouses, raising money or simply giving advice, philanthropy became the principal, if largely unpaid, occupation of a great number of middle-class Irish women in the nineteenth century. Motivated by Christian duty, women, regardless of their denominational status, made a significant contribution to the perception of poverty and the poor in Irish society. Through their charitable work they enhanced and expanded the social role of women and made social work a legitimate occupation for them. Ultimately, some of these women claimed that the importance of their contribution earned them the right to take part in the political process. Voluntaryism not [only] allowed women to exercise their religious and moral duty to society, it also gave them the opportunity to shape the provision and direction of philanthropic enterprise and to guide it into those areas which they considered to be of major importance. As a consequence charitable provision for women and children developed on a much broader scale than that provided for men. Women philanthropists believed implicitly in the moral and spiritual superiority of women. It was, many of them believed, principally through work by women, with women, that the social and moral regeneration of society could be attained.

The myriad of philanthropic associations, societies and institutions established by women catered for specific needs and had limited objectives. The narrowness of their operations was determined by practical issues, primarily by their financial solvency. Few of these organisations dispensed charity unconditionally and one of the major concerns of women philanthropists was to channel relief to the 'deserving poor'. In many cases they initiated a system of selection in order to guarantee 'worthiness' and since many of the relief agencies provided work for their inmates they not only justified the existence of the charity by making the inmates 'deserving', in the sense that they worked for their keep, but also at the same time helped to place the charity on a sound financial footing. The majority of women's voluntary organisations not only embraced narrow goals, but remained localised and rarely developed any network of similar societies to extend their function. All of the lay penitent asylums, for example, were separately managed by committees which appear to have had few links regarding membership, nor do the various committees appear to have communicated with each other regarding advice on management or policy. Similarly the myriad of clothing, Bible and refuge organisations were also quite distinct and operated separately.

Many philanthropic societies were also exclusivist. Membership was determined by social background but to a greater extent by religious affiliation. Philanthropic effort was organised on distinct religious grounds and this proved to be both a cohesive and divisive force in regard to those institutions established by women. There is almost no evidence of any interaction between lay Catholic women or female religious with their Protestant sisters. Exceptionally, one author writing in 1875 notes that Catholic women began the visitation of the sick in an unnamed workhouse, when a Protestant woman, who had already initiated a visitation scheme for Protestant inmates, asked them to do so.[1] The elements of evangelicalism and proselytism, which were found in many charitable organisations, caused tensions between various organisations and this was particularly true of those societies which looked after orphaned or destitute children.

The denominational basis of many charitable societies with similar objectives prevented women from uniting to create larger, more extensive and perhaps more efficient organisations. Religious bias inhibited women from pooling their financial resources and also from building upon each other's experiences as charity workers. Some form of network appears evident between organisations which were run by particular denominations. Thus children and 'fallen women' were often referred from one charity to another, but referrals were never made across the religious divide. In the Catholic sphere, female religious were separated from lay women by being allowed almost the sole right to provide charitable services. Female religious communities controlled a vast network of welfare organisations. They built the infrastructure of social welfare which bound the people to the Church and the Church to the people. It is obvious that the Catholic hierarchy offered fewer opportunities for lay women to organise and women in lay organisations were at numerous disadvantages when compared to the freedom allowed nuns, especially in gaining entrance to public institutions. It may be that convents, which were so successful in attracting entrants because they allowed for a practical expression of religious commitment, actually damaged the position of women in society by undertaking work based on vocation rather than a committed desire to alter the position of women in society. Nuns, in their work, exemplified the ideal image of women. They devoted themselves, without complaint, to meeting the needs of others. Although they brought many improvements to the institutions they ran, for example by reforming the nursing care provided in workhouse hospitals, it was a reform brought about by example rather than a determination to ensure that public officials or government provide support for such reform.

The religious basis of many charitable societies also hindered the development of a critique of the social origins of poverty and destitution. Religion, while it gave many women the impetus to organise voluntary societies, also in many cases defined the limits of their approach. Those societies concerned with moral reform, the penitent asylums or criminal refuges, sought to change values by example and persuasion and a belief in the possibility of spiritual regeneration. Even though the women who ran these benevolent societies sought the moral reform of their inmates they were in effect remoulding the 'sinner' rather than questioning or eradicating those conditions which gave rise to the 'sin'. Refuges for the destitute and penitent asylums were offering institutional solutions to social problems, as were the reformatories and industrial schools established for delinquent children after mid-century. Within these institutions, lay and religious women attempted to alter the social, moral and often religious behaviour of their charges. The screen of philanthropy gave them the moral authority to control those who sought their aid. For the majority of women philanthropists the perpetuation of class differences was an implicit part of their work. They were primarily serving their own class interests.

Two traditions of philanthropic activity are discernible, a benevolent and a reformist one. The reformist tradition was a continuation of the benevolent tradition and differed from it in the level of public and political action which women were willing to undertake rather than in a radical shift in philosophy or perception of women's role in society. It is also significant that the reformist tradition owed its existence, principally, to Quaker and Nonconformist women. Reformist societies such as the Dublin Aid Committee (later the National Society for the Prevention of Cruelty to Children) and the Philanthropic Reform Association, for example, were organised by committees of men and women. In these organisations women formed alliances with men in attempting to ensure that the state take responsibility in legislating for change, either in workhouse conditions, or with regard to the protection of children. Women in reformist societies were most likely to become involved in the suffrage issue and to fight for the right to sit as poor law guardians. For many of these women the vote, at local or national level, was intended to provide the most direct means to initiate philanthropic and social change. The acquisition of the vote was also essentially the means for middle-class women to extend their own individual rights.

Philanthropic societies offered women a sense of identity and community, whether on a small scale, as in the lay societies, or as reflected in the larger communities of female religious who engaged in charitable activities. Such societies gave women a sense of purpose and achievement and allowed them to play a role in expressing their concern for the less fortunate in society. Altruism certainly played a major role in female philanthropy but women within charitable organisations also exerted considerable power on a personal basis. The multiplicity of voluntary associations established by women reflects a desire on the part of women for autonomy. From the beginnings of voluntary service women were not content to remain as mere auxiliaries to male-run societies. Women also gained a number of practical skills from organising charitable societies. Organising committees, raising funds, keeping accounts, writing annual reports, and, in reformist societies, petitioning local and central authorities, proved women to be capable of successful organisation. Philanthropic involvement also allowed some women, like their British and American counterparts, to develop professional careers in social work. It further granted them some political influence, especially in organisations like the Philanthropic Reform Association. Charitable involvement did not always have positive outcomes. In Ireland the nature of nineteenth-century philanthropy was sectarian, reflecting the sectarianism which existed in society itself. Women's work in philanthropy, particularly their work with children, helped to entrench this sectarianism further.

Many changes occurred over the nineteenth century which altered the position of women in society. Some of these changes were due to the changing expectations of women brought about through improved educational and work opportunities. Women had initiated many of these changes themselves, challenging those systems which attempted to control and confine them. Those who benefited most from women's philanthropic activities in this respect were the middle- and upper-class women who organised the societies. For the poor they aided, no alteration in the social or class systems was advocated. For a small number of philanthropic women their involvement in charity work had a politicising effect. They became passionate and articulate reformers of a political and social system which they successfully challenged and altered over the century. The last half of the nineteenth century was, arguably, the time of greatest change in the lives of middle- and upper-class women. The expansion of female religious congregations altered the expectations of Catholic women who decided to become nuns. Lay Catholic women were also affected by these changes, and while opportunities were expanding for nuns they were, ironically, contracting for lay Catholic women. Women of other religious denominations found their voices to speak against injustice, to demonstrate publicly against the double standard of sexual morality and to confront the inequalities which existed towards women in society. Because of women's action these injustices were gradually altered. Women's involvement in philanthropy brought many of them to an awareness of injustice and also to the belief that only formal political power would enable them to make the changes necessary to create a more just, though not necessarily more equal, society for everyone. Many of these hopes for change were dashed by the political realities of early twentieth-century Ireland, which divided women just as much as religion had in the nineteenth century.

Note

1   Anon., 'Rounds of visits', *The Irish Monthly*, 3, 1887, p. 80.

Chapter 28

Joanna Bourke

■ from 'THE BEST OF ALL HOME RULERS':
THE ECONOMIC POWER OF WOMEN IN IRELAND,
1880–1914, *Irish Economic and Social History*, XVIII,
1991, pp. 34–47

THIS ARTICLE EXAMINES THE ECONOMIC power of rural women in Ireland during the late nineteenth and early twentieth centuries. Historians concerned with the position of Irish women have concluded that powerlessness was characteristic of women's lives. [. . .] Should this story of female impotence be accepted? Irish women have been portrayed as progressively forfeiting whatever power they may have inherited from earlier times. This loss of power has been linked to changes in female labour: the movement of women into the unwaged domestic sphere allegedly disarmed them. As 'dependents', performing housework, they were rendered powerless. This portrayal of female powerlessness as housewives may serve an important ideological function but it does not reflect the reality of the lives of those women choosing in this period to become full-time houseworkers. For these women, patriarchy was not the problem and threats to the individual woman's power were liable to come from other sources. [. . .]

In the last half of the nineteenth century, the position of women within the paid labour markets in Ireland deteriorated. Married women were increasingly dependent on the husband's wage. Economic opportunities for unmarried women collapsed. Except during periods of peak agricultural demand, the labour of rural women in the fields was increasingly not required.

According to the censuses, from the last few decades of the nineteenth century to 1911, paid employment for men remained stable, in contrast to female employment, which was rapidly declining. In 1861, 846,000 women in Ireland were employed; 815,000 were employed by 1881, dropping further to 550,000 by 1901. By 1911, only 430,000 women were employed. In 1891, 27 per cent of women in Ireland were said to be engaged in employment; declining to less than 19 per cent within twenty years. The number of female agricultural labourers dropped from 27,000 in 1891 to just over 5,000 by 1911. Eighty per cent of all female workers were found in ten occupations. In 1891, 22 per cent of all men were working in occupations where not one woman was employed; by 1911,

34 per cent of all men were working in occupations where not one woman was employed.

[. . . W]hat is overlooked is the booming economic importance of female labour in another sector of the economy: the household. There are two sides to this. First, in communities experiencing a contraction of employment, women might choose to maximise their possible economic contribution by focusing their energies into unwaged domestic work. Second, and more significant, there was simply more housework to do. The agricultural changes released capital (as well as labour), and investment in housing, furniture, diet and household technologies increased the amount of housework that had to be performed. The release of child labour from agriculture and the introduction of new forms of child care also meant more work for women within the home.[1] Economic growth changed the material and labour requirements of the home. [. . .] It is difficult to estimate the number of waged and unwaged houseworkers in Ireland. Using my estimate of the number of houseworkers in Ireland, and looking only at full-time workers, in 1861 nearly 56 per cent of women doing housework were unwaged: that is, they were houseworkers. This percentage increased to over 65 per cent by 1881, then rose to 78 per cent in 1891. In 1901, 81 per cent of women doing housework were houseworkers. This had increased further to 85 per cent by 1911.[2]

[. . .] Why were women choosing housework? What is striking is the fact that many women thought that housework was a good – even the best – option. Notions of false consciousness can be dismissed and there is no reason to assume that women were more altruistic than men. The chance of finding employment as an agricultural labourer does not seem to have caused rural women any great pleasure in this period. Offers of employment in paid domestic service were greeted with weary sighs. Merely the absence of a wage did not cause young women accustomed to working for free on the family plot to purse their lips. The intensification of the two spheres of labour was acceptable to women in this period because it maximised their power. This is not to argue that the search for economic power was what motivated women moving into full-time housework, rather that it was not against their interests to make the move. There was a price to pay for the movement of large numbers of women into full-time housework; but the benefits were perceived as being cheap at the price. [. . .]

It must be admitted that the alternatives to housework were often unattractive. Working for an exacting mistress or a grumpy overlord does not automatically confer a good deal of self-esteem on a person. Wages may increase female power, widen their number of choices and provide access to status outside the family. The extent to which this actually did occur is doubtful: female employment options in rural Ireland were customarily based on the social standing of the male 'head' and opportunities to move beyond this depended more on geographical mobility than on the labour market.

At the same time, it must be stressed that women were not moved to toil within the home through reading a stirring tract on blissful domesticity. It was not simply a matter of domestic ideology. After all, waged domestic service was being rejected wholeheartedly, precisely because it did not confer the benefits of unwaged domestic service. In 1911, 72,000 fewer women worked as indoor domestic servants than in 1891. [. . .]

In contrast, the housewife controlled not only her time, but also a large chunk of the household money. Her control over expenditure on food was crucial to her power. Since around 70 per cent of the money being spent by the household was spent on food, the ability of a housewife to cite the rise and fall of food prices and the possible location of bargains was important.

Women were able to increase their power within the household in this period. Power has a lot to do with the replaceability and dispensability of the skills or resources of individuals. The refusal of a wife to cook a meal, apparently trivial, can be an important mechanism by which to enforce decision-making. It is no coincidence that a large number of stories focus on the wife refusing to continue performing domestic labour because she is not appreciated sufficiently – and exchanging the tasks with her husband: in these stories, his work in the fields is found to be replaceable while he (predictably) makes a mess in the home.

It is never enough, though, simply to be appreciated. Men had to be increasingly excluded from the higher levels of domestic management. Houseworkers in Ireland (and England) were becoming very conscious of the need to increase the skill component of their work. They proposed to do this through education in housework. [. . .] Education in housewifery was necessary in order to dispel the idea that housework was 'natural' and therefore simple. Promoters of domestic education declared that 'womanhood' was 'a profession for which very careful training is required [. . .] a woman wants something more than her sex to qualify her for her profession'.[3]

Hundreds of thousands of women attended the courses which were established in every district.[4] The Congested Districts Board, the Department of Agriculture and Technical Instruction, and the Irish Agricultural Organization Society all instituted education in housewifery. One by one, their classes in lace-making, knitting, poultry, and butter-making were converted into domestic education classes. Women supported this move and attended in ever-increasing numbers. The most important classes were those set up by the Board of National Education. From the early years of the 1890s, the Board employed itinerant teachers in cookery and housework. By 1900, cookery and laundry were a recognised and examined part of the curriculum and pressure came to be exerted on all schools to teach domestic skills to the students. Cookery was popular amongst the students and there was widespread comment that the classes increased enrolments and attendance of girls at school.[5]

Education in housework was an exclusion tactic. Housework became more specialised and skilled: as the housewife took over these skills, the male 'head of the family' was gradually excluded. Thus the bargaining power of women was enhanced. The exclusion of men was not based merely on biological or psychological differences between men and women. It was an exclusion based more on the need of women to ensure their underlying eminence within the household. While none of the mainstream domestic classes included men, classes in cookery established for men working on ships and boats caused no comment. Men were able to learn domestic skills, but only in contexts which did not threaten the predominance of women within the home.

[. . .] One crucial component is missing: power is not fixed, and it fluctuates over the life-cycle. For many houseworkers, power increased with age, peaking during the child-rearing period, then declining with physical weakness. Each of these stages, however, must be examined more closely.

The young unmarried houseworker was in the worst position. Her power was extremely limited. Over and over again we hear of mothers excluding their grown-up daughters from housework. [. . .] For the young unmarried woman whose chances of either snatching the household reins from her mother or of establishing a household of her own were slim, emigration was an option. Emigration was not necessarily the 'best choice': many young women found that they could express a satisfactory level of control over their own and other people's lives by performing housework for unmarried or widowed male relatives. The unmarried woman unable to become a substitute wife for a relative might do better to emigrate instead of attempting to find paid employment within Ireland. Employment lowered their status.[6] Their choices, as we have already noted, were increasingly limited. Because their pay was low, they were liable to have to live within another house-hold and provide domestic services to help pay for their keep. The sensible woman recognised that paid employment simply doubled her exploitation and was exhausting.

The married woman's power depended to some extent on whether her husband or his father held the authority in the household. A wife living within a household headed by her husband could wield some influence in her early married years. [. . .] A wife in the unfortunate position of living within a household headed by a relative could wield little power until her husband gained power, or until she could displace the mother-in-law.

The wife had the potential to produce the most precious product on the market: labour power. With the birth of children, a wife gained power rapidly. Furthermore, she controlled the labour power of both her male and female children until they reached a certain age; it was the mother who directed the children to run to the shop, fetch water and sweep the floor. The effect of increased dependency of children (partially a result of declining employment opportunities for the young and partly due to increased pressure for regular school attendance) was to reduce the immediate value of children to the household, while simultaneously increasing their long term value for the housewife. The more intensive child care being given to children cemented her influence over them. Protracted childhoods in households where the mother was the main bestower of child-love and care, and where the father was absent for much of the day, potentially provided the mother with immense power.

Furthermore, children cemented the economic contract between the couple. The rights of a woman to the property of her husband's farm was established by the birth of children. Thus there was an acute loss of economic power and security if a woman remained childless.[7] If she were childless and made a widow, she might be forced to leave the farm, the collateral kin of the dead simply returning the cash equivalent of her dowry. Once she had children, her power increased dramatically. If widowed, she was allowed to hold the land in trust for her husband's heirs. Male children were an immensely important long-term invest-ment for married women. As the probability of women living to old age improved, and age of marriage for both men and women retreated, it became increasingly likely that it was the widow (rather than the married couple or the widower) who would be able to decide what would happen to the dowry brought in by the son's wife.

A decline of power was liable to be experienced by a woman in her old age. First, there was the inability to perform many of the economic tasks that had earned her power. Second, the older woman had invested a lot of time and energy in securing the loyalty of her son: the young bride was a serious threat. Third, there was the arrival of the daughter-in-law. [. . .] However, daughters were preferred to daughter-in-laws if physical incapacity rendered it necessary for the elderly mother to hand over the reins of power to some other houseworker. No wonder old age was often a painful period: as Peig Sayers says when it became clear that a daughter-in-law would be brought in: 'My mother was in very low spirits'.[8] [. . .]

The elderly widow who had handed over the keys to the parlour may have been in a stronger power position than the elderly widower who had signed over the land. Elderly women remained productive by performing those domestic tasks from which elderly men were increasingly excluded. [. . .] Indeed, elderly men were more liable to end up in workhouses than elderly women. Seven per cent of all men over the age of sixty-five years were living in workhouses in 1911, compared to 4 per cent of elderly women. [. . .]

What did unmarried, unemployed and so-called 'dependent' women have to gain in a country where a popular female route to power was through house-keeping? [. . .] Most of these women were the unmarried daughters or sisters of the 'head of the family'. Irish households provided adequate substitutes for the marital bed and counting house. The unmarried houseworker's labour as a substitute farm-wife was crucial to the economic survival of the household. Less than 5 per cent of households could do without it. Unmarried men always needed a woman – a *relative* – to perform those activities men seem incapable of providing for themselves: washing clothes, sorting socks, baking cakes and so on. A large number of women chose not to emigrate precisely because Irish society provided powerful positions for women, even if they did not marry or earn a wage. Indeed, women in Ireland considered themselves more powerful within their sphere than houseworkers in other countries. A man simply called Frank was attacked by a woman with the words:

> You mistake the word wife for slave. I am afraid it would be unnec-
> essary to have the words 'for better' in your marriage ceremony, but
> there is very little probability of your ever being married unless to an
> Australian May, or some other darkie who is not very particular.[9]

[. . .] The increased sexual division of labour was an attempt to minimise risk of conflict and powerlessness. The returns in terms of power may not have been earth-shattering. If a woman wanted higher possible returns, accompanied with a higher risk of absolute failure, she could emigrate and try her hand in the American, Canadian or Australian employment and marriage markets. But, for many women, the lower-risk route to power was more than sufficient. Tombstones over the country spell out the words: 'Rest in Peace, my Darling Wife, the Best of all Home Rulers.'

Notes

1   In this paper, I can only provide a brief sketch of these changes. The chief changes occurred in the areas of food, housing, child care, health requirements, clothing, fuel, care of the elderly, shopping and washing. I trace these rapid changes in 'Women working: the domestic labour market in Ireland, 1890–1914', *Journal of Interdisciplinary History*, winter, 1991.

2   The estimate of houseworkers was made on the following assumptions: (1) only women between the ages of twenty and sixty-five years do housework; (2) women not designated an occupation in the census were full-time houseworkers; (3) every 'unoccupied' women doing full-time housework relieved an 'occupied' women from doing housework; (4) 'occupied' women who do not have an 'unoccupied' woman to substitute for her labour do half the housework of 'unoccupied' women; (5) the presence of a domestic servant in the household supplements rather than substitutes for the work of at least one other houseworker. [. . .]

3   'Notes of the week: fresh aid for rural reformers', *Irish Homestead*, 3 December 1910, p. 992, speech at the meeting of the United Irishwomen. [. . .]

4   For a further description and discussion of these classes, see my 'The health caravan: female labour and domestic education in rural Ireland, 1890–1914', *Éire-Ireland*, XXIV, winter 1989, pp. 21–38.

5   Appendix to the *Seventy-Fifth Report of the Commissioners of National Education in Ireland, School Year, 1909–1909, Section One: General Report of the State of National Education by Inspectors and Others*, House of Commons Papers, 1910, xxv, p. 78 [. . .]

6   See my *Husbandry to Housewifery: Women, Economic Change and Housework in Ireland, 1890–1914*, Oxford, 1993 [. . .]

7   For an example, see Canon P. A. Sheehan, *Glenanaar. A Story of Irish Life*, New York, 1905, p. 26 [. . .]

8   Peig Sayers, *An Old Woman's Reflections*, translated by Seamus Ennis, Oxford, 1962, p. 24.

9   Letter from 'Insistioge', 'The ideal girl and the ideal man', *Ireland's Own*, 25 February 1903, p. 18.

Chapter 29

Anne O'Dowd

■ from WOMEN IN RURAL IRELAND IN THE
NINETEENTH AND EARLY TWENTIETH
CENTURIES: HOW THE DAUGHTERS, WIVES AND
SISTERS OF SMALL FARMERS AND LANDLESS
LABOURERS FARED, *Rural History*, 5/2, 1994, pp. 171–83

THE SURGE IN WRITING BY AND ABOUT women in recent decades in Ireland is contributing to a good understanding of the place of women in Irish society. [. . .] It is research which shows that women had to be exceptionally good at their chosen or allotted role in life in order to be recognised and noted, or had to be capable and highly efficient at tasks ordinarily and traditionally done by men. This is especially true of the women who were the wives, sisters and mothers of the labourers and small farmers of nineteenth-century Ireland [. . .]

A questionnaire was circulated by the Department of Irish Folklore in University College Dublin in the 1950s, at a time when there were both recent memories and many actual cases of women who were still making a very significant contribution to the work on the land, as distinct from improving the family's level of comfort within the home. From the replies to the questionnaire which came from all over Ireland, women certainly did their share, especially in emergencies. They carried loads on their backs and on their heads, they bound oats, saved hay, weeded, thinned, cut seed potatoes, planted and picked potatoes, pitched sheaves, stacked corn, footed and drew out turf, drew seaweed and kelp from the shore to dry land, pounded furze for feed for animals, shaped mud turf, spread and tied flax, picked mussels, baited lines and gutted fish. In short, their work was arduous and back-breaking, involving, it is suggested, much more bending and stooping than their male co-workers in the field or on the shore, and in nearly all of the above-mentioned tasks the women were helping men in what was essentially defined as men's work. The traditional female work role was centred nearer the home, and it was in the yard and the house that exclusively female tasks – caring for the family, dairying and rearing pigs and hens – were to be found. Just as women may have been excluded from what were perceived as 'manly' tasks, so also were men 'prohibited', by society's collective attitude and convention, from 'women's' work. In many places men would not milk cows, and hiring arrangements were made on the specific understanding that milking cows was not included in the bargain. Some men, it is said, were ashamed even to handle eggs, and nicknames and derogatory phrases assisted to check men's possible interference. Names such as Cissy, Sheila, Judy and Betty, etc. have been recorded from around the country for men who worked with hens, and they were described as misers, odd and tyrannical and the 'butt of the neighbours' if they interfered with the profits derived from the sale of hens and their eggs. It is the money which is the main issue here, for the profits were for the woman to spend as she wished. It was invariably spent on the household and through time began to be seen as lucky, especially if used in card playing, as part of an investment, or to buy raffle tickets.[1]

The introduction of creameries to the Irish countryside at the end of the 1880s effectively and swiftly removed milking and butter-making from the female environment of the home to a factory milieu run and managed by men. This move was severely criticised for many years, especially in Munster, the dominant province in creamery development, as it removed butter-making from women and took traditional work away from girls, especially in west Cork and Kerry, who had been employed as dairymaids on farms in Limerick and Tipperary. When the Irish Agricultural Organisation Society campaigned for the proper instruction in poultry keeping and egg marketing in the 1890s, the bitter pill of the creamery experience of the previous decade was not forgotten. Women fought to hold on to the profits from the sale of eggs and would not allow them and their business to become swallowed in the male affairs of the creamery. In effect, egg co-operatives were not a success and women managed, despite the Agricultural Produce Eggs Act of 1924, to maintain control of the production of eggs, which could then be used to barter for groceries, as late as the 1950s.[2]

The Congested Districts' Board (CDB) was set up at the end of the nineteenth century, as a form of development board to assist so-called congested areas, which stretched along the west coast from Donegal in the north to Cork and Kerry in the south. The baseline reports produced by the CDB contain the results of investigations by board inspectors, and the estimated expenditure and cash income tables [. . .] leave no doubt that women's contribution to these communities was highly significant.[3] [. . .]

Teelin, Killybegs and Tory are all fishing communities in which women played an active and important role. If they were prohibited by tradition from working on the boats, they did work baiting the lines, sorting, gutting, curing and drying the catch, cleaning the nets and lines for storage and, in some communities, marketing and selling the fish and working in fish curing stations. In Teelin, women's work contributed the profit from eggs, the pig, knitting and sprigging. Women also prepared the wool for the weaver who produced the flannel cloth noted in the budget, and they helped their menfolk at fishing. Scouring and finishing the cloth prior to selling was largely done by women, but they were often assisted by men, so that the profit from the sale of the cloth cannot be included as an exclusively female contribution. For our purposes here, we will reckon the female contribution as 75 per cent of the work involved in producing the finished cloth. Women's contribution to the fishing industry in these fishing communities made up at least £12. 6s. 3d. of the profits of the household income. Comparable figures for Killybegs and Tory might be calculated at £22. 14s. 10d. and £13. ls. 8d. The figures are, of course, only rough estimates because they are based on estimated receipts, and because women's work in farming activities, turf saving and kelp making are here considered to be worth only a third of that of men. Considering the amount of time spent by men in their fishing boats, women's contributions may have been a great deal more. The Donegal Congested Districts must also be noted for the considerable income earned by women at the home industries of sprigging (mentioned in four Congested Districts), cloth preparation (mentioned in eight Congested Districts) and knitting (mentioned in five Congested Districts.)

In the Congested Districts of County Mayo especially, another factor enters any discussion on the contribution by women as daughters and spouses living on small to medium-sized holdings in the nineteenth century. Attempts to eke out a satisfactory living on the holding proved an impossible task for many thousands who annually migrated to other parts of Ireland, and to farms in England and Scotland to earn enough money to pay the rent. The numbers of Irish migratory labourers travelling to Great Britain probably reached a peak in the 1860s when there were an estimated 100,000 people making the annual journey. In the early years of the nineteenth century the established pattern was for the whole family to make an exodus from the home for the summer months – the men to find work and the women to beg or enter asylums for refuge and shelter, a pattern which had already been established in at least the seventeenth century. By the middle of the nineteenth century the women begged less and began either to work as seasonal workers themselves or to stay at home to mind the holding. [. . .]

Some of the CDB's inspectors noted the enormous economic contribution by women at the end of the nineteenth century. This contribution covered the full round of the agricultural year: assisting in the springtime; getting the potato and oat crops in the ground before the men left for the seasonal work; cutting and saving turf and reaping, when necessary, in September before the men's return. More real evidence of their contribution at this time can be seen when we look at the percentage of family income derived from seasonal earnings. Achill Island off the coast of Mayo was the home of great numbers of potato pickers who travelled annually to the potato fields of Scotland. Men, women and children left the island for up to six months of each year, from May to September, causing witnesses to the Bessborough Commission in the 1870s to comment: 'It's the only place I know where they go off and lock the doors', and 'they simply pay for these houses as lodgings for the winter'.[4]

In the 1890s, 73 per cent of the cash income from an Achill family in ordinary circumstances was from migratory earnings: £9 earned by the man of the house, another £9 by his son and £6 by his daughter. A further £6 was contributed from the profit of the sale of eggs and a pig. However, for many other families in Congested Districts in Mayo, it was a tradition for only the man to leave on an annual work journey. In thirteen of the remaining eighteen Mayo Congested Districts, which account for most of the county, more than one-fifth (the percentages ranged from 23 per cent to 52 per cent) of the family income was derived from migratory earnings. In these Congested Districts the higher the percentage the longer the period spent by the man away from home, and the greater the load of farm work done by the woman. In nearly all the cases cited, this involved looking after cattle, sheep, potato and oat crops, in addition to the more traditional women's work of tending pigs and poultry.

No figures can show the non-monetary contributions, by both men and women, to the household. These would have included primarily the use of natural materials found in the environment to make household furnishings, e.g. straw for seats, mats and mattresses and a variety of sally and osier rods to make an array of baskets. Straw and rushes were used to make horse and donkey collars and many materials including straw, hay, rushes, bog wood, horsehair, sally rod and heather were used to make ropes. Men were traditionally basket- and rope-makers, but the use of materials available on the farm to produce homely comforts was the work of women. They made most of the family's clothes and bedding from wool and linen and fed the family from home produce, particularly milk, oats and potatoes. With both limited ingredients and accoutrements the woman of the house, as the cook, managed to produce an extraordinary array of food. Most cooking was done over the open fire – boiling in a pot or skillet, roasting on tongs or a grid iron and baking in a pot oven. From potatoes alone, for example, boiled potatoes, potato bread, stampy, colcannon and boxty were made. Bread was made from quern-ground and mill-ground meal; wheaten and oaten being the most popular, but rye, barley and Indian-meal bread were also eaten. The woman as housewife and cook had to deal with contingencies as they arose. When there was a shortage of potatoes at the end of spring and the beginning of summer, various forms of porridge, including brose, *praiseach*, *leite* and stirabout were made from yellow meal and oatmeal. When there was a shortage of milk for making soda bread, a supply of sour flour or *plúr géar* was made up from flour, salt and the water from boiled potatoes. When there was a shortage of milk to drink, a concoction known as bull's milk was made from oatenmeal and water left steeping in a crock for up to two weeks. The liquid so produced was a refreshing drink, especially in hot weather.

Condiment, or what was frequently known as *annlan* or dip, for potatoes, consisted of a variety of ingredients. It might have been a piece of boiled meat, fish or cabbage; the gruel which remained from boiling oaten dumplings with salt or sugar; thin porridge with butter, pepper and onions; or boiling water with some flour and an onion for taste. The furnishings in the homes were sparse and limited and often consisted of no more than a table, one or two chairs, straw seats and a dresser or clevvy in the kitchen and roughly made beds in the one or two bedrooms. It has been suggested that as a result women had very little cleaning to do in the house. Apart from providing shelter for adults and children, the dwelling might also have housed two cows tethered at one end of the kitchen, two goats tethered at the side of the kitchen and several hens and some geese. In this context consider the following reminiscences from two women who lived in different parts of the country. The first excerpt is from a recording in Irish made in 1939 by Padraic Bairéad of Brigid Ó Maolfhábhaill (from the parish of Kilmore, Erris, Co. Mayo . . .)

> Then when people got up in the morning first they had to prepare the fire and when they finished breakfast the woman of the house or her daughter had to take out the ashes. When they had that much done, they would put down a good turf fire again as they had to boil potatoes for pigs and hens. After doing that much, the woman of the house

took her heather brush and she would sweep the floor, under the bed and table and every other corner in the house. [. . .] The dung produced by the cows, calves and horse had to be taken out of the house after that. The woman of the house then got her grape and shovel and she had to take out that much dirt to the manure heap that used to be a couple of feet from the door. Indeed the house used to be all covered and drowned but when she had this much done she would put a good coating of sand on the floor to dry it again. [. . .][5]

Peig Sayers is the most renowned of Irish story-tellers and she related the following to Seosamh Ó Dálaigh, the folklore collector, in 1951 when she was seventy-nine years of age and living in Baile Bhíocáire, Dún Chaoin, County Kerry [. . .]

The houses were small and narrow and there was a houseful of people in them and it is no wonder if there were insects and fleas on the people in the houses. There were housewives who were diligent in their efforts to keep the houses and beds clean, but there were some who made no effort so that there were insects and nits in the children's heads and on the people's clothes. [. . .]

Long ago the floors got very little brushing when a horse was tethered at one end of the kitchen and perhaps two calves tethered to the side walls of the house [. . .] When the animals were put out in the summer, the houses were cleaned and lime was put on the floor and the house-wife was in better charge. The floor was swept a couple of times daily and bright dry sand from the strand was spread on it. The walls were cleaned of dirt and they were whitened with lime. When there was a fine sunny day the feather mattresses and the straw from the beds were put out and the boards of the beds were taken to the river and washed. The bedclothes were also spread out in the sun every fine day in the summer. The loft and the back loft were also to be cleaned and tidied as also were the rafters.

Whenever it was necessary clothes were washed, but there was a big wash once a fortnight, but when the people were working with seaweed and with fish they had to wash their clothes once a week because the salt would be in their clothes. Monday was generally wash day because they changed their clothes every Sunday. [. . .][6]

[. . .] In many areas of the country, improvements to make housework less burden-some and laborious were only introduced when rural houses were electrified in the 1940s, 1950s and 1960s.[7] While much of the hard work was taken out of housework with electricity and running water supplies, its load actually increased with the higher standards of cleanliness and comfort demanded by changing customs. By Peig's time it was possible to buy soap, and from the evidence in the CDB budgets small farmers did expend part of their income on soap purchases. There is some evidence, however, that wood ashes were still being used at this time to clean clothes, especially those which were particularly soiled. It was the woman's work to make the household's supply of soap from ashes and if a cash profit was made from its sale it was hers to spend.[8] It was also her responsibility to make the necessary supplies of starch from potatoes and she provided the artificial light for the house in the form of rush lights and tallow candles and such requisites as polish from soot and goose fat or seal oil, and scouring emollient for cloth finishing from the urine collected from family members.[9]

The most important part of work connected with the house which the woman both made and had to uphold was its reputation. It was her responsibility to see that the myriad of customs and beliefs connected with the house was observed. [. . .] Countless such beliefs and customs were observed, but the last word here is Peig's and only further research on the contribution of women as wives, daughters and sisters of small farmers and labourers in rural Ireland will test the veracity of her words:

> *Dá feabhas fear tí agus dá croíúla má bhíonn bean tighe dhoicheallach aige túrfaí sí dro-ainm air féin agus ar an dtig ach dá olcas é fear tí túrfaig bean mhaith tí dea-cháil air.*[10]

(However good and cheerful the man of the house is, if the woman of the house is churlish to him she will give him and the house a bad name, but however bad the man is, a good housewife will give him a good reputation.)

Notes

1   The replies to this questionnaire are in IFC (Irish Folklore Commission) MSS 1523, 1828 and 1829. (. . . I am grateful to the Head of the Department of Irish Folklore, UCD, Dr Séamas Ó Catháin, for permission to quote from the manuscripts).

2   Patrick Bolger, *The Irish Co-Operative Movement*, Dublin, 1977.

3   Congested Districts' Board, *Baseline Reports*, Dublin, 1892–1898.

4   *Report of H. M. Commissioners of Inquiry into the Working of the Landlord and Tenant (Ireland) Act, 1870, and the Acts Amending the Same (Bessborough Commission)*, P.P. 1881, xviii, 17407–10, pp. 560 and 578.

5   IFC MS 669: 40–1.

6   IFC MS 1201: 504–31.

7   Michael Shiel, *The Quiet Revolution*, Dublin, 1984.

8   Hely Dutton, *Statistical Survey of the County of Clare*, Dublin, 1808, pp. 76–7; IFC MS 1146: 570–1.

9   A. T. Lucas, 'Cloth finishing in Ireland', *Folklife, Journal of Ethnological Studies*, 6, 1968, pp. 18–67.

10   IFC MS 1201: 352.

Chapter 30

Mona Hearn

■ from LIFE FOR DOMESTIC SERVANTS IN
DUBLIN, 1880–1920, in Maria Luddy and Cliona Murphy
(eds), *Women Surviving: Studies in Irish Women's History in
the 19th and 20th Centuries*, Dublin, 1989, pp. 148–79

DOMESTIC SERVICE WAS THE MAJOR employment for women
in Ireland in the nineteenth century; in 1881, 48 per cent of employed
women were in the domestic class. Between 1881 and 1911, years for which
comparable statistics are available, there was a steady decrease in the number of
indoor servants in each successive census, 39,000 less in 1891 than ten years previously, 35,500 less in 1901 and 40,000 fewer in 1911. In that year domestic service
was surpassed by manufacturing industry, but it was still the second largest
employer of women, with 125,783 female indoor servants.[1] The numerical significance of domestic service is reflected in the fact that a separate occupational class
in the census was devoted to it. [. . .]

Domestic service was, in the period under review, an inevitable part of life
for many thousands of girls. The expected pattern of existence for middle- and
upper-class girls was life in father's home followed by life in their husband's home;
for working-class girls it was life in father's home followed by employer's home
and finally husband's home.[2] Girls went into domestic service because it was very
often the only thing for them to do. It appealed to parents, especially as a career
for daughters, because it offered board and lodgings as well as money wages.
Domestic service was also acceptable to the ideology of the time which considered the home, albeit someone else's home, the natural place for a girl or woman;
the work was what any woman would do in her own home; also, it was considered the obvious destiny for those without families of their own – those from
orphanages, industrial schools and reformatories.

Taking up a 'situation' as it was called for an indoor servant was a more fundamental step than taking up a position in most other industries. It involved a
complete break with home, friends and a familiar way of life; it entailed living in
a dependent and subordinate position in the home of people who were not only
strangers, but who were also of a different social class with different habits, values
and lifestyle. The employer's household embraced the servant's whole life. Total
loyalty to master and mistress was expected. Apart from some limited free time,

the servant was always available to see to the wants and comfort of her employer. The total control of servant by master, which was in fact reinforced by legislation, meant that the domestic servant had little discretion over the day-to-day conduct of her life.

The vast majority of Irish servants were children of small farmers, estate workers, the semi-skilled and the unskilled. The lack of alternative employment in Ireland was a crucial factor in limiting career choice for these girls; in fact the usual choice facing them was domestic service or emigration.[3] [. . .] The ratio of servants was high in towns and cities in which there were only traditional occupations available to women; Dublin had 50 servants for every 1000 of the population. Cork had 49 per 1000[4] and Belfast, where there were manufacturing jobs for women, only 22.[5] [. . .]

Wages of domestic servants compared very favourably with wages in other industries.[6] [. . .] The servant had very few expenses and could save, or send money home to help relations.[7] In addition to wages, domestic servants had free board and lodgings and many appreciated this advantage.[8] Other reasons which might have attracted people to domestic service were a desire to improve their social position – working in a 'good place' in Merrion or Fitzwilliam Square, for instance, was considered desirable – and the fact that service provided a relatively simple way for girls to enter urban life. Certainly the attractions of town or city life and the desire to escape from the poverty and hardship of subsistence farming and crowded tenements would have played a part. Parents welcomed the control and security which they felt service offered their daughters.[9] Being part of a household where one's 'comings and goings were matters of interest and moment' [. . .] was considered preferable to living on one's own in rented accommodation.[10] [. . .]

The majority of servants were young single women working in houses where only one servant was employed. They were usually called general servants and were responsible, with the help of the housewife, for all the work of the house. The general servant was the only one for whom Mrs Beeton had any sympathy, describing her life as 'solitary', and her work as 'never done'. [. . .] Houses at this time were often poorly planned and were usually devoid of labour-saving appliances and there was indeed a vast 'amount of daily menial labour' involved for the general servant. Chores included: lighting and tending the coal range in the kitchen, fires in the living rooms and perhaps the bedrooms; carrying hot water for shaving and bathing to the bedrooms and emptying slops; trimming and lighting the oil lamps; cleaning the steel knives with bath-brick. Quite elaborate meals were prepared and cooked on the temperamental coal range and served in the dining room, which was often on the floor above the kitchen; dishes were washed in a dark scullery with water heated on the range and washing soda to help remove the grease. In addition, the servant had to mind the children. Flagged and tiled floors and passages, common in those days, were frequently scrubbed, and the granite steps leading to many Dublin houses scrubbed regularly. Every room was cleaned thoroughly once a week and lighter chores, for example cleaning the silver or brass or ironing the clothes, were done in the afternoons. Some general servants also did the weekly wash while in other households a char woman was hired.

In two-servant houses the most common servant employed was a cook; the second servant, whose function it was to look after the cleaning of the house, was usually called a general servant, housemaid, house/parlourmaid or was given no specific title. This was the beginning of specialisation in the service hierarchy. Not all two-servant houses had a cook; presumably the housewife did the cooking herself or it was done by the general servant. The second servant was often a nursemaid for the children. The usual three servants employed in Dublin houses were a cook, parlourmaid and housemaid. 'With three servants – cook, parlour-maid and housemaid – a household is complete in all its functions. All else is only a development of this theme.' In larger households the cook had an assistant, a kitchen maid or perhaps a second assistant, a scullery maid; the parlourmaid's duties were taken over by the butler, and the housemaid had the assistance of other housemaids who might be called upper and lower housemaids.[11]

[. . .] Domestic service was an occupation for young people and the old family retainer was probably a rarer phenomenon than her appearance in literature suggests. In 1911, 47 per cent of indoor female servants in Ireland were under twenty-five years of age and only 18 per cent were over forty-five.[12] [. . .] The majority of servants were single, they either married comparatively late and left service, or they did not marry at all.[13] That employers preferred unmarried servants is clear from newspaper advertisements, which often either stipulated that an applicant must be single or asked for a declaration of marital status. In Dublin in 1911, 92 per cent of female servants were single, 6 per cent were widowed and only 2 per cent were married. [. . .] Conditions of service and the attitude of employers did not facilitate the meeting of the sexes in circumstances conducive to courtship and marriage. Servants worked long hours and had very little freedom; they therefore had limited opportunities to meet each other.[14] This was especially true of those working in one or two-servant households, which included the majority of servants. These girls tended to marry milkmen, breadmen, butchers, roundsmen, or small shopkeepers, probably the only men they met regularly. Marriage was looked on by many servants as a way of escaping from service.[15]

The process of acquiring a spouse was actively discouraged by many masters and mistresses. The disparaging term 'follower' was used to describe a servant's boyfriend; it was the subject of jokes and cartoons. A 'no followers' rule pertained in many households.[16] [. . .] This rule isolated servants further from their own social class. The low status of their occupation also made it harder for them to acquire an eligible young man. A number of former servants said that they pretended to boyfriends that they worked in factories.[17] One woman who used to go to dances with two other servants said that one of them who was 'very grand' always told the men she had an office job; she used to arrange to meet them in places like Grafton St.[18] [. . .]

There were great variations in wages from one household to another and from one servant to another. This is stressed by many writers.[19] The wage was affected by the income level of the employer, the age and experience of the servant, the number of staff employed, the location, supply and demand. [. . . W]ages were highest in Belfast where there was more alternative employment, and [. . .] rates were higher in Dublin than in Cork or Limerick. Servants in capital cities earned higher wages than those working in other parts of the country as there was greater demand for servants [. . .] and more wealthy employers. The wage paid was finally a personal one – that agreed between employer and servant. [. . .]

Servants usually slept in the attic or top-floor bedrooms, which they may have shared with one, or sometimes two others. These rooms were generally sparsely furnished.[20] Many former servants were content with the accommodation provided for them; the majority had a single room though some shared with another servant. These rooms were plainly furnished with an iron bed, chest of drawers, wardrobe and perhaps a wash-hand basin.[21] Servants in small houses rarely had a sitting room; the kitchen was used by the servants, and, could be 'quite equal the house-place of the cottages of their own mothers'.[22] [. . .] Most former servants stated that the food in service was good or very good, and in many cases the same as that eaten by the family. It was in households that really could not afford servants that shortage of food was usually experienced. [. . .]

Domestic servants were particularly vulnerable to exploitation by their employers. Being predominantly female – in the 1911 census, 93 per cent of servants were women[23] [. . .] – they were more easily intimidated. They were usually young and the vast majority were untrained when they entered service. Moreover, most worked in one- or two-servant households and lacked the support which membership of a larger workforce would supply. Servants spent twenty-four hours a day in their workplace and were generally in constant daily contact with their mistresses. All these factors gave employers an unusual amount of control over servants.

Servants never achieved the collective power which membership of an effective trade union could have supplied. Attempts to organise them in trade unions in Ireland met with very little success; this was also the experience in England, France and the United States. The fact that servants worked alone or with one other undoubtedly made unionisation very difficult. Other reasons for the failure were the close relationship between employers and servants, the constant movement of servants from one situation to another, the fact that unmarried women looked on service as only a temporary occupation and the fears of servants of losing their places and being deprived of references.[24] Servants were afforded very little protection by the law while the employer had extensive rights to protect himself against his servant.[25]

The master was obliged to supply food and lodgings but not medical attention or medicine for his servants. He could dismiss a servant without the customary one month's notice for 'a good and valid reason'. Obviously 'good and valid reason' could be interpreted in many ways. Reasons for dismissal without notice were: wilful disobedience to a lawful and reasonable order, theft, drunkenness (habitual or on one occasion only), insolence [. . .] immorality [. . .] illness, but only if permanent or prolonged. A servant had to obey lawful orders, exercise care in the performance of his duties and 'abstain from doing that which he ought not to do'. A master was under no legal obligation to give his servant a character.[26] This was very serious, as a reference was absolutely essential when a servant was seeking work. Many efforts were made in the early twentieth century to compel employers to give references to their servants but without success.[27]

Domestic servants, however, benefited from general legislation: the provision of old age pensions in 1908, sickness benefits in 1911, and the Workman's

Compensation Act of 1906. The National Insurance Act of 1911, which was designed to give workers free medical treatment and cash benefits while ill, met with strong opposition from both employers and servants – though principally from the former in Ireland and England. A threepenny weekly contribution was required from mistress and servant. [. . .]

Employers could and did exploit the unequal situation. The very low money wages paid to some servants – as little as £4 a year up to the 1920s – is testimony to this. Food was rationed by some mistresses and food supplies kept in a locked cupboard; sleeping accommodation could be very poor.[28] Some servants had no half-day.[29] Others had no holidays.[30] Servants were sometimes physically assaulted by their employers. Special legislation to safeguard young people under eighteen years of age was brought in in England in 1851 as a result of a couple of cases of extreme cruelty against servants.[31] Sexual exploitation of servants by masters and sons of the house was not uncommon. [. . .]

The ability to change jobs was the only real power servants had when work conditions were unfavourable. It was one which was used frequently. [. . .] The threat to change jobs was also, it seems, an effective weapon. Servants who demanded rises, with or without threats of departure, usually had them granted. [. . .] Advertisements for servants also showed that inflexibility existed. Employers evidently found it necessary to mention certain chores specifically, such as: washing, minding children, sewing, waiting at table. [. . .]

The capacity of servants to control, to a certain extent, their own destiny shows a workforce which was far from powerless. The power came from the ability to disrupt the household by withdrawing their labour permanently. However, servants could disturb the peace of the home without leaving. This power derived from the close personal relationship which existed between mistress and maid especially in small households. Servants were exposed to the moods and humours of the mistress but the opposite was also true. This close association very often led to the growth of mutual respect and perhaps affection; even when there was lack of empathy between the two, the mistress was very much aware of the satisfaction or dissatisfaction of the servant with her 'position'. Apart from treating the girl well because she knew and liked her – after all a maid was not an anonymous pair of hands in a factory – it was in the interest of the mistress and her family to have a happy and contented servant in the home. Servants were of the utmost importance to the employing class in the nineteenth and early twentieth centuries, their domestic well-being depended on servants, and while [the employers] sometimes used their positions in society to block or try to block legislation favourable to servants, on an individual basis, this dependence favoured domestic servants.

Notes

1   *Census of Ireland, General Reports*, 1881, 1891, 1901 and 1911.
2   Leonore Davidoff Lockwood, 'Domestic service and the working class cycle', *Society for the Study of Labour History*, bulletin no. 26, Spring 1973, p. 10.
3   A Donegal woman who wrote to the author said of the 1920s that whole families

of girls from small farms went into service. Boys and girls, she added, were at their 'wit's ends' for any kind of work (from Fohan, Co. Donegal on 26 February 1980).

4   *Cost of Living of the Working Classes. Report of an Enquiry by the Board of Trade into Working Class Rents, Housing and Retail Prices*, H. C. 1908 [Cd 3864], cvii, pp. 359, 372

5   Ibid., p. 366.

6   'Except amongst the lowest class of domestic workers, wages (with which must be estimated cost of maintenance), have for many years been higher than those of workers in comparable occupations, such as clerks, shop assistants and factory employees, and they continue to rise.' Ministry of Reconstruction, *Report of the Woman's Advisory Committee on the Domestic Service Problem*, H. C. 1919 [Cmd 67], xxix, p. 29.

7   Rowntree, in his study of York, states that it was well known that Irish and Welsh children not living at home and working as domestic servants sent considerable sums home to their parents. Seebohm Rowntree, *Poverty: A Study of Town Life*, London, 1902, p. 112.

8   A former servant said that she gave up her job as a shop assistant and became a servant for this reason (from former servant at Leighton Road, Crumlin to author on March 23 1980). [. . .]

9   Lockwood, 'Domestic service', p. 10. [. . .]

10 Brighid, 'Domestic service as a profession for women', *The Irish Homestead*, viii/6, February 1902, p. 113.

11 Charles Booth, *Life and Labour in London*, London, 1903, p. 218.

12 *Census of Ireland*, 1911.

13 This is also pointed out by Theresa McBride, *The Domestic Revolution*, London, 1976, pp. 56, 84, and by L. Davidoff and R. Hawthorn, *A Day in the Life of a Victorian Domestic Servant*, London, 1976, p. 86.

14 This is also stressed by many writers. See McBride, *Domestic Revolution*, pp. 56, 90. [. . .]

15 Miss C. E. Collet, *Report on the Statistics of Employment of Women and Girls*, H. C. 1894 [C7564], lxxi, pt. 11.

16 'This meant that you could not ask anyone in' (former servant at Dublin Central Mission, Marlborough Place to author on 12 March, 1980).

17 A former employer said that she told her servants to tell boyfriends that they were housekeepers (employer at Eglinton Park, Dublin to author on 18 April 1980).

18 'Kathleen' wrote to author in 1980.

19 Pamela Horn, *The Rise and Fall of the Victorian Servant*, Dublin, 1975, p. 124. McBride, *Domestic Revolution*, p. 60.

20 Horn, *Rise and Fall*, p. 111; Davidoff and Hawthorn, *Day in the Life*, p. 82; Flora Thompson, *Lark Rise to Candleford*, London, 1973, p. 173.

21 A former servant stated that she had white furniture in her room, 'it had to be different' (telephone conversation on 26 March 1980).

22 Booth, *Life and Labour*, p. 219. A former servant described the kitchen where the servants played cards as warm and comfortable (to author at Terryglass, Nenagh on 29 August 1980).

23 *Census of Ireland*, 1911.

24   Davidoff and Hawthorn, *Day in the Life*, p. 84. [. . .] Minutes of evidence of the ITGWU to the Commission on Vocational Organisation in 1940, Mss 922–41 (National Library of Ireland), vol. 7,928. p. 2345, par. 14423.

25   McBride, *Domestic Revolution*, pp. 15, 25.

26   *Mrs Beeton's Household Management*, London, 1923, pp. 1518–20.

27   Horn, *Rise and Fall*, p. 46.

28   Booth, *Life and Labour*, p. 219.

29   A former servant, an orphan, who worked in the west of Ireland in 1936.

30   'Holidays were never heard of' (former servant in Fenner, Slane to author on 5 March 1980). An employer explained that she did not give her servants holidays as they generally lived nearby (former employer from Oughterard to author, 27 February 1980).

31   Horn, *Rise and Fall*, pp. 118–20.

Chapter 31

Mary E. Daly

■ from **WOMEN AND IRISH TRADE UNIONS**,
in Donal Nevin (ed.), *Trade Union Century*, Cork, 1994,
pp. 106–16

T HE EARLIEST INVOLVEMENT OF IRISH WOMEN in trade
union activities probably occurred when wives, sisters or daughters of male
trade union members acted in support of their striking relatives in protests or
demonstrations. There is a long history of women participating in such activities
but otherwise they were relative late-comers to the trade union movement both
in Ireland and elsewhere. Early trade unions were dominated by skilled artisans
who were determined to protect their status against attacks by employers and by
outside workers. Women by definition were outsiders who were excluded from
most apprenticeships and from the overwhelming majority of skilled trades. Not
only did these pioneering trade unions represent occupations which women were
not permitted to follow, but their overall ethos was utterly opposed to women
working outside the home. Nineteenth-century craft unions regarded working
women as synonymous with cheap labour. They argued that women only worked
because their menfolk were unable to support them, and that by working outside
the home for low wages women further undermined male earning-power, setting
in motion a vicious circle of increased working-class poverty and undermining the
family in the process. The solution, according to this line of reasoning, lay in
paying men a Family Wage and excluding women from the labour market. Such
views were not unique to Ireland, in fact they were widespread throughout Europe
and the United States and persisted well into the twentieth century. As a result
the relationship between women and the trade union movement, in Ireland and
elsewhere, was a complex and occasionally an uneasy one.

Organising women workers into trade unions proved a difficult task. In late
nineteenth-century Ireland the overwhelming majority of women worked in either
domestic service or in agriculture.[1] Domestic servants, who worked in ones or
twos in private homes under a wide variety of conditions proved virtually impossible to organise in any country. Most female agricultural labourers were in their
teens, intent on earning enough money to emigrate; others worked for relatives
– again, unpromising trade union material. A high proportion of women in industry

worked either in small workshops or within their own homes. Whether employed in workshops or in large establishments such as the Belfast linen or Derry shirt factories, women rarely worked at tasks carried out by men. Most did not serve formal apprenticeships; consequently their work was regarded as unskilled or semi-skilled. The typical female industrial worker was young and single, with a low level of political consciousness. She tended to regard work as a transient experience prior to marriage and was unlikely to make a long-term commitment towards trade union membership. With wages often less than half those of a general male labourer and perhaps only one-sixth those of a skilled worker, she was often reluctant to pay a weekly union subscription of even a few pence. Older women who worked outside the home generally did so because of difficult family circumstances: they were widows with dependent children, wives of casual labourers or chronically ill men; if single they often supported parents or siblings. Dual burdens of work and family left them little time for attending union meetings. Such women saw work as a necessary evil; many saw the solution to their plight, not in the higher wages or improved working conditions which a trade union might offer, but in securing an adequately paid job for a husband, son, father or other male relative which would permit them to abandon paid work for domesticity. Many of these women would have endorsed the traditional views of male trade unionists: that a woman's place was in the home and that better pay for men or adequate welfare provisions would permit them to retire there.

In most countries the organisation of women into trade unions coincided with the unionisation of unskilled labourers. In Ireland the 1890s witnessed both the first serious efforts to organise labourers and the first trade union activity among women in the Belfast linen industry. Both the women's unions and the labourers' unions proved short-lived and by the time the Irish TUC (Trades Union Congress) was founded in 1894 the trade union movement was firmly dominated once more by traditional skilled unions. The first sustained breakthrough in recruiting women members came in the early years of the new century when Michael O'Lehane's Drapers' Assistants' Association became the first trade union in Ireland (with the exception of the INTO [Irish National Teachers Organization]) to admit both men and women. By 1914 it had 1,400 women members among a total membership of 4,000. The upsurge of trade union militancy associated with Larkin and Connolly also impinged on women. During the Belfast docks strike of 1907 women from the linen mills demonstrated against blackleg labour; other women organised door-to-door collections. The first, and only long-lived Irish all-women's trade union, the Irish Women Workers' Union, (IWWU) was founded in 1911 against a backdrop of labour militancy in Dublin. Delia Larkin, its first general secretary, was a sister of Jim Larkin, the ITGWU (Irish Transport and General Workers Union) leader who became the first president of the Irish Women Workers' Union. During its early months the IWWU sheltered under the wing of the ITGWU. By 1913 they had recruited many of the women in Jacob's biscuit factory; during the 1913 Lock-Out, the right of these women workers to belong to a union was challenged by the company in a manner similar to William Martin Murphy's assault on the ITGWU and they too were locked out.

The aftermath left both unions impoverished; membership had fallen and both Jim and Delia Larkin were no longer in Ireland. Helena Molony, an actress and committed nationalist, and James Connolly took on the task of reorganisation. When Molony was imprisoned for her part in the 1916 Rising, Louie Bennett, a suffragist from a prosperous Dublin family and Helen Chenevix, daughter of a Church of Ireland bishop, took charge.[2] Unlike the typical male trade union leaders these three women, who were to lead the IWWU for many decades, were not members of the working class who rose into leadership roles, a characteristic they shared with the first generation of British women trade union leaders. This occasionally led them to treat the union rank and file with a degree of pity, perhaps even condescension.

The establishment of a separate union for women in 1911 reflected the conventions among British and Irish unions at the time, which excluded women from membership of male unions. In Britain however, the First World War brought a sharp increase in women's waged employment and the intrusion of women into traditional male jobs. As a result male unions appear to have relaxed their hostility towards women members, if only for reasons of self-interest. Although women's employment in Ireland during the First World War showed much less expansion, Irish unions appear to have followed their British counterparts in deciding by the 1920s to admit women. The decision probably reflected a belief that having won the right to vote, women's struggle for equality was almost over. However, despite overtures towards amalgamation from the ITGWU, the IWWU survived as a separate union until 1984, when it was decided to merge with the Federated Workers' Union of Ireland. From the 1920s most of the growth in female trade union membership took place in mixed general unions and in clerical and white-collar unions rather than the IWWU. This suggests that women workers were giving priority to class solidarity over gender interests. However, although these mixed unions undoubtedly protected women's working conditions and sought improved wages, until the second half of the twentieth century, they rarely articulated the point of view of women workers, nor did they do anything to reduce inequalities in pay and career prospects for women workers. Women came to account for up to one-quarter of the membership of the Irish Transport and General Workers' Union. However, the first woman was not elected to the national executive until 1955 and Sheila Williams, better known as Sheila Conroy, was the only female member of the executive of the ITGWU before the 1970s. For many decades therefore, the IWWU remained the sole voice within the trade union movement which spoke for women's interests.

The 1920s proved a difficult period for Irish trade unions. After the rapid growth of membership in the aftermath of the First World War, the number of both male and female members slumped as many industries either closed down or reduced the size of their workforce. In marked contrast, the 1930s saw steady expansion both in overall trade union membership and in women's participation.[3] [. . .] Whether they were employed in factories, shops or offices, most women workers tended to be young and single; marriage bars were the norm for most white-collar jobs and many women in industry resigned voluntarily on marriage. Women's jobs offered lower pay than comparable jobs for men. Yet despite this, aggregate statistics showing rising female employment in industry and services aroused considerable disquiet among male trade unionists – disquiet which was shared by the Fianna Fáil government, whose industrial policy was geared to maximising male employment. Many male trade unionists believed that women were supplanting men in industrial and service employment; in fact there was no evidence to support such beliefs; instances of men and boys taking over jobs previously done by women in laundries and factories are much more readily documented. Often this occurred because of the ban on women's night work, which was enforced both by Irish law and by the International Labour Organisation with full support from all Irish trade unions with the qualified exception of the IWWU. However in an era when complaints of women taking jobs away from men were rife, women trade unionists were necessarily put on the defensive. In 1932 Louie Bennett's presidential address to the Irish TUC described the growing number of women working in industry as 'a menace to family life', and argued that 'in so far as it has blocked the employment of men it has intensified poverty among the working class'. Bennett and other trade unionists of the 1930s tended to defend women's work, not as a right but as a necessary evil. Further evidence of the vulnerable position of women trade unionists and the hostile climate in which they had to survive emerges from the INTO's acquiescence in the government's imposition of a ban on married women teachers despite having a majority female membership,[4] and the trade union response to the Conditions of Employment Act [. . . of 1936 which granted] the power to prohibit women from working in designated industries and to set quotas for women workers in individual industries. Senator Thomas Foran, President of the ITGWU, a union containing approximately 36,000 members at that time, was thoroughly supportive of the proposed legislation and roundly denounced women who opposed it. His speech in the Irish Senate asked: 'Do the feminists want here what occurs in certain industrial countries across the water where the men mind the babies and the women go to the factories? Do they want that in this holy Ireland of ours?'[5]

When confronted with such viewpoints women trade unionists were in a vulnerable position: a weak and financially vulnerable minority in a predominantly male movement. The IWWU sought in vain to modify the clauses which discriminated against working women; however, their opposition was tempered by a recognition that they could not afford an open dispute with the Irish trade union movement. For that reason, despite strong personal reservations concerning the clauses relating to women in the 1937 Constitution, IWWU leaders such as Louie Bennett felt themselves constrained from uniting openly with an Irish feminist movement, which was dominated by women graduates, in outright opposition to the Constitution.

However, while it is important to record the existence of tensions between women's rights and the trade union movement, we should beware of presenting an unduly negative picture of women's status. If male trade unionists showed little sympathy with demands for equal rights, they were often gracious towards individual women trade unionists: both Louie Bennett and Helen Chenevix served as presidents of Congress, the former on two occasions.[6] Women trade unionists led the way in campaigns for a cleaner, safer working environment; during the Second World War the IWWU campaigned for more effective food rationing and assisted in the formation of the Irish Housewives Association; in 1945, following a three-month strike, they negotiated an agreement which gave Dublin laundry workers two weeks' holidays with pay; this was the landmark decision, which eventually made two weeks holidays with pay the norm of most industrial workers.

None of these campaigns broached controversial issues such as disparities in pay between men and women or women's exclusion from many areas of employment. Indeed health, hygiene and consumer issues could be seen as part of a woman's traditional role. Contentious issues such as equal pay tended to be avoided, perhaps because they might split the trade union movement, or because they were not necessarily supported by the majority of women trade union members. In 1953 the IWWU supported a demand for equal pay at Congress, but wished to 'debar the young married women or "the single girl" from its terms'.[7] For the overwhelming majority of women, who worked in single-sex occupations, equal pay was an irrelevance. The depressed state of the Irish economy throughout most of the 1950s, resulting in a falling level of employment and record emigration, meant that workers' interests became focused on protecting their jobs and standard of living and [they] showed little interest in apparently unattainable goals such as equal pay. In addition, Irish society was preoccupied with the low marriage rate and particularly with rural population decline; many commentators saw the employment of women in towns and cities as a factor which contributed to this crisis. Such a climate was not conducive to advancing the status of women. In addition the pioneering generation of Irish women trade union leaders was fading from the scene; a new female leadership was only beginning to emerge.

In contrast, the 1960s and early 1970s were a period of optimism and economic growth, a time when the trade union movement looked anew at women workers. The number of women employed in manufacturing industry fell as many of the protected industries established in the 1930s crumpled in the face of competition from imports. Although overall employment in manufacturing industry rose, the new jobs tended to be male jobs; government policy dictated that the industrial promotion agencies give preference to creating male employment. As a result, women's share of jobs in manufacturing industry in the Republic fell from 35 per cent in 1951 to 30 per cent in 1971 and 27 per cent in 1981. Although no similar policy existed in Northern Ireland, the sharp decline of the traditional textile and clothing industries brought a similar trend, with women's share of manufacturing jobs falling from 43 per cent in 1951 to 33 per cent in 1981.[8] At the same time overall employment in the public service and in the financial sector rose significantly as did the percentage of jobs in these sectors which were held by women. Thus the profile of women workers changed; the importance of industrial workers declined, white-collar workers came to assume a greater prominence. The Irish female labour force continued to be dominated by young, single women to a greater extent than in any other western economy. However, from the early 1970s, with the disappearance of the marriage bar in both the public service and the private sector, the percentage of married women increased suddenly.

Changes in trade union membership reflected the pattern of female employment. The number of women trade unionists showed little increase during the 1950s, rising only from approximately 55,000 in 1950 to 60,000 ten years later. By 1970, however, numbers had grown to 100,000; by 1977 there were over 158,000 women trade union members: approximately two-thirds of all female employees.[9] Although male trade union membership was also on the increase, growth was faster among women. By the end of the 1970s men and women were equally likely to be members of trade unions, a dramatic change from previous

generations, when women were significantly less likely than men to become trade
union members. [. . .]

From the 1960s equal pay and promotion prospects began to feature to a
greater extent among the demands of women trade union members. The fact that
an increasing number of women members worked in white-collar occupations,
side by side with men who often had significantly better pay and promotion possibilities, brought a sharper focus on inequality in the workforce than was possible
for women who worked in occupations where an all-female workforce provided
no basis for comparison. [. . .]

The trade union movement proved relatively adept at responding to the changes
in women's demands; whether this reflects a change of mind, or simply a pragmatic awareness that women constituted an important growth market for trade
union recruitment cannot be known. The decision by the newly reunited Irish
Congress of Trade Unions in 1959 to appoint a Women's Advisory Committee
proved particularly fortuitous. Although its initial impact was slight, the
Committee's annual report to Congress provided a platform for raising issues of
specific interest to women. Congress had provided women members with a voice
and they were not slow to use it. The first evidence of a new female assertiveness emerged in 1964, when the annual motion in favour of equal pay – a
long-standing token gesture of no practical significance – gave way to protests
against the failure to award women the same minimum pay increase as men under
the centralised agreement of that year [. . . and in 1965] pressure from women
members led Congress to establish a Committee on Equal Pay. This may well have
been a delaying tactic; the report was still outstanding in 1968 when the
committee's brief was extended to examine the wider question of women and
work. In the same year Congress passed a resolution calling on the government
to set up a Commission on the Status of Women, a demand which had also emerged
from a number of independent women's organisations who were responding to a
1967 United Nations directive. The Commission's interim report on equal pay,
which was published in 1971, forced trade unions seriously to confront the position of women in the labour market for the first time; its proposals for legally
enforceable equal pay, investigation of women's promotion prospects and the
opening of a wider range of careers for women marked a new era for the Irish
trade union movement. [. . .] Perhaps the Commission's greatest contribution was
in raising consciousness about women's issues and setting an agenda for achievement. The 1974 Anti-Discrimination (Pay) Act provided a framework for the
pursuit of equal pay and anti-discrimination claims, as did the work of the
Employment Equality Agency, which was founded in 1977. The succession of
National Wage Agreements throughout the 1970s also gave the unions scope for
including equal pay provisions as part of the overall negotiations. Trade unions
have also played an important role in developing women's leadership skills and
have provided many women members with opportunities for further education.

The pace of change in recent years has proved breathtaking in comparison with
previous generations; most remarkable is the fact that much of this has been
achieved at a time of high unemployment, when a backlash against working women
might have been anticipated. In fact women have weathered recent decades better
than men. [. . .] Despite these positive trends, progress towards equality has proved

more onerous than many would have anticipated in the 1970s. The removal of measures which formally discriminated against women has not proved sufficient to attain this goal. [. . .]

Notes

1   Mary E. Daly, 'Women in the Irish workforce from pre-industrial to modern times', *Saothar* 7, 1981, pp. 74–82.

2   Mary Jones, *These Obstreperous Lassies: A History of the IWWU*, Dublin, 1988, pp. 6–22.

3   Mary E. Daly, *Industrial Development and Irish National Identity, 1922–1939*, Syracuse and Dublin, 1992, pp. 120–1.

4   Eoin O'Leary, 'The Irish National Teachers' Organisation and the marriage ban for women national teachers, 1938–58', *Saothar*, 12, 1987.

5   *Debates Seanad Éireann*, 27 November 1935.

6   Mary E. Daly, 'Women, work and trade unionism', in Margaret MacCurtain and Donncha Ó Corrain (eds), *Women in Irish Society: The Historical Dimension*, Dublin, 1978, pp. 72–3.

7   *Report of Irish Trade Union Congress*, 1953–4.

8   Liam Kennedy, *The Modern Industrialisation of Ireland 1940–1988*, Dublin, 1989, p. 45.

9   Membership figures from Registrar of Friendly Societies. See also F. O'Brien, *A Study of National Wage Agreements in Ireland*, Dublin: ESRI Paper No. 104, 1981, and *Report of Commission of Inquiry on Industrial Relations*, Dublin, 1981, pp. 21–4.

Conclusion: Irish women's history – a challenge

■   Alan Hayes

There has long been an involvement by women in writing history . . .
But there were decades of history-teaching where women's history played
no part. Then in the 1970s women's history arrived, partly as a search
for roots on the part of the second-wave women's movement who wanted
to find out where they got lost and what had happened, and method-
ologically, because the tools of social history, particularly economic
history, began to be widely used at that time and these were the best
tools for researching women's history'.[1]

THUS SAID MARGARET MACCURTAIN, pioneer of the history of
women in Ireland, in an interview published in 1994. MacCurtain has long
been a facilitator for a wide range of historical themes and topics and, amongst
her numerous publications, she was co-editor, with Donnchadh Ó Corrain, of the
first collection of modern Irish women's history, *Women in Irish Society: The
Historical Dimension*, published by Arlen House in 1978 – a collection which has
influenced most works of Irish women's history. Indeed, she considers this work
to be her most significant, stating that 'its essays [. . .] are an expression of the
vitality of the intellectual and creative energy of the 1970s'.[2] That work consisted
of essays by young dynamic female and male scholars who have since played an
important role in Irish academic writing and teaching, and indeed in political life.

To consider the current state of women's history in Ireland and its growth
since that first major development which arose from the second-wave feminist
movement, it is necessary to look particularly at the developments of recent decades
and the debate on integrating women's history into mainstream, both nationally
and internationally.

Since the 1960s, women's history has emerged internationally as a specialist
subject offered in a huge number of educational establishments either as an optional

or compulsory subject for undergraduates, and as an increasingly chosen option for postgraduate research. It has developed alongside 'traditional' history, which presents itself as neutral but actually isn't, since many aspects of the historical past are absent or misrepresented, including that of gender. The pursuit of women's history attempts to give back some of this neutrality to mainstream history, by working towards achieving equity in the curriculum and in historical writing, by helping to make history more meaningful for all readers and by giving them a more balanced perspective when exploring historical events and themes.

In Ireland we are still at an early stage in the development of women's history in third-level institutions, let alone in tackling its introduction into second-level history courses (apart from the few token examples). Although most institutions now offer courses at undergraduate level in the history of women these courses are unfortunately often marginalised as optional, can be regarded by many students as being directed mainly towards female students, and indeed appear to be largely taken by women. Likewise women's history courses offered within the discipline of women's studies are overwhelmingly taken by female students. The presentation of these courses is largely based on the research and personal interest of mainly female members of staff. This dependence is a fragile foundation, which can lead to the termination of the course if the lecturer is no longer available. While this is true of many options which rely on specific focused research by a particular academic, should the history of half the population be seen as 'optional'?

In a debate on the integration of women's history into mainstream history courses in late 1997, mainly concerning the history of the United States, a number of interesting views were exchanged over the H-Women (Women's History) email discussion list. A correspondent on the list brought forward an experience she had had while teaching a course in 'World Civilisation'. After assigning some outside reading which dealt with women for this mainstream course, she met with some antagonism:

> I find that many students feel as if I have some agenda because I attempt to integrate women's history. I understand that this may have something to do with the rural/traditional background of my students, but I would like to have feedback from those who have had similar experiences with students who are reluctant to learn women's role in history.[3]

One student commented that 'your teacher must be a woman' because she had disseminated material relating to women. The responses which this request received crossed many divides and reported hostility from both male and female students from different walks of life to the integration of women's history into mainstream history courses. Responses from students claimed that lecturers in courses which integrated themes of sexuality, gender and family were either 'PC', 'revisionist', 'dykes' or 'feminists' ('which they saw as a terrible thing!'). Another lecturer was told that she had a clear 'agenda', which is true of all teaching and not necessarily bad, although in this example it was clearly meant to be a criticism, and not an acknowledgement of another's differing politics. One response referred to a male colleague, who was considered 'enlightened' because he lectured about gender relations, while a female colleague was assumed to be speaking from either bias or self-interest when lecturing in this area. Another respondent suggested that the best option was to be open from the start and to state directly that the aim of the course, 'to explore the interdependence and differing perspectives of all peoples in society', necessitates an examination of women as well as minority groups and white men. This is a prime example of a way forward which we could explore in Irish history, in the continuing development of women's history and in the integration of new specialisms into mainstream history teaching, research and publishing.

The pursuit of history and its writing is a marginal affair, as indeed are all academic pursuits. No matter what area of history one chooses to study it is marginal to another in people's perception. Women's history is seen by many historians as a particularly marginal subject to study. Also, since the 1970s, a number of specialist publishing houses, run under feminist politics, have been at the forefront in publishing women's history. This endeavour, even among some women historians, is seen as marginalising women's history. Finally the publishing of women's history in special edited historical collections focusing on women, either thematic or not, and the submitting of individual articles to feminist journals and magazines, is seen again by some historians as another form of marginalisation. These three beliefs are untrue.

Firstly, in terms of numbers and output, women's history is a substantial area of study. For example, the previously mentioned H-Women email discussion list is part of the H-Net humanities and social sciences website system and email discussion lists. These contain over a hundred different pages and lists covering a wide range of historical themes from the history of Britain and Ireland, to African history and culture, and the history of childhood and youth to the history and culture of Catholicism, ranging from a couple of hundred subscribers to almost 3,500 subscribers. The H-Women list has the largest number of subscribers out of all these hundred different subjects.

Secondly, in terms of publishing houses, specialist publishers are an ideal choice as they have a particular interest in what they are publishing, as opposed to larger publishers who may publish by numbers. A particular passion for a special subject or book creates more dedication and interest from that publisher, and can result in a more motivated and stimulating relationship. Rather than marginalising women's history these publishers, with their specialist knowledge, can possibly locate target audiences better than larger publishers and thus create a more focused and potentially higher readership for the work. Also, in this electronic information age marketing rarely distinguishes between the biggest and the smallest. All publishers can market and distribute their books internationally.

Finally, the pursuit of history, and indeed many other academic pursuits, necessitates their being organised into particular themes. As academic life becomes more specialised it seems inevitable that we tend to compartmentalise our work and our interests. This is a natural way to go. There are currently plans to establish a journal of Irish women's history. This will follow along the paths made by other thematic journals – since there are journals for social history, political history, ecclesiastical and rural history, American history and indeed a number which specialise in general Irish history. So why not a specialised Irish women's history journal? Any concept of marginalisation is just an illusion.

The process of writing women back into history challenges the validity of past centuries of history writing and necessitates a thorough reworking and re-evaluation of 'knowledge' as it stands at present. Women's history is more than writing about the 'great women' of history (much as mainstream history is more than the 'great men' approach) and it must also avoid stereotyping and trivialisation. We will be regularly rewriting the historical record as new evidence is uncovered and analysed (and then re-analysed!) and all our perceptions will constantly need to be re-evaluated. Thus all scholars, both female and male, will need to keep their eyes open and be aware of new developments which will alter traditionally held beliefs.[4]

The first major development in women's history in Ireland, *Women in Irish Society: The Historical Dimension*, threw down challenges to Irish academia to acknowledge and incorporate women into scholarship and teaching. Many of these challenges have been taken on board to date. A large amount of gender-related research has been carried out in Ireland since the 1970s and published both nationally and internationally. The one challenge which has largely failed to be met has been the participation of men in the writing of Irish women's history. The first history of women which I have uncovered from the last century written by a man is James F. Cassidy's *The Women of the Gael*, which was published in Boston in 1922 with intriguing chapters on 'the social dignity of women' and 'womanly morality and honour from the sixteenth century onwards'. Whilst certainly not suggesting that this approach is the ideal way to proceed, I think it was an important start, and joins other significant twentieth-century historical works on women by women, including those by Helena Concannon, Alice Curtayne, C. J. Hamilton, Crissie M. Doyle and Katherine A. O'Keefe O'Mahoney amongst others.

Nevertheless, since the rise of second-wave feminism, apart from a few dozen examples, there has been no substantial effort from the majority of historians, who are male, to incorporate the experiences of women into their writing and research. The challenge from MacCurtain and Ó Corrain to all scholars, both male and female, to examine gender and explore its implications still needs to be *cohesively* addressed by the entire academic community. The women's history community also needs to accept male participation in this field, even if that participation may not be written from a feminist political perspective. Indeed women's history written by women is not necessarily written from that particular political agenda either. Histories of women written by men can be either feminist or not, it just shouldn't matter what the author's political bias is as long as the work is of an acceptable standard.

The history of women and of gender must be integrated into all aspects of historical teaching, research and publishing in order to more accurately represent the past. Much evidence has already been discovered and there is much more to write and research. What is needed is the understanding and interest of the entire historical community, both female and male, to acknowledge that the history of half the human race is a worthwhile endeavour and integral to our continuing quests to understand the past. As Helena Concannon felt, in her *Daughters of Banba*:

> To understand any nation we must understand its women. But in the case of Ireland, the necessity is particularly great. It is always as a woman that her lovers have thought of her.[5]

Notes

1   Thomas O'Loughlin, 'Sister Act' interview with Margaret MacCurtain, *History Ireland*, 2/1 (Spring 1994), pp. 52–4.
2   Ibid., p. 54.
3   For a transcript of this discussion see the H-Women home page and email list at www.h-net.msu.edu/~women/
4   For a sample of new primary material recently uncovered see the CD-Rom produced by the Women's History Project, *Directory of Sources for Women's History in Ireland* (Dublin, 1999).
5   Mrs Thomas Concannon, *Daughters of Banba* (Dublin, 1922), p. ix.

Index